PERFORMING BRECHT

In 1969 Peter Brook wrote: 'Brecht is the key figure of our time, and all theatre work today at some point starts from or returns to his statements and achievement.' Twenty-five years later the same still holds true. Sooner or later every theatre student, whether theory- or practice-based, will study Brecht. But the relationship between Brecht and British theatre has always been a problematic and controversial one.

Performing Brecht sheds light on this relationship in an unprecedented history of the productions of Brecht's plays in Britain over the last forty years. Margaret Eddershaw surveys all aspects of Brecht in performance, from his methodologies to his place in postmodernist theatre and beyond. She focuses on key productions by directors including George Devine, Sam Wanamaker, William Gaskill, Howard Davies, John Dexter and Richard Eyre. Eddershaw also provides in-depth case studies of three productions of the 1990s, incorporating her own exclusive access to the rehearsals and interviews with the directors and performers. The case studies are:

- *The Good Person of Sichuan*, directed by Deborah Warner, starring Fiona Shaw
- *The Resistible Rise of Arturo Ui*, directed by Di Trevis, starring Antony Sher
- *Mother Courage*, directed by Philip Prowse, starring Glenda Jackson

This unique work will be indispensable for students, teachers and theatre practitioners, and enlightening and accessible reading for anyone interested in the theatre and in Brecht.

Margaret Eddershaw was a founder member of the Department of Theatre Studies at Lancaster University, and during her twenty-five years there she combined an academic career with professional performing, directing and playwriting. She now lives in Greece, where she continues to write on and for the theatre.

PERFORMING BRECHT

Forty years of British performances

Margaret Eddershaw

London and New York

First published 1996
by Routledge
11 New Fetter Lane, London EC4P 4EE

Simultaneously published in the USA and Canada
by Routledge
29 West 35th Street, New York, NY 10001

Routledge is an International Thomson Publishing company

© 1996 Margaret Eddershaw

Typeset in Garamond by LaserScript, Mitcham, Surrey
Printed and bound in Great Britain by
TJ Press (Padstow) Ltd, Padstow, Cornwall

British Library Cataloguing in Publication Data
A catalogue record for this book is available from the British Library

Library of Congress Cataloguing in Publication Data
Eddershaw, Margaret.
Performing Brecht/Margaret Eddershaw.
p. cm.
Includes bibliographical references and index.
1. Brecht, Bertolt, 1898–1956 – Stage history – Great Britain.
2. Brecht, Bertolt, 1898–1956 – Dramatic production. 3. Theater–
Great Britain – History – 20th century. I. Title.
PT2603.R397Z5935 1996
792.9'5'0941 – dc20   95-52603
CIP

ISBN 0–415–08010–X (hbk)
ISBN 0–415–08011–8 (pbk)

For Keith

How long
Do works endure? As long
As they are not completed.
Since as long as they demand effort
They do not decay

Bertolt Brecht

CONTENTS

CONTENTS

ACKNOWLEDGMENTS

I should like to thank all the actors, directors and writers who have given so generously of their time and insights and have allowed me access to their work.

I am indebted in particular to Professor Keith Sturgess of the Department of Theatre Studies, Lancaster University, who has been a constant source of support and encouragement throughout the writing of this book.

ABBREVIATIONS

B on T: Brecht, B. (1964) *Brecht on Theatre*, trans. John Willett, New York, Hill & Wang

MD: Brecht, B. (1965) *The Messingkauf Dialogues*, trans. John Willett, London, Methuen

INTRODUCTION

The aim of this book is to examine how Brecht's ideas on the function of theatre and dramatic performance, his own practice and productions and a changing view of the meaning of the plays themselves, have influenced and shaped productions of his work in Britain over the last forty years. An attempt is made to analyse how, why and with what results practitioners in this country have sought to understand the varying pulls of aesthetics, politics and dramatic theory in their presentations of the Brecht texts. While trying to avoid suggesting that there is a definitive 'model', this book asks what has been and what is the practice of British Brecht, and what should or might it be? The account focuses on the challenges and problems set by Brecht's dramaturgy, theatrical theory and politics for British practitioners working within a very different context and set of theatrical traditions from those that Brecht himself enjoyed and helped subvert.

In 1969, Peter Brook wrote in *The Empty Space*: 'Brecht is the key figure of our time, and all theatre work today at some point starts from or returns to his statements and achievement' (Brook, 1972, p.80). Twenty-five years later this is still partly true, though a fact probably less widely acknowledged than it was in the late 1960s and early 1970s. Today, however, Brecht's plays and his theatrical theories are studied for British school examinations, and the term 'Brechtian', while it might be variously interpreted and inappropriately applied to mere borrowings of his staging techniques, is readily used by or known to anyone even only mildly interested in theatre. (Indeed, as the reader will note here, 'Brechtian' is a tautologous adjective that is difficult to avoid.) But there has always been, and there remains today, an uncertainty about the relationship between Brecht and British theatre.

Initially, when Brecht's work was first beginning to be known in Britain, there was the traditional British xenophobia to overcome, not to mention a particularly strong resistance to things Teutonic, a result, obviously, of the experiences of two world wars. The reasons why Brecht might, indeed, have remained complete anathema are many. As a German writer he was

1

seen (as he often still is) as characteristically 'heavy', boring and lacking in a sense of humour, or at least irony – in fact the kind of playwright he himself deplored in his own, rational theatre. Furthermore, he was a Marxist and thus his ideas were (and are) unlikely to be suited to the mainly bourgeois institution of British theatre and theatregoers.

Since Brecht's ideology has so often been a barrier to a full appreciation of his work in Britain, and consequently appears regularly in this book, it is worth briefly spelling out here the basis and implications of his political beliefs. Brecht's commitment to the classic Marxist tradition of 'dialectical materialism' (the idea that the individual is created by socio-political and economic factors and is, therefore, able to change his circumstances and environment) provided a 'legitimacy' (in his view at least) for an interventionist form of theatre. Brecht's 'discovery' of Marxism (in 1928/9) confirmed his already well-developed idea that theatre should have a social function. As he said, he 'had written a whole pile of Marxist plays without knowing it' (Völker, 1979, p.110). His 'epic theatre' was based on the concept of the primary importance of *production* in social life and it was intended to demonstrate socialism as the constant revolutionising of the forces and relations within the processes of production. Brecht often spoke of his form of theatre as one designed to make a contribution to 'the full unfettering of everybody's productivity' (Suvin, 1984, p.20). He would admit, however, that in order for epic theatre to work fully, the actors involved in the production needed to share a Marxist view of the world.[1] Certainly many theatre critics and historians would agree that without a knowledge of Marxist philosophy and aesthetics, it is virtually impossible to grasp the full meaning of Brecht's plays.

For example, Marxist philosophy is fundamental to Brecht's dramaturgical exploration of the relationship between the individual and society. As a playwright, he builds up a complex framework of social, political, economic, historical and personal factors, which determine the character as an individual; his phrase for this is 'statistical causality'. This approach to characterisation enables Brecht to demonstrate through his plays a wider range of possibilities for human behaviour than is the case with more 'naturalistic', psychologically-based drama.

Brecht's politics have, of course, been used frequently against him – as a reason for rejecting his artistic achievements, and as a 'stick' with which to beat him and expose the apparent hypocrisy in his personal behaviour. His detractors often draw attention to the fact that he never actually joined the Communist Party and that, after returning to East Berlin in 1949, he obtained an Austrian passport (1950), gave exclusive publishing rights to his writing to a *West* German publisher, and maintained a Swiss bank account. Equally notably, Brecht even refused to sign a binding contract with his own company, the Berliner Ensemble, until 1953, when he signed a form of 'open' agreement. In extenuation, it might be claimed that after his years in exile, when his artistic ambitions and activities had been inevitably limited, he was determined to ensure that he and his work would be available to both East and West, and thus his commitment to Communism was made on his own terms.

Brecht also drew criticism from some of his supporters for appearing to condone Stalin's barbaric form of Communism in Russia, and again for failing to criticise the East German government's use of Russian tanks to restore order after the Berlin uprising of June 1953. As Peter Thomson says in his account of Brecht's life:

> There is much about him, what he did and what he failed to do, that makes him vulnerable. He was a man who lived untidily, but who combined timorousness and combativeness as few people have.
>
> (Thomson and Sachs, 1994, p.38)

Crucially, the corollary of Brecht's Marxism was his creation of play-texts that were based on a social, economic and historical understanding of the development of human life and behaviour and its institutions, and which expressed Brecht's passionate concern for the poor, the disempowered and the disenfranchised in society. His aim was not just to reflect the real world in his drama but to contribute to its change and improvement. While his deeply felt pacifism was readily acceptable to many at the time of and immediately after the war of 1939–45, his anti-capitalist stance was more of a problem in the capitalist West. The ideals and heartfelt beliefs expressed in his plays were put into theatrical practice by Brecht operating through a working method and process that was open, experimental and collaborative, and which placed emphasis on the ensemble rather than on the individual performer. And this method and process were (and are) as much a stumbling block to his full acceptance in Britain's theatre environment as was and is his Marxism *per se*.

To compound the problem, much of his creative work appeared to arrive here already wrapped in the brown paper of Brechtian dramatic theory. There has always been an unwillingness in Britain to contemplate or work via a theoretical basis for art. British theatre, it might be argued, has never paid open respect to the intellectual approach; instead, it has thrived on traditional approaches and instinct, not on revolution and theoretical debate. Those approaches include an eclectic manner in the creating of the professional actor ('training' is not a prerequisite for membership of the profession), though the predominance of a 'naturalistic' performance style in mainstream theatre (supported by television and film) results in the fact that a 'psychological' approach to character has been (and is) the dominant approach to a part for most actors. However, the paucity of rehearsal time in the British professional theatre, and the frequent concern on the part of directors to create 'scenes' rather than motivation, has encouraged the actors' reliance on their own instinctual understanding of what a part requires rather than on the development of a systematic process based on training. This, plus a basic distrust of the intellectual, typical of British art circles, and other factors of British theatrical life, has led to the assumption by many that to 'think' about performing will inhibit the 'feeling' necessary to the creative act. To cap it all, of course, Brecht actually set himself against naturalism as a style or intent, and thus (or so many practitioners assumed for some time) also set himself against the development of a clear emotional line in performance – another black mark for him from a theatre that prided itself on its ability to 'move' an audience by a truthful display of deep sentiment. The great British actor Alec Guinness wrote in 1949 in answer to an article by Brecht on acting:

> I find his theories cut right across the very nature of the actor, substituting some cerebral process for the instinctive and traditional accumulation of centuries . . . I believe in the mystery and illusion of the theatre which Brecht seems to despise.[2]

And yet the part of the British theatrical tradition that is built on the performing of Shakespeare so often brings the performer very close to Brechtian notions of theatre. Brecht's own generous accolade to the bard – that his was a truly epic form – is a strong testimony here; and as many practitioners acknowledge (and are quoted in subsequent chapters of this book), the natural inclination of British actors towards ironic story-telling, so familiar to us from Shakespeare, makes them easy converts to Brechtian practice.

Until the mid-1950s, only among a small band of left-wing enthusiasts was Brecht's work actively supported in Britain. The great boost to the development of a public for the playwright came from the first visit to London by his company, the Berliner Ensemble, in 1956 – shortly, that is, after his death. Since the Berliner performed in German, it is not surprising that the major impact they had was on 'theatrical style', on the visual and physical aspects of production, rather than on thematic content. A number of British directors and designers were immediately struck by the bareness and simplicity of the company's staging, the careful detail lavished on and produced in costumes and props, and the robust clarity and exuberance of the acting. These responses led to a small crop of British productions of Brecht plays in the late 1950s and early 1960s, but these received somewhat mixed reviews. The feeling persisted that there was something wrong with the plays themselves, acceptability of which was certainly not helped by the difficulties of translating Brecht's specialised verbal language. The archaic words and phrases, unusual rhythms, poetic word order, and so on, proved, and continue to prove, a challenge to any translator. And the early British productions of Brecht appeared to suffer from either an over-fidelity to 'Brechtianism' as understood by the performers, or from a lack of understanding of the essential combination in Brecht of socio-political meaning and theatrical fun. Even critics who admired these early productions sometimes felt (and declared) that they had to overlook or ignore Brecht's politics in order to enjoy the performance. Reviews were often either antagonistic to this new form of theatre or baffled by it. In both cases it frequently resulted in dismissive reviews and a rejection of the playwright.

Gradually, however, the tide of anti-Brecht feeling was beginning to turn and it was given a following wind when the Berliner Ensemble made their second visit to London in 1965. Ideas in the British theatre were on the move; the arts in general in the 1960s were in a time of change and expansion. Then the 'politicisation' of theatre in the post-1968 period, which led to the development of the 'fringe' theatre scene, provided a perfect context for the rehabilitation of Brecht. His plays – including their politics this time – were ideal material for that rather un-British event, the construction of an 'alternative' theatre discourse.

As with so much that starts artistic life as 'alternative', Brecht's plays were soon absorbed into the mainstream of British theatre, and less than a decade later his work featured in the programmes of even the most conservative of repertory theatres and was hailed as 'classic' by the British national companies. Brecht had been appropriated. But the problem with appropriation, of course, is that its very purpose is to pull sharp teeth and nullify political bite. And Brecht's political message would be sanitised for a British establishment's flirtation with socialism.

As British political theatre was itself eroded by the Thatcherite 1980s, Brecht's status within British culture – never completely convincing – became unsure. In the 1990s, Britain blinks, uncertainly and with nostalgia, in a post-cold war, post-industrial and postmodern light. Not only are the political enemies no longer identifiable, authors, too, have gone largely the way of cultural relativism. Whether there will be a meaningful place and function again for Brecht in British theatre remains to be seen.

The first chapter of this book considers the context and development of Brecht's ideas and theories on theatre performance, focusing in particular on the differences and similarities between Brecht and the 'naturalistic' actor/director Constantin Stanislavski – 'measuring the distance' between them. It then considers Brecht's choice of actors and his methods of working with them, and how these illuminate his theoretical ideas on performance. Material is drawn from published interviews with and performance reviews of key performers such as Helene Weigel, Ekkehard Schall, Angelika Hurwicz and Charles Laughton.

In Chapter 2, the subject is the penetration of British theatre by Brecht material in the 1950s. The chapter explains how both early British productions of Brecht and new playwrights in Britain were influenced by the work of the Berliner Ensemble. Two tendencies are highlighted: that of some practitioners to imitate the outward appearances of Berliner productions, thus placing the emphasis on theatrical 'style' rather than process, and that of others to attempt to follow Brecht's precepts for the rehearsal process in a context ill-suited to them. Examples of British Brecht discussed here include George Devine's production of *The Good Woman of Setzuan*, Sam Wanamaker's *The Threepenny Opera* and William Gaskill's *The Caucasian Chalk Circle*. (Throughout this book all the play titles given reproduce exactly the translations used for the particular productions discussed.) The chapter also includes a brief assessment of the relationship between the work of Brecht and that of key British playwrights: John Arden, Arnold Wesker, John Osborne, Robert Bolt and Edward Bond.

Chapter 3 describes the ways in which the political upheavals of 1968 and the social and artistic developments in Britain made Brecht eminently suitable and accessible to radical theatre groups. It analyses the impact of politically committed theatre practitioners' attempts to take on all aspects of Brecht's dramatic theory, political philosophy and, as far as possible, theatre practice. Detailed analyses of Brecht productions by some key radical companies (e.g. Foco Novo, Belt and Braces Roadshow, Liverpool's Everyman Theatre, Manchester's Contact Theatre and Glasgow's Citizens Theatre) demonstrate how their commitment to the integration of political meaning and aesthetic expression contributed to the growing understanding and acceptance of Brecht's theatre in Britain.

This achievement is contrasted in Chapter 4 with the ways in which Brecht's plays were incorporated into the classical repertoire by the national companies – the Royal Shakespeare Company and the National Theatre – in the 1970s and 1980s. Here there is an assessment of the damaging impact on these Brecht productions of the companies' hierarchical structure and organisation, the all-too-frequently non-collaborative approaches to production, and the undue emphasis placed on performance style and set design, often in isolation from a genuine commitment to the intrinsic, socio-political meaning of the texts. The chapter centres on the productions of Brecht in the 1970s and 1980s for the Royal Shakespeare Company directed by Howard Davies, and on those at the National Theatre directed by John Dexter and Richard Eyre.

Chapter 5 presents three case studies, that is, detailed accounts based on access to rehearsals and on interviews with the relevant directors and performers, of three major British productions of Brecht plays in the early 1990s. The first case study is of the award-winning production of *The Good Person of Sichuan* at the National Theatre in 1989/90, directed by Deborah Warner, with Fiona Shaw as Shen Te/Shui Ta. The second is of the Citizens Theatre's 1990 production of *Mother Courage*, directed by Philip Prowse, with Glenda Jackson in the title role. And the third is of the National Theatre's *The Resistible Rise of Arturo Ui*, directed in 1991 by Di Trevis, with Antony Sher as Ui. The main focus of this chapter and its case-studies is the relationship in practice between Brechtian theory, and the aesthetics and the politics of the texts, in both the rehearsal process and the finished performances.

The book concludes with a chapter that considers Brecht in the light of recent, postmodernist and other developments in theatre. It draws on contemporary ideas on performance of significant practitioners such as Augusto Boal, Eugenio Barba, Howard Barker, David Hare and, in particular, Edward Bond, and assesses ways in which Brecht's plays may be performed now. Finally, it speculates about the future and the continuing need for Brechtian theatre. As the man himself said:

> We need a type of theatre which not only releases the feelings, insights and impulses possible within the particular historical field of human relations in which the action takes place, but employs and encourages those thoughts and feelings which help transform the field itself.
>
> (B on T, p.190)

1

BRECHT AND THE PERFORMER

Measuring the distance

Show that you are showing! Among all the varied attitudes
Which you show when showing how men play their parts
The attitude of showing must never be forgotten.
(Brecht, 1976, p.341)

Of all Brecht's ideas about theatre, his concept of the appropriate emotional distance between performer and role and between audience and performance is probably the best known. A full understanding of its implications, however, is not easy, and reaching it is not assisted by Brecht's determination to present his theatre as the opposite of 'naturalistic' theatre and, therefore, of the approach of its arch-exponent, Constantin Stanislavski. This simple 'binary opposition' is neither an accurate representation of Brecht's practice nor a helpful approach for those wishing to perform his plays in a sympathetic manner. Furthermore, this opposition has frequently created a barrier for British actors to understanding the performance demands of a Brecht text.

On the assumption that an examination of Brecht's dramatic theory and actual theatrical practice will provide clues, not only to a proper appreciation of his theatre, but to appropriate ways of tackling his dramatic work some four decades after his death, this chapter focuses on how his ideas on performance were influenced and developed, on his subsequent theorising and the formulation of his 'epic theatre' in opposition to the naturalistic form, and, finally, on how all this relates to his specific ways of working with performers in the Berliner Ensemble.

While it is neither feasible nor appropriate to make a detailed analysis of Brecht's personal, social and political background in this study, one cannot overlook its significance in the development of Brecht's practice both as a playwright and director in his early years in Germany, and during the fifteen years of exile that followed. Marks of the social and cultural upheavals of the 1920s and early 1930s, and the stresses and artistic limitations of his period of exile, are everywhere evident in Brecht's poems, plays and theoretical writings. In the 1920s it was as a poet that Brecht was best known in Germany, and it remains important to recognise the significance of his poetry within his work as a whole. John Willett puts it succinctly, as well as reminding us of the proper sequence of events: 'the poems led into and permeated the plays, from which the theories in turn sprang' (Brecht, 1976, p.vii). In the eponymous hero of Brecht's first play, *Baal*, one can recognise the bohemian and rebellious poet/playwright, who was in part Brecht himself; and it quickly becomes evident that Brecht's personal experience as poet, singer and visitor to the cabarets of Berlin had an important influence on his writing, and, as significantly here, on his ideas of what constituted an appropriate and meaningful theatrical experience.

PRACTITIONERS WHO INFLUENCED THE YOUNG BRECHT

Among the many cabaret performers that the young Brecht admired was the young singer and fellow playwright Frank Wedekind, of whom he wrote:

> I have never been so excited and so deeply moved by a singer. It was the man's enormous vitality, his energy, that enabled him, overcome by laughter and scorn, to bring off his indomitable song to humanity, and this also gave him his personal magic.
>
> (Völker, 1979, p.148)

This description appears to conflict, of course, with notions of emotional distancing that he appears often to value in his theoretical writings, but Brecht always responded positively to a performer's energy. Crucial here is the implication that Wedekind made contact with his audience; there is full awareness of the performer's and the audience's presence by both parties, and open acknowledgment by the audience of the performer's skills – important features, of course, of all cabaret. Thus this kind of performance is immediately different from that of 'naturalistic' theatre, where mutual acknowledgment is absent by definition. There is also the matter of personality; Brecht clearly revelled in the performer's exploitation of self. When Wedekind died in 1918, Brecht wrote a telling obituary for an Augsburg newspaper:

> He filled every corner with his personality. There he stood, ugly, brutal, dangerous, with close-cropped hair, his hands in his trouser pockets, and one felt that the devil himself couldn't shift him.
>
> (*B on T*, p.3)

Another of Brecht's favourite performers in the 1920s was Karl Valentin, a popular Munich slapstick comedian, whose act contained songs, monologues and comic mime, all of it expressing the naïve wisdom and proverbial pathos of the 'little man'. In *The Messingkauf Dialogues*, it is acknowledged by Brecht that he 'learnt most from . . . the clown Valentin, who performed in a beer-hall' (*MD*, p.69). And, as with Wedekind, Brecht in particular admired Valentin's energy and ability to provide social comment through comedy:

> This man, one of the most penetrating spiritual forces of the period, brings vividly before our eyes the complexity of the interconnections between imperturbability, stupidity and *joie-de-vivre*, it's enough to make horses laugh and take deep inner note.
>
> (Hayman, 1983, p.49)

Furthermore, in a programme note for the Munich Playhouse in 1922, Brecht praised Valentin for his 'virtually complete rejection of mimicry and cheap psychology', one of his many disparaging references to what he perceived as the characteristic features of 'naturalistic' acting.

In the same programme note, Brecht compared Valentin favourably with the film actor Charlie Chaplin. The latter had become the object of Brecht's admiration since the showing in Berlin, during 1921, of the film *The Face on the Bar-Room Floor*. On seeing this film, Brecht had recorded in his diary that it was 'the most profoundly moving thing I've ever seen in the cinema: utterly simple . . . it's unadulterated art . . . of a quite alarming objectivity and sadness' (Brecht, 1979, p.140). Again, Brecht draws attention to both the emotional quality of the performance for the audience, and a sense of objectivity, which the performance generated, thus registering early the idea that 'distance' and emotion were not mutually exclusive features of the actor's art. He later described more fully how he thought Charlie Chaplin's acting fulfilled a large part of the Brechtian ideal:

> If Chaplin were to play Napoleon, he wouldn't even look like him; he would show objectively and critically how Napoleon would behave in the various situations the author might put him in. . . . In my view the great comedians have always been the best character actors.
>
> (*B on T*, p.68)

And here, in his appreciation of the character portrayal of comic performers, Brecht gives us another vital clue to his definition of what constitutes a good actor. This is an issue to which we shall return. Chaplin, meanwhile, adds his weight to Brecht's view that the film comic's approach to acting was essentially non-naturalistic and instinctual by stating in his autobiography:

> I abhor dramatic schools that indulge in reflections and introspections to evoke the right emotion. The mere fact that a student must be mentally operated upon is sufficient proof that he should give up acting.
>
> (Chaplin, 1964, p.227)

Brecht's admiration for Chaplin led him to draw on ideas and scenes from the latter's films in his own writing. For example, he admitted that the sequence in *The Caucasian Chalk Circle* in which Grusha hesitates over and finally takes up the baby was influenced by Chaplin's film *The Kid*. In fact, of course, the cinema in general and silent-film acting in particular had a significant impact on Brecht while he was working in pre-war Berlin, the film capital of Europe at that time. The medium of film seemed to him to allow the spectator the opportunity for a greater degree of objectivity than was current in the theatre. As Frederic Ewen explains: 'Film, in Brecht's eyes, dispenses with "empathy and mimesis" – the human being is seen as "object" in his behavioural activity' (Ewen, 1970, p.191). There is, however, a problem here. While it is true that the camera allows the film director greater control over focus and selectivity in what the audience sees, thus rendering the film persona as object, film acting, nonetheless, in other ways encourages closer identification for the audience with on-screen characters than might be appropriate for Brecht's ideal kind of theatre.

However, the possibility of film as a significant socio-political tool within theatre was impressed upon Brecht in the late 1920s by his collaboration with the well-known German director Erwin Piscator. Brecht joined Piscator's 'dramaturgical collective' for one year (1927/8), as writer and director. It is likely that Brecht's lifelong and important commitment to working as part of a creative team dated from this time. Certainly his debt to Piscator was enormous. Many of his most fundamental theatrical concepts were either borrowed or adapted from those of Piscator. As Brecht admits in *The Messingkauf Dialogues*: 'The theatre's conversion to politics was Piscator's achievement, without which the Augsburger's [Brecht's] would hardly be conceivable' (*MD*, p.69). It was, as is well-known, Piscator who first coined the term 'epic theatre', which implied for him the inclusion of social and historical background within a production and led him to make use within the theatrical performance of film (in the form of newsreel clips and cartoons), and of statistics and diagrams, narrators, music and large choirs, and multiple settings. The intentions of Piscator's epic theatre were revolutionary, both politically and theatrically. But Brecht criticised Piscator's deployment of film on the grounds that he was using it as propaganda rather than as a contribution to rational argument. Thus, he thought, Piscator properly failed to challenge accepted political views of the audience or to create the genuine possibility of an objective assessment by it of issues raised. Brecht's concept of epic is most distinguished from Piscator's, perhaps, in its unwavering intention to encourage the spectator to view the stage events critically. On the other hand, Piscator's ideas on acting bore a close resemblance to those of Brecht:

We do not require a professional naturalness, but a performance so scientific and so clearly analyzed by the intellect that it reproduces

11

naturalness on a higher level and with a technique just as intentional and calculated as the architecture of the stage.

(Piscator, 1980, p.121)

In other words, nature (naturalness) becomes the object of analysis, not a technique for achieving convincingness. Because of the scenic and technical innovations of Piscator's theatre, it is not surprising that he was frequently criticised for not being an 'actor's director', but, rather, for caring more about the spectacle of performance. When he defended himself against those critical of the way he handled actors, by describing the rehearsals for his production of *Hoppla! Wir Leben!* (1927), the words could be mistaken for Brecht's own:

> Each actor had to be quite conscious of the fact that he represented a particular social class. I remember that a great deal of time was spent at rehearsals discussing the political significance of each role with the actor concerned. Only when he had mastered the spirit of the part in this way could the actor create his role.

(Piscator, 1980, p.214)

Piscator and Brecht also shared a common admiration for the work of the Soviet director Meyerhold, who visited Germany in 1930 with several productions by his own company. Brecht would later describe Meyerhold as the greatest Russian director, and the most cursory glance at the aims and style of the latter's work demonstrates easily why Brecht was an admirer. Meyerhold had begun his career as an actor with Stanislavski's company at the Moscow Art Theatre, but found naturalistic performance too restrictive a mode. He engaged his company, therefore, in a project to develop a non-naturalistic form of acting that was founded on a socio-political view of theatre, and he drew on, among other things, the broad, physical style of performance of the *commedia dell'arte*. Not surprisingly perhaps, Meyerhold, too, admired the work of Charlie Chaplin, and he recommended to his actors that, since they were attempting to exploit the full expressive power of movement, they should study Chaplin's 'so-called "momentary pauses for aim", that peculiarly static style of acting, the freeze' (Braun, 1969, p.321). Such clarity and concentration of physical expression, as Chaplin deployed in his film work, were fundamental to Meyerhold's form of acting, which he called 'bio-mechanics'. His idea was that each action should be preceded by its opposite impulse ('pre-acting'), thus creating a dialectical mode of performance. This, of course, is in some ways analagous to Brecht's idea of the dialectical alternative (which is discussed on p.16). Meyerhold was also fascinated by Chinese theatre, holding up the actor Mei Lan Fang as a model to his company. When invited to Moscow in 1935, Brecht had the opportunity to see this Chinese actor at work. He was immediately impressed by the simplicity and clarity of Fang's stage work and by the essential 'distance' that was built into his kind of performance. This resulted, of course, in Brecht's essay on the relationship between Fang's performances and Chinese acting in general and epic theatre. Entitled 'Alienation Effects in Chinese Acting' (1936), the essay reports that, in watching Mei Lan Fang, Brecht was struck not only by the distance maintained between the actor and the role and between the character and the audience, but by the fact that the actor portrayed intense emotions without 'becoming heated'. He concluded that this approach was more healthy than Western naturalistic performance, and, equally significantly, that it indicated 'a keen eye for what is socially important' (B on T, pp.93 and 95).

THE PERFORMER'S DISTANCE IN EPIC THEATRE

Brecht's much-discussed concept of 'distanced' acting, or 'demonstrating' a role, or 'alienation', has fuelled many heated debates as to what the actor is intended to do. Peter Hall, a major British director, has a simple view of the matter:

> Brecht's theories of alienation for actors only make sense in the heavily sentimental and excessive tradition of German acting before he began his work. . . . I study theories and I even utter them. Only theorize after you have created.[1]

The point about a sentimental tradition of German acting is well made. Certainly, Brecht was reacting strongly against a prevalent style, as he saw it. Equally, he himself did not create his work on the basis of theory but rather developed a theoretical base retrospectively to explain and analyse his practice.

Roland Barthes, in his article on *Mother Courage*, offers perhaps the clearest explanation of 'distance' and emotional commitment for both the director and actor of Brecht's plays:

> The verisimilitude of the acting has its origin in the objective meaning of the play, and not, as in 'naturalist' dramaturgy, in the truth inherent in the actor. That is why, in the long run, distancing is not a problem for the actor, but for the director. . . . Put differently, to distance is to cut the circuit between the actor and his own pathos, but it is also, and essentially, to re-establish a new circuit between the role and the argument; it is, for the actor, to give meaning to the play, and no longer to himself in the play.[2]

Without an appreciation of this kind of relocation of the actor's focus, 'naturalistic' performers of Brechtian roles may well find the work unsatisfying, and conclude that somehow Brecht is asking them to act 'less'.

13

(This will be discussed more fully in later chapters.) Brecht is at pains to stress, however, that epic acting should not be unnatural, nor, on the other hand, what is often called – somewhat vaguely – 'stylised'. On the contrary, he says, 'the success of the alienation effect is dependent on the lightness and naturalness of the whole procedure'.[3]

On the other hand, the Brechtian style of playing aims to 'remove from the incident or character all that is taken for granted, all that is well known and generally accepted and . . . generate surprise and curiosity about them' (Patterson, 1981a, p.160). In other words, the natural is distilled to the point where it again seems strange to us. In an effort to clarify further, Brecht famously, and perhaps unhelpfully, called this 'acting in quotation marks', developing the idea in his 'Street Scene Essay', by drawing an analogy between the epic actor and the witness to a street accident, who describes what took place. What Brecht sought was quite simply a 'cooler' mode of performance, not less acting but one based on a different premise. The crucial element, of course, is the reduction in the importance and contribution of empathy on the part of the audience, or between actor and role, performance and audience – a deliberate attempt to prevent the cathartic experience of emotional fulfilment.

This was not, however, entirely to eliminate emotional experience for either the actor or the spectator:

> Neither the public nor the actor must be stopped from taking part emotionally; the representation of emotions must not be hampered, nor must the actor's use of emotions be frustrated. Only one out of many possible sources of emotions needs to be left unused, or at least treated as a subsidiary source – empathy.
>
> (*MD*, p.57)

Furthermore, the Brechtian actor is actually intended to exploit the tension created between the cooler 'showing' of epic theatre and the warmer 'experience' of more naturalistic forms; it is, Brecht states, 'a matter of two mutually hostile processes which fuse in the actor's work' (*B on T*, p.278).

In order to assist this process, he builds such juxtapositions into the dramaturgy of his plays, so that much of the intended distancing is achieved by the text itself rather than by the work of the actor. An example of this would be Brecht's dialectical use of comedy and tragedy, and his expression of admiration for an analogous technique he perceived in the painting of Brueghel makes clear how he saw this working:

> Even though Brueghel manages to balance his contrasts, he never merges them into one another, nor does he practise the separation of comic and tragic; his tragedy contains a comic element and his comedy a tragic one.
>
> (*B on T*, p.157)

The intermingling of tragedy and comedy in Brecht's plays contributes, in large part, to their satirical stance. Criticism through fun (*Spass*) is a vital element in Brecht's notion of effective theatre, and the actor must remain aware, moment by moment, of the contrasts of comic and tragic in performance. The Brechtian performer's playing in this sense is aided not just by the text's wholesale changes in dramaturgical style but by, for example, the detailed distancing effects created through the use of unusual vocabulary and linguistic structures that are designed to catch the spectator's ear and make them take special note. Brecht's use of music is, of course, another such device. He considered that 'serious music' could not provide the opportunity for the expression of social attitude as well as feeling because 'it clings to lyricism and cultivates expression for its own sake' (*B on T*, p.87). So he turned for musical styles to incorporate into his plays to the contemporary music of his day, namely jazz and cabaret. This music Brecht regarded as 'gestic' in that it was able to convey or underscore the social relationships between characters. He expected the performer to contribute to this effect when performing a sung element in the text by developing a stance or attitude different to his/her performance norm:

> The actors
> Change into singers. They have a new attitude
> As they address themselves to the audience, still
> Characters in the play but now also undisguisedly
> Accomplices of the playwright.
> (Brecht, 1976, p.426)

And so, too, Brecht reminds us, the songs always contain significant parts of the dramatist's message.

Brecht's concept of gestic music is obviously the equivalent of his idea of gestic acting (for which he had admired Charlie Chaplin). Not only the single actor's body language but actors' physical groupings on stage are used to highlight the social relationships in the plays. As Brecht explains:

> The epic theatre uses the simplest possible groupings such as express the events' overall sense. No more 'casual', 'life-like', 'unforced' grouping; the stage no longer reflects the 'natural' disorder of things. The opposite of natural disorder is aimed at: natural order.
> (*B on T*, p.58)

These groupings should make each moment so explicit in its social meaning as to enable the audience to 'read' it without the assistance of the spoken text; in effect, as though one were interpreting the scene, perceiving the *social attitudes* between the characters, from behind glass or from a still culled from a film. This idea is, of course, summed up by the term *Gestus*. However, even Brecht acknowledged that this gestic performing is not the easy conveyance of single meanings or ideas:

15

These expressions of gest are usually highly complicated and contradictory, so they cannot be rendered by any single word and the actor
must take care that in giving his image the necessary emphasis he
does not lose anything but emphasizes the entire complex.

(*B on T*, p.198)

This sense of the basic contradiction within *Gestus* led Brecht to formulate
the idea of the actor's playing what he called 'the dialectical alternative', an
idea which, as indicated earlier, bears a close resemblance to Meyerhold's
'pre-acting'. Brecht's intention was to invite actors to explore, at moments
in the play of decision for their characters, possible alternative decisions to
that ultimately taken. This became known as the 'not . . . but' technique:
character A did *not* do this, *but* that. Furthermore, it was essential that the
actors should find ways of indicating to the audience what those alternative
possibilities for behaviour were. Brecht's view was that in some instances
it was sufficient simply to alert the actors to the alternatives in rehearsal;
this was then in their minds whenever the scene was performed. At the very
least such a technique would highlight for the audience the moment of
decision, and draw attention to the essentially contradictory nature of
human behaviour. More importantly, it forcibly enacts the potential for
making changes. Whether it is necessary or, indeed, feasible for an actor to
convey more at such moments, and how more is actually achieved, remain
issues to which we shall return later.

THE EPIC THEATRE AUDIENCE

We know, of course, that Brecht intended his spectators to remain largely
objective during a performance, but, as with his precepts for the actor, his
intentions and methods are often misunderstood. Unhelpful in Britain at
least has been the frequent mistranslation of *Verfremdungseffekt* as 'alienation', which has the unfortunate additional meaning in English of 'turning
against' (which, indeed, is what many British critics of Brecht did). Even
translating the term as 'distancing effect' promotes the notion that Brecht
meant the audience to be detached from their feelings during a performance. However, the real point which he strives to make clear is not that an
audience should not feel, but that he intends them to feel *different*
emotions from those being experienced by the characters on stage. If, for
example, a character expresses sadness, the audience might experience
anger at the social causes of that sadness. Perhaps it is, in the end, largely
a matter of degree. Sympathy is acceptable in Brecht's theatre but not
empathy. The former is legitimate because it stops short of total identification. When the spectators' feelings turn into empathy, the character as
object is lost, so the argument goes, and the audience is disempowered
from analysing clearly the social and political forces at work in the fictional
world of that character.

Many critics have taken issue with Brecht over an audience's very capacity to 'think through' the issues raised in a play during the performance, as opposed to some kind of 'recollection in tranquillity' after the play is over. Equally contentious, it seems, is Brecht's theory of sustaining distance between the actor and role and between the spectator and the performance by means of emphasising the story-telling and of narrating the past. Demetz argues that this idea

> disregards the psychology of the audience and the pragmatic relationship of stage to spectator. Brecht cannot alter the fact that his epic theater creates the past event *here* and *now*. The artful immediacy of presentation endangers the entire technology of pastness.
>
> (Demetz, 1962, p.4)

But here Demetz ignores the other aspect of Brecht's idea of epic performance, which is a shared acknowledgment and enjoyment of the performance itself by both the actor and the audience. Thus the spectator can say: 'The actor knows that I know he knows I am watching him tell me a story.' This is vastly different from the 'he knows that I know he is pretending I am not watching him experience an event' of naturalistic theatre.

Brecht himself, even in the late stages of his career, was still trying to find an effective formulation of the immediacy of performance, on the one hand, and the achieving of an objective understanding on the part of the spectator on the other. Manfred Wekwerth, a director with the Berliner Ensemble, reports that in 1956 (the year of his death) Brecht expressed the view that 'narrating a story on the stage was really at the same time a "dialecticizing" of the events' (*B on T*, p.282). Brecht by then, according to Wekwerth, normally referred to his form of theatre as 'dialectical' rather than epic, and in the last collection of his theoretical writings, published posthumously under the title 'Dialectics in the Theatre', we read:

> If we now discard the concept of EPIC THEATRE, we are not discarding that progress towards conscious experience which it still makes possible. It is just that the concept is too slight and too vague for the kind of theatre intended; it needs exacter definition and must achieve more. Besides, it was too inflexibly opposed to the concept of the dramatic, often just taking it naïvely for granted, roughly in the sense that 'of course' it always embraces incidents that take place directly with all or most of the hall-marks of immediacy.
>
> (*B on T*, p.276)

It is to this 'inflexible opposition' to dramatic (Brecht's term for 'naturalistic') theatre that we now turn, in an attempt to measure the distance between Brecht and Stanislavski. This is, of course, a map of familiar territory, but a quick summary and lay-out of the key areas of opposition may help us to find greater clarification for the British actor of the significant differences (and similarities) between these two great practitioners and thus to sharpen perceptions of Brecht's concepts of performance.

BRECHT AND STANISLAVSKI

In 1930, when writing notes to accompany his opera *The Rise and Fall of the City Mahagonny*, Brecht set out a table showing 'certain changes of emphasis as between the dramatic [naturalistic] and the epic theatre' (*B on T*, p.37). This list serves to highlight his idea that by drawing spectators emotionally into the performance, naturalistic theatre inhibits their ability to think during the performance and to act subsequently upon the issues explored. For the actor, Brecht sets out the ways in which the character in naturalistic theatre is presented as a complete, fully conceived and unalterable human being, with inevitable behaviour and an inexorable fate. In epic theatre, on the other hand, man is shown as being in the process of formation and susceptible to change.

Of course, Brecht's most sustained attack on naturalistic theatre in general, and on Stanislavski in particular, is contained in *The Messingkauf Dialogues*, which he worked on between 1939 and 1942, before abandoning them. Here, for example, he pours scorn on Stanislavski's efforts to stimulate the actor into a 'truthful' performance through the use of improvisation:

> There's an account of some well-known exercises for actors, designed to encourage natural acting, which includes the following drill: the actor places a cap on the floor and behaves as if it were a rat. This is supposed to teach him the art of inspiring belief.
>
> (*MD*, p.4)

Obviously it was easy for Brecht to deride rehearsal techniques taken out of context. He himself recognised that one of the main reasons for the differences of approach between himself and Stanislavski was that their interest in the performance came from contrasting perspectives: 'Stanislavski when directing is first of all an actor. When I direct I am first of all a playwright'.[4] He also acknowledged that Stanislavski's 'System' of acting was an improvement on what had gone before, simply because it was a system. However, his fundamental criticism of Stanislavski and, therefore, of the Moscow Art Theatre, rested on his perception that their work lacked a political function. The Russian director appeared to abhor such a function, writing in his autobiography, *My Life in Art*: 'the very least utilitarian purpose or tendency brought into the realm of pure art, kills art instantly' (Stanislavski, 1924, p.390). Later, he expressed the subtly different view that any political messages in the performance had to be gleaned by audiences without the overt help of the actor:

For a social and political play to have an effect on the audience, isn't the
secret for the actor to think as little as possible of the social and political
intentions of the play, so as to be perfectly sincere and perfectly honest?

(Benedetti, 1982, p.14)

Clear differences, then, emerge for the actor between Stanislavskian and
Brechtian precepts in two very fundamental aspects of performance: the
relationship between the actor and the role, and between the actor and the
audience.

THE ACTOR AND THE ROLE

In the actor/role dynamic, the key difference in the two theories lies
between the Stanislavskian 'embodiment' of the character and the Brechtian
'demonstration' of it. To some extent this comes down to a contrast
between what the character *is* and what the character *does*. Furthermore,
the Brechtian actor creates the role by means of 'montage' rather than
through the linear, logical development of psychological continuity
followed by his Stanislavskian counterpart. The latter is urged to find and
express a 'through line' for his/her role that may be summed up in a
sentence, that conveys the main motivating force that drives the character
through the play. Thus all his/her actions are capable of being viewed as
logical and coherent. Brecht, on the other hand, exhorted actors to make
an 'inventory' of the role and thereby to emphasize the contradictions, the
lack of logic and consistency, in the character's behaviour.

Naturally, these differences of approach also had an impact on the
contrasting ways in which the actor would construct the actual performance of
his/her role throughout the play. Brecht wanted the actor to play each scene
for its own sake (rather than building one scene on the previous one). Indeed,
his own episodic dramaturgy helped to ensure that this mode of playing was
necessarily adopted. Stanislavski, on the other hand, made every effort in
rehearsal to link one scene to the next, and where a jump in time or place
occurred, the Moscow Art Theatre actors would improvise connecting scenes
and events in order to create what Stanislavski called 'the unbroken line of life'.
This last technique undoubtedly reinforces what most actors instinctively want
to achieve: continuous engagement with their character and the placing of that
character in a kind of time-flow. Much less familiar and comfortable for such
an actor is Brecht's emphasis on the character's ongoing contribution to the
narrative, rather than the consistent development and presentation to the
audience of a psychologically conceived 'human being'.

A similar divergence of approach occurs in relation to the actor's
identifying and conveying the meaning that lies underneath the words of
the text. Stanislavski explored with his actors the 'sub-text' of the lines, the
characters' true feelings, which may often not be expressed overtly by the
words, and may, indeed, be denied by them. To Brecht, the meaning

beneath the text is one of social attitudes rather than of feelings, and the expression will come about through the use of *Gestus*. Thus, the 'truth' of the actor's performance of the role is based, for Stanislavski, on a *psychological* understanding of character, whereas for Brecht it draws on a *sociological* one. As Brecht himself saw, the 'success' of the first is correctable only from 'inside', but that of the second from 'outside' (by reference to external reality):

> When the actor comes to examine the truth of this [Brechtian] performance – a necessary operation, which gives Stanislavski a lot of trouble – he is not merely thrown back on his natural sensibility. He can always be corrected by reference to reality. Does an angry man really speak like that? Does a guilty man sit like that? He can be corrected, that is, from without, by other people.
>
> (*B on T*, p.33)

This external checking by the Brechtian actor also helps prevent him/her from attempting to transform him/herself into the character (and thus losing sight of the significance of the performance), an idea for which Brecht strongly criticised the Russian director. But Stanislavski was careful to point out at various times in his books that, while attempting to achieve inner, psychological truth for and emotional involvement in the character, the actor must not 'lose' him/herself entirely in the part. Perceiving that it is of both artistic and practical value to maintain a kind of dual consciousness, Stanislavski quoted one of his favourite actors, Tommaso Salvini, on this theme:

> An actor lives, weeps, and laughs on the stage, and all the while he is watching his own tears and smiles. It is this double function, this balance between life and acting that makes his art.
>
> (Stanislavski, 1937, p.267)

This is obvious enough; as any actor knows, there has to be a part of the mind available during performance to cope with the unexpected, such as a missing prop.

However, Stanislavski considered it fundamental that the actor find and sustain the appropriate emotions throughout a scene. He/she could do this by drawing, for example, on personal, actual experiences via the technique of 'Emotion Memory', a favourite occupation of the American 'Method' actor. In contrast, Brecht required the actor not only to step back from total emotional involvement during performance but to remain keenly analytical of the situation:

> When your son is shot you feel it, ummph, directly in the belly, like Weigel in *Mother Courage*, but the actress is not feeling it at that moment; she is thinking.
>
> (Marowitz *et al.*, 1965, p.201)

20

At that moment when Courage sees her dead son, Weigel is repeating that part of the story, she is narrating a past event, not reliving the experience. Nonetheless, Brecht was aware that too much thinking could adversely affect his kind of theatre, that it could become too detached from genuine feeling and betray a lack of humanity:

> Our mistakes are different from those of other theatres. Their actors are liable to display too much spurious temperament; ours often show too little of the real thing. Aiming to avoid artificial heat, we fall short in natural warmth. We make no attempt to share the emotions of the characters we portray, but these emotions must none the less be fully and movingly represented.
>
> (*B on T*, p.248)

The key phrase here is 'spurious temperament'; the Brechtian actor is invited to be more selective in the use of emotion and constantly to turn down the volume. But that, ironically, might also be advice that Stanislavski would give in order for an actor to avoid the false and the cheap.

THE ACTOR AND THE AUDIENCE

Looking now at the second main difference between the theorist–practitioners' precepts for the actor, that is, the relationship between the performer and the spectator, it is obvious that the context for the actor's performance, including not only the immediate stage environment, but the whole concept of the theatrical art, has a crucial effect on that relationship. Stanislavski (with his partner Danchenko) had, in setting up the Moscow Art Theatre, been highly critical of the lax, uncreative atmosphere of many Russian theatres at the end of the nineteenth century. His company, therefore, intended to encourage a kind of audience behaviour that would contribute to the aesthetic, concentrated and 'special' occasions they wanted theatre performances to be. Stanislavski reveals his own, 'holy' view of theatre when writing about the problems of handling the new, post-revolutionary Soviet audiences of 1917:

> We were forced to begin at the very beginning to teach this new spectator how to sit quietly, how not to talk, how to come into the theatre at the proper time, not to smoke, not to eat nuts in public, not to bring food into the theatre and eat it there, to dress in his best so as to fit more into the atmosphere of beauty that was worshipped in the theatre.
>
> (Stanislavski, 1924, p.554)

Interestingly, and sadly, this chimes to some extent with attitudes to audiences in late twentieth-century British theatre. Programmes of the Royal Shakespeare Company exhort patrons not to eat sweets or make other noises that might disturb the performances. (So much for Shake-speare's own 'nut-cracking' audiences.) Brecht set his face against such bourgeois notions. Famously, he drew on the other hand an analogy between his own epic theatre and a sporting event, at which spectators were not only encouraged to smoke but to express their opinions of the skills on display. Thus a Brechtian performance would be enjoyed and judged like a game of football:

> The rotten state of our theatre audiences stems from the fact that neither stage nor audience has any idea of what is supposed to happen. In sports arenas people know, when they buy their tickets, exactly what is going to happen, and it is precisely this that happens when they are sitting in their seats; in other words, trained people with the keenest sense of their responsibility, display their particular skills in the manner best suited to them, but in such a way that one is forced to believe they do it mainly for their own enjoyment.
>
> (Völker, 1979, p.89)

Brecht's notion of sporting theatre also acknowledges the audience as a participant, an *educated* participant, in the event. More than that, the spectator's presence is carefully exploited in that the actors in a Brecht performance frequently address the audience directly: and so they become implicated. In naturalistic theatre, of course, the actor pretends the audience is not there, and spectators become privileged *voyeurs* who peep through the 'fourth wall' at the self-sustaining 'life' on stage. Stanislavski writes in *An Actor Prepares* about the problem for the actor of that gaping fourth wall, the black hole beyond which the audience sits, full of a destructive potential to distract the performer. He consequently created a number of exercises in his 'System' to help actors maintain their onstage concentration and to create the necessary 'public solitude': 'During a performance, before an audience of thousands, you can always enclose yourself in this circle [of attention] like a snail in its shell!' (Stanislavski, 1937, p.82). By contrast, Brecht wanted his actors to come out of their shells and make contact with the spectators. He especially tried to ensure that they avoided treating the audience as 'a single emotional lump' by asking them

> to think of their audience as a divided group of friends and enemies, rich and poor, and to divide their audience accordingly by addressing them-selves to one part of the audience now, to another part the next moment.
>
> (Marowitz et al., 1965, p.148)

Kenneth Tynan, the British theatre critic, developed this idea further, noting that the actor in a Brecht play was inclined to treat the spectator as an equal, 'in a sort of dialectic, rather than as people to be sweetened or flattered'.[5] The American actor/director Joseph Chaikin agreed and saw the implications of this for the actor's focus:

The actor's attention, which might otherwise be on the character, is here connected to the spectator. Moment to moment, the play is between actor and audience, as the actor's attitude changes about the character and his circumstances . . . yet the actor should not – and does not have to – wink, woo or pander to the audience: there is a tacit understanding.[6]

In all of these ways, Stanislavski and Brecht were and are ideologically and practically apart. Nevertheless, their positions can be seen to converge.

DECREASING THE DISTANCE BETWEEN BRECHT AND STANISLAVSKI

Late in his career, Stanislavski came to hold a different view of the relationship between art and politics from that quoted earlier. He wrote that he now saw politics as having

an integral part of our lives now. This means that the director's horizon includes the government's structure, the problems of our society. It means that we, the directors of the theatre, have much more responsibility and must develop a broader way of thinking.

(Gorchakov, 1968, p.16)

Perhaps a significant indication of his revised view lies behind his admiration for his erstwhile colleague Meyerhold. Of a production by the latter in 1925, Stanislavski said: 'Meyerhold has accomplished what I myself was dreaming of' (Braun, 1969, p.196); and then, shortly before he died in 1938, he described Meyerhold as 'my sole heir in the theatre here or anywhere else' (Braun, 1969, p.251). Stanislavski's lately expressed admiration of Meyerhold might, however, be less an embracing of political theatre than a recognition of a more 'theatrical', less realistic style of production.

While sharing an admiration for Meyerhold, Brecht and Stanislavski came, in fact, to occupy much common ground in their practice. In the last five years of his life (1933–8), Stanislavski decided that in some respects his System's approach of working from the actor's inner feelings to outward expression was not necessarily the best or only way. He recognised that the detailed analysis of role and text, the collection of a mass of information on the character to be played, personal relationships within the text, and social background of the action and so on, might be overwhelming for an actor in the early stages of rehearsal, on both an intellectual and emotional level. He therefore devised a new and radical approach, known as the Method of Physical Actions (or, more accurately, the Method of Analysis through Physical Actions). (Interestingly, this last development in the 'System' is often overlooked by British drama schools offering 'Stanislavski' training.)

This method set the actor to begin the rehearsal process by building up a sequence of the most important physical actions as required by the text, and thus create a physical structure or score for the whole play. The effect of this, probably unintentional, was to move the emphasis in the early rehearsal work from character towards narrative. Inseparable from this new emphasis on the sequence of physical actions is a foregrounded awareness of rhythm and, of course, the perception that body rhythms are able in themselves to trigger emotions related to them, rather than the recall of emotion finding expression in the natural (spontaneous) action. Thus Stanislavski was now requiring his actors to reverse the original idea of the System. That is, via the Method of Physical Actions they were now working from the outward expression towards the inner feeling. In just the same way, Charlie Chaplin explains in his autobiography how he analysed and experimented with ways of moving to gain access to a particular character. For example, he describes making use of a drunken London cab-driver's walk: 'I followed him and observed him. The fellow interested me, and he showed me the way to that character which I finally found within myself' (Chaplin, 1964, p.144).

Brecht recognised that this modification in Stanislavski's thinking moved the Russian director's practice closer to his own, and he went so far as to claim: 'Stanislavski's "method of physical actions" is most likely his greatest contribution to a new theatre'.[7] On another occasion (in *Theaterarbeit*, 1952) he made a list entitled: 'Some of the Things that can be learnt from Stanislavski'. He includes here the feeling for a play's poetry, the sense of responsibility to society (seeing the actor's art as having social significance), the importance of ensemble playing and of truthfulness, the need for unity of style and the importance of the further development of the theatre as an art form (*B on T*, p.236). Since this article of Brecht's was occasioned by a visit made to Moscow, it is often regarded as an insincere and conciliatory gesture towards a director who was still very much in Soviet favour. Nonetheless, all this evidence of 'proximity' between Brecht and Stanislavski gives weight to the argument that in many aspects of their practice (as opposed to artistic purpose and political intentions) they were not at the opposite ends of a theatrical gamut. Rather, it is more helpful to see that Brecht works over some of the same ground as Stanislavski and then takes the ideas much further, and in his own particular direction.

Such an idea is supported by Brecht's essay called 'Building a Character', a title borrowed with, no doubt, an ironic purpose from Stanislavski's famous book of the same name. In this essay Brecht outlines three phases of the actor's work: in the first phase the actor loses him/herself in the character; in the second he/she searches for the subjective truth of the character; and in the third he/she attempts to see the character from the outside. The Stanislavskian actor also works through the first two of these phases. However, though Stanislavski stressed that the actor must also be able to observe the character he/she plays from the outside, the actor was not required to make this observation evident to the audience, except in a comic or satirical play. Of course, most of Brecht's plays are intended to be satirical.

A major actor of the Berliner Ensemble, Angelika Hurwicz, informed Brecht that on reading Stanislavski's first book, *An Actor Prepares*, she discovered 'parts which appeared quite important, which I have made use of for years now'.[8] And she went on (in an interview for the book *Brecht As They Knew Him*) to support the idea that these two great directors were not really in opposition in a practical sense, and that (despite *The Messing-kauf Dialogues*) Brecht was not 'hostile to drama exercises aimed at ensuring the truth to life and the warmth of the presentation of the role; in fact, he regards them as a pre-requisite' (Witt, 1975, p.132). Hurwicz pointed out, too, that Brecht began his rehearsal of the play-text by determining with the actor the super-objective or through-line for the character, and that he, in effect, required the actor to go a stage further, to move beyond the realistic portrayal that Stanislavski sought, and to add a socio-critical dimension to the psychological reality of that character. She was aware, though, of the problems caused by the characteristic mis-understandings of Brecht's theoretical writings with regard to the actor's emotional commitment, and gave a useful perspective on the main issue of the relationship between the actor and the character:

> All that he [Brecht] said in the *Small Organon* against the possession of the actor by his role, which has caused so much confusion and indignation, is aimed against actors who forget about their super-task, who only see their own parts, and who offend against the content of the play as a whole, even when they give their parts interesting details and great acting ability.
>
> (Witt, 1975, p.133)

The decreased distance in approaches to performance between himself and Stanislavski became apparent to Brecht when he visited the Soviet Union in 1955. He saw a production at the Moscow Art Theatre, which, although Stanislavski had died in 1938, was still operating according to his System. Brecht was, it is said, astonished by the degree of 'alienation' which he saw in the performance. As he left the theatre he is reputed to have remarked:

> Now I shall have to defend Stanislavski from his supporters. . . . Now I shall have to say about him what people say about me – that the practice contradicts the theory.
>
> (Witt, 1975, p.213)

And it is to this possible contradiction of theory by Brecht's practice that we now turn.

· CHOOSING HIS ACTORS

The reasons for Brecht's early admiration of Wedekind, Valentin and Chaplin underlie his choices of actors with whom he worked throughout his career. Writing in the *Left Review* in 1936, Brecht described his early attempts of the 1920s to create his own theatre company by 'the training of a whole generation of young actors, for the new style of acting, the epic style' (*B on T*, p.79). These actors included Helene Weigel, Lotte Lenya, Oskar Homolka, Ernst Busch and Peter Lorre. The individual and collective performance skills, physical and emotional qualities and temperaments of these actors give further vital clues to the necessary skills and talents of the Brechtian performer.

Brecht first worked with the Hungarian-born Peter Lorre in 1929 on a production in Berlin of Marieluise Fleisser's *The Pioneers of Ingolstadt*. One day the theatre manager, Aufricht, 'found a small actor waiting impatiently for an interview. He told the man that he looked like a tadpole, but he could go down to the stage and ask Brecht to cast him as the village idiot' (Hayman, 1983, p.138). Lorre was given the part of the village idiot and Brecht soon afterwards advised Aufricht to offer him a three-year contract. As a small, unprepossessing 'tadpole' of a man (not physically unlike Chaplin), Lorre was good casting for his most successful pre-war Brechtian role, that of Galy Gay in *Man is Man*. In this play the character of Gay is increasingly 'dehumanised' by the group of soldiers who force him to change his identity. The critic Ihering remarked on Lorre's mixed style of performance in this role, describing him as going 'from personality to mask, from an identifying acting technique to reporting, from the dynamic to the static' (Hayman, 1983, p.156). Brecht had directed the actor to speak in a broken and disjointed manner in order to convey the contradictions within the character's actions and attitudes, and while Lorre's delivery seems to have puzzled some critics and audience members, Brecht himself commented: 'This way of acting was perfectly right from the new point of view, exemplary even' (*B on T*, p.53). On the other hand, Lorre's instinctive way of performing was more realistic, more emotional, a style that led to his success in the cinema. It was said, for example, that in his playing of the central role in Fritz Lang's film *M* 'in appearance, voice and expression, Lorre captured the inner torment of the perverted killer' (Ott, 1979, p.156). Appropriately, when Brecht was in exile in the United States (at the same time as Lorre), he wrote a film adaptation of *Macbeth* for him, but the project did not come to fruition.

Oskar Homolka, in contrast to Lorre, was 'a burly, ambitious, temperamental Viennese' (Hayman, 1983, p.103) and he always seems to have exploited his strong physical presence on stage. During his first production with Brecht in 1924, when he played Mortimer in *Edward II*, Homolka displeased his director by getting drunk during the opening performance, and, as a consequence, gesticulating too much. However, Brecht's admiration for the actor's broad style of playing overcame this inauspicious start and they subsequently co-directed *Baal*, in which Homolka played the lead. Here, he looked like an enlarged version of Chaplin, in a suit with trousers that were too short and a battered round hat. Later, when in exile, Brecht was to create both the roles of Azdak in *The Caucasian Chalk Circle* and of Galileo with Homolka in mind. He subsequently wondered (in a letter to Piscator) about asking him to consider playing Arturo Ui (Brecht, 1990, p.341).

It was, however, another of those early trainees, Ernst Busch, who was to play both Azdak and Galileo (in the Berliner productions). Like Homolka, Busch was a large actor, both physically and in terms of stage presence. Initially his main skills were as a singer and cabaret-performer, which made him good casting for his role as the Morität-Singer in *The Threepenny Opera* (in 1928). Accounts of Busch's acting suggest that one of his strengths was an ability to draw on and exploit his working-class background. Consequently, when he appeared in the Berliner revival of *The Mother* (1951), Brecht was able to describe his performance of Semion Lapkin as 'the first great characterization on the German stage of a class-conscious proletarian' (Hayman, 1983, p.353). Another possible role for Busch being considered at the time was Marcius in *Coriolanus*. Fellow director Peter Palitzsch had suggested that Busch, 'the great people's actor who is a fighter himself . . . won't make the hero too likeable' (*B on T*, p.263). Brecht had responded that Busch would find the balance between being liked and disliked. (Unfortunately, Brecht did not have the opportunity to confirm this as the Berliner production of *Coriolanus* was not mounted until after his death.) The relevance of Busch's temperament, personal background and experience was also vital in his portrayal of Azdak. Brecht praised the characterisation thus:

> This Azdak is the product of Busch's whole life, including his childhood in proletarian Hamburg, his struggles in the Weimar Republic and in the Spanish Civil War, and his bitter experiences after 1945.
>
> (Hayman, 1983, p.374)

All of that suggests in part the kind of drawing on personal experience that Stanislavski advocated. But there is, too, the political *cachet*, sensed by Brecht, of Busch's own, authentic social background. For an English critic, the effect was less successful. John Willett suggests that Busch was miscast as Azdak, precisely insofar as the actor's exploitation of himself was unhelpful to the role:

> Busch does not seem to fit in the Brechtian theatre at all: he is far too conscious of his audience and inclined to play up his own personality. An admirable Narrator, he upset the whole play as soon as he took up the part of Azdak.
>
> (Willett, 1984, p.231)

27

Nevertheless, Willett here undervalues the vital talent in a Brechtian actor of playing consciously to the audience. Brecht himself not only liked Busch's acting, but continued to promote his actors' exploitation of their personalities in their performance.

Although Willett did not like Busch's Azdak, he did admire his portrayal of Galileo, which, 'given that he is so far from any conceivable academic or intellectual type [was] surprisingly good' (Willett, 1984, p.233). Here, Willett forgets the Brechtian precept of casting against type:

> Parts are allotted wrongly and thoughtlessly. As if all cooks were fat, all peasants phlegmatic, all statesmen stately. As if all who love and are loved were beautiful. As if all good speakers had a fine voice. . . . It is pure folly to allot parts according to physical characteristics.
>
> (*MD*, p.87)

Busch may not, as Willett said, have been the obvious casting for an academic, but his preparation for the role of Galileo included thorough research into history, physics and astronomy, subjects on which Brecht encouraged the actor to 'lecture' the company during rehearsals. This serves to emphasise, of course, that the character of Galileo, as conceived by Brecht, is in no sense a caricature, despite his obvious sensual enjoyment of eating and drinking. Rehearsals of *Galileo* at the Berliner were suspended in April 1956, because of Brecht's illness, and he did not complete his direction of the production.

The Galileo role was originally played by Charles Laughton, whom Brecht had met in America. He, like Busch, was a physically large actor, so much so that Brecht wrote a poem entitled *Laughton's Belly*:

> Here it was: not unexpected, but not usual either
> And built of foods which he
> At his leisure had selected, for his entertainment –
> And to a good plan, excellently carried out
>
> (Brecht, 1976, p.393)

Both Laughton's size and his obvious love of food made him appropriate casting for Galileo. Other well-known features of his performance style, especially its strongly, even excessively emotional basis, for instance, make him seem an unlikely candidate for Brechtian theatre. However, Brecht saw in Laughton an ability to act truthfully and without sentimentality. The actor himself had a simple and direct attitude to his profession. Once, when asked why he acted, Laughton replied: 'Because people don't know what they're like and I think I can show them' (*B on T*, p.164). Brecht's view of the proper outcome of acting was similar to that, if expressed in a more complex way:

> It is less a matter of the artist's temperament than of the notions of reality which he has and communicates, less a matter of his vitality

than of the observations which underlie his portraits and can be derived from them.[9]

Laughton admired Brecht's talent, too, and in 1943 he agreed to help him prepare his English translation of *The Life of Galileo* (the German text having been completed in 1938). Laughton spoke no German and Brecht's English was uncertain, but they established an immediate and effective rapport. With the aid of dictionaries, they acted out and demonstrated the text for each other until the meaning satisfied both. Subsequent translators of Brecht would do well to take note of his comments on this process:

> This system of performance-and-repetition had one immense advantage in that psychological discussions were almost entirely avoided. Even the most fundamental gests, such as Galileo's way of observing, or his craze for pleasure, were established in three dimensions by actual performance. . . . We were forced to do what better equipped translators should do, too: translate gests. For language is theatrical in so far as it primarily expresses the mutual attitude of the speakers.
>
> (Hayman, 1969, p.54)

Laughton's biographer claims that, through his contribution both to the translation and in performance, the actor was very much responsible for making the character of Galileo more human, 'making him touchingly and harshly a real man instead of a saintly martyr' (Higham, 1976, p.140). And Brecht acknowledged that Laughton helped to clarify the role and 'to show things as they really are' and that 'despite all his indifference (indeed timidity) in political matters he suggested and even demanded that not a few of the play's points should be made sharper'.[10] Laughton was also concerned to make the production both comic and narratively clear. Brecht reports:

> Laughton became set on the idea of getting a good draughtsman to produce entertaining sketches in the manner of Caspar Neher, to expose the anatomy of the action. 'Before you amuse others you have to amuse yourself', he said.
>
> (*B on T*, p.166)

The actor's determination to highlight the narrative led him to work with the younger cast members of *Galileo*, teaching them the play's structure and how to play it in order to make it clear for an audience. Brecht was impressed, however, that Laughton avoided imposing his own acting style on the other actors. Yet, in spite of all this apparently detailed, Brechtian work in rehearsal, Laughton claimed that he did not understand what Brecht was talking about and in the end he 'just went on the stage and acted'.[11] Nonetheless, Laughton was so concerned about the possible effects of the prevailing heatwave at the time of the production, that he proposed, apparently in all seriousness, that trucks filled with ice should be parked by the walls of the theatre 'so that the audience can think' (Hayman, 1983, p.380).

Brecht summed up the extraordinary experience of working with Laughton in an essay, 'Building Up a Part: Laughton's Galileo', and he placed the actor's achievement in the broader context of theatre history:

> We seem to have lost any understanding and appreciation of what we may call a *theatrical conception*: what Garrick did, when as Hamlet, he met his father's ghost; Sorel, when as Phèdre she knew that she was going to die; Bassermann, when as Philip he listened to Posa. It is a question of inventiveness. The spectator could isolate and detach such theatrical conceptions, but they combined to form a single rich texture. Odd insights into men's nature, glimpses of their particular way of living together, were brought about by the ingenious contrivance of the actors.
>
> (*B on T*, p.163)

This emphasis on theatricality and inventiveness goes some way to explaining why Brecht admired such 'larger-than-life' performers like Laughton, like Busch, and like many other Brechtian actors: he enjoyed their exploitation of their performance skills, their imagination, their obvious enjoyment of handling an audience, and their ability to be bold and take theatrical risks. These elements of Brecht's theatre seem diametrically opposed to the grey, heavy and dour image that has so often characterised others', and frequently British, perceptions of it.

Brecht's choice of female performers tells a similar story. One early Brechtian actress was Therese Giehse, who appeared in her first Brecht role, Mrs Peachum, in the 1929 production of *The Threepenny Opera* in Zurich. She also subsequently appeared in *Herr Puntila and His Servant Matti* (in which The Plum Song was specially written for her), and *The Good Person of Setzuan*, and she played Mother Courage in the first production in Zurich in 1941. In this last role, Giehse achieved great success. When Brecht worked with her on the revival for Munich in 1950, he wrote to his collaborator, Elisabeth Hauptmann: 'Rehearsals are going well. Giehse is wonderful, a tough business woman' (Brecht, 1990, p.496). However, Ronald Hayman suggests, in his biography of Brecht, that the author/director might have felt in retrospect that her performance was rather too tragic, noting that it had given 'the bourgeois press occasion to talk about a Niobe tragedy and about the moving endurance of the female animal' (Esslin, 1959, p.204). After that production he gave Mother Courage a new hard line at the end of the play – 'I must get back into business' – to undercut any audience empathy with the character in the final moments.

Giehse's comment on actors, that 'they must have souls and imagination, above all imagination' (Drews, 1965, p.11), appears to conflict with the view of many critics that her own acting style was gritty and unsentimental, and that her strength in performance was the truthful playing of characters rooted in reality. She returned to playing Brecht late in her career, taking the lead in a revival of *The Mother*, directed by Peter Stein in 1970. Michael Patterson relates the realism of her acting technique to that of a Stanislavskian actor:

> To the part of Wlassowa Giehse brought a reticence of style and an attention to detail that would have been the pride of a Stanislavskian actress. But the function of accurately observed detail was here motivated by quite different considerations from those of the naturalistic performer. The latter would use detail to render the character more *realistic*, to make the illusion more credible; Giehse used it to make Wlassowa more *real*, not creating the illusion of being the character but showing how a mother in Wlassowa's situation would really behave.
>
> (Patterson, 1981b, p.50)

The best-known female Brechtian performer is, of course, Helene Weigel, who not only played many major Brecht roles but was also in charge of the Berliner Ensemble for many years. Weigel, a Communist Jewess, had been educated at a school run by a militant suffragette, who was at pains to prove that girls could reach the same intellectual level as boys. Thus, Weigel's renowned 'toughness' of character, her willingness to take on challenges, was built on an early foundation. She began her professional theatre career in Frankfurt in 1919 and developed a relationship with Brecht in the early 1920s. She bore him a son in 1924, and they were married in 1928.

Weigel's first Brecht role was Widow Begbick in the première of *Man is Man* (1926). She soon came to exemplify for Brecht the power of unsentimental acting. He praised, for example, the way she announced the death of Jocasta in *Oedipus Rex*, in which she appeared in 1929. He wrote that she called out:

> 'dead, dead' in a wholly unemotional and penetrating voice . . . without any sorrow, but so firmly and definitely that the bare fact of her mistress' death carried more weight at that precise moment than could have been generated by any grief of her own.
>
> (*B on T*, p.28)

Weigel's presentation of the role of Vlassova in *The Mother* (1932) helped to confirm Brecht's growing conviction that the actor should 'demonstrate' character (rather than embody it) in order to create 'distance' and objectivity in the audience. He describes the first scene of *The Mother* and the way in which Weigel delivered her opening lines:

> she spoke the sentences as though they were in the third person; and so she not only refrained from pretending in fact to be or to claim to

be Vlassova (the Mother), and in fact to be speaking those sentences, but actually prevented the spectator from transferring himself to a particular room, as habit and indifference might demand, and imagining himself to be the invisible eye-witness and eavesdropper of a unique, intimate occasion. Instead what she did was to introduce the spectator to the person whom he would be watching acting and being acted upon for some hours.

(B on T, p.58)

A reviewer of that performance (Ihering) remarked that this detached, unsentimental form of theatre really brought out Weigel's best abilities: 'She was more playfully relaxed than ever. . . . It was not only masterly, it showed that certain acting talents are released only in this style' (Hayman, 1983, p.166). Weigel had developed the character of Vlassova from the physical characteristic of a drooping left shoulder. She explained: 'Someone who grows like that is not very pushing' (Hayman, 1983, p.348). Her approach here anticipates Stanislavski's Method of Physical Actions.

Weigel's attention to physical detail, in characterisation, in stage business and in the handling of props, was always a significant factor in the construction of her performance. In an early poem, called *Weigel's Props*, Brecht writes of the careful way each item is hand-picked by the actress:

> Selected for age, function and beauty
> By the eyes of the knowing
> The hands of the bread-baking, not-weaving
> Soup-cooking connoisseur
> Of reality.

(Brecht, 1976, p.427)

Weigel understood as well as anyone that stage objects related to eating, drinking, working or the handling of money should be used in such a way as to make social and historical, as well as personal, statements to the audience. Her loving handling of Vlassova's pot of lard, for example, was said to show the 'reverential attitude towards food of those who live close to starvation' (Hayman, 1983, p.348). The original production of *The Mother* was the occasion of a significant moment in Brechtian history, in that the performances were banned by the Nazis, resulting in the company's presenting 'readings' instead. These 'readings', ironically, in their flattening of a realistic presentation, confirmed Brecht in his developing judgment that there should be a separation, some distance, placed between the performer and the role in the kind of theatre he wanted to create.

After her next major Brecht role, Señora Carrar, performed in 1937 while she and Brecht were in exile, Weigel was praised by the playwright for producing acting that was 'the best and purest that could so far have been seen anywhere as part of Epic Theatre' (Hayman, 1983, p.203). In particular, he admired the demonstrative clarity of her performance, in that she showed everything

> That was needed for understanding
> A fisherwoman, but did not transform herself fully
> Into this fisherwoman and she played
> As if partly absorbed with thinking
> At the same time, always asking herself:
> What was it really like?
>
> (Brecht, 1961, p.58)

Exile in non-German speaking countries meant, of course, that it was virtually impossible for Weigel to exercise her talents as an actor. When Brecht wrote *Mother Courage* in 1938/9 (while in Scandinavia), he developed the role of dumb Kattrin specifically with Weigel in mind. She did not, however, appear in the play until the two of them returned to Berlin in 1948. Then, as the company's leading female player, she took the title role. For the opening night of that production, Brecht wrote a poem, *For Helene Weigel*, which concludes with the lines: 'to the unteachable now show / With some slight hope / Your good face' (Brecht, 1976, p.415), a reminder that an extraordinarily strong face was one of Weigel's many theatrical 'weapons'. Brecht even told her that she only needed to be aware of her own facial expressions 'in order to be able to convey the various moods without always having to feel them' (*MD*, p.76). When it came to playing Mother Courage, however, Weigel argued with Brecht about how emotionally the character should be presented, and it was claimed that she displayed a greater emotional range within the role when she knew Brecht was not present in the theatre. We shall return to Weigel's views on Brechtian acting later.

As with Vlassova, Weigel applied her usual care and attention to the finding and use of the apt props for Mother Courage. In particular she demonstrated the mercenary aspect of the character by her (Weigel's) skilful deployment of a purse. She researched this by experimenting with different ways of closing the purse, such as the making of a loud 'snap' at the end of a transaction. The clarity of her physical portrayal of key moments was most notable in the scene where Mother Courage is forced to deny knowledge of her dead son, Swiss Cheese. Weigel famously conveyed the character's pain at her loss by means of a totally silent scream that was underscored by a sequence of powerful gestures and body movements. As John Rouse puts it, this was the supreme example of 'distanced' performance:

> the very physicality of the movement moves it beyond the level of naturalistic grief with which an audience can empathize. We are shocked, stunned, shaken by Courage's grief, but we are not allowed

to share it on the plane of petty emotional titillation. The technically accomplished extremity of Weigel's acting, in short, defamiliarizes Courage's grief through the very demonstration of that grief.[12]

Consequently, we can see Weigel as a good example of Brecht's ideal actor. She had a strong political commitment to theatre as a social force and as a collaborative and collective enterprise. Her preparatory work for the playing of a role included close attention to physical and character detail but this was balanced by an understanding of the broader, social perspective represented by that role. And she had a range of technical skills and an ability to exploit, in an appropriate way, personality and stage presence to enable her to be dynamic and memorable.

ACTING AT THE BERLINER ENSEMBLE

It is often said that one of the key skills of any theatre director is the ability to choose the right actors. Certainly it is true that significant decisions about the way characters will be played are made when actors are assigned to roles, even, or especially when, as Brecht proposes, actors are required to play 'against type', or at least are cast in roles seemingly outside their range. Brecht's choice of performers undoubtedly had a fundamental impact not only on the final shape and texture of his productions but, just as importantly, on his working methods during rehearsal.

When, after fifteen years in exile, Brecht returned to Berlin in October 1948, he attempted to gather round him many artists with whom he had worked previously. He tried, without success, to entice Piscator to return in order to direct, and he invited Peter Lorre to join the acting company. Lorre resisted, despite Brecht's offer of the role of Hamlet and special poetic pleading:

> You are being summoned
> To a country that was wrecked
> And we have nothing to offer you
> Beyond our need for you.
>   (Hayman, 1983, p.344)

Brecht's new company, however, did include a number of earlier actors: Helene Weigel, obviously, Ernst Busch and Therese Giehse (the latter as guest artist); also the two designers, Caspar Neher and Teo Otto; two composers, Hans Eisler and Paul Dessau; and Erich Engel, the director. The company was based at the Deutsches Theater (sharing the building with the resident company) and it was given substantial funding and theatrical resources by the state. Their first production, *Mother Courage*, opened on 11 January 1949 and was very well received. Brecht wrote simply in his diary: 'Helli's [Weigel's] Courage character now superb. Great boldness in

34

it' (Hayman, 1983, p.331). On the strength of this initial success, Brecht and Weigel began to develop plans for a permanent company with its own theatre. They were authorized (and further financially subsidised) by the East German State to set up the Berliner Ensemble, which formally opened in November 1949. Four years later they moved to the Theater am Schiffbauerdamm as their theatrical home.

From the outset of the new regime, as soon as he started work on the production of *Mother Courage*, Brecht established an exploratory method of rehearsal in which outsiders were made welcome. Unlike many directors, he rejected privacy on the assumption that he, the actors and the production would all benefit from the input and comments of people not engaged in the production. One visitor remarked: 'Never have I seen a director who guarded his secret less jealously than Brecht. Anyone who wanted could come in' (Ewen, 1970, p.445). Manfred Wekwerth, who joined the Berliner Ensemble as a young trainee director, recalls that immediately after being introduced to Brecht at a rehearsal, he was told by him to 'Watch this and write down everything you disagree with!' (Hayman, 1983, p.351). Nothing could be further from the strictly enforced privacy usually operating in the rehearsal room of a contemporary British theatre.

Carl Weber, who also joined the Ensemble as a director, describes seeing his first company rehearsal. He thought, to begin with, he was watching a break in the proceedings:

> It was typical of the loose way Brecht worked, of his experimental approach and of the teamwork the Ensemble was used to. . . . The actors also took an experimental attitude. They would suggest a way of doing something and if they started to explain it, Brecht would say that he wanted no discussion in rehearsal – it would have to be tried.[13]

While Brecht's rehearsal method may have seemed loose or casual to Weber, reports of the painstaking, detailed and lengthy rehearsal of the briefest moment, word or gesture by Brecht and his actors are legion. An observer of one of Brecht's early post-war rehearsals wrote:

> The directorial method was based on investigation and varied experimentation that could extend to the smallest gestures – eyes, fingers . . . Brecht worked like a sculptor on and with the actor.[14]

Such physical separation of one moment from the next enabled, of course, the undercutting of emotion and the insertion of the necessary distance between the actor and the role. The subtlety and detail of Brecht's work with his actors on these moments indicates the importance he placed on precision and clarity in performance. Hurwicz, again, describes how Brecht worked in rehearsals in order to help actors to highlight important moments while retaining an overview of the whole play:

With actors who fail to produce a certain nuance necessary at a
key-point in the plot, Brecht takes all possible measures to achieve
his ends. He replaces emphasis by gesture, gesture by a pause, a look
by a throat-clearing, and so on. In this way Brecht trains actors to be
exact, to be responsible with regard to their parts and the whole play
without forcing them.

(Witt, 1975, p.133)

Within all these processes lies another crucial aspect of Brecht's ideas
about the business of acting: that it must be part of a collaborative,
collective process, all the actors working towards a common goal, and that
the specific intention and style of performance should be allowed to
emerge during this interactive rehearsal process in which the whole
company participates. This approach was unusual in Brecht's day. Also, it
is fair to point out that it is seldom discernible in Western theatre today with
its frequent hierarchical working structures and the unequal power relationship that exists between actor and director. On the other hand, the
generous funding accorded to the Berliner Ensemble enabled Brecht to
enjoy very long rehearsal periods for each production, sometimes as long
as a year. A shorter rehearsal period makes ensemble work less easy,
sometimes impossible. These are issues to which we shall return in
subsequent chapters.

Actors at the Berliner Ensemble were aware that Brecht did not begin
rehearsals with preconceived ideas on staging or style for that particular
production. Ekkehard Schall, who worked as a young actor with Brecht and
became a leading performer at the Ensemble after the playwright's death,
explains: 'A Brecht production does not start with a style; the style emerges
during rehearsals in the sequence of situations, in which attitudes are
assumed and then played' (Kleber, 1987, p.84). Equally, the actors knew
that Brecht was not overly concerned about the techniques that individual
actors deployed or what means they used to achieve a performance. As Carl
Weber emphasizes:

He didn't tell them to go home and do this or that or to go behind the
set and concentrate. He didn't give a damn about the mechanics they
used, he just cared about results.[15]

Equally, it seems that Brecht the director almost never made reference
during the practical process of mounting a production to even the best
known of his theories. Lotte Lenya, the great singer-actress, who first
worked with Brecht on the premiere of *The Threepenny Opera*, gives an
amusing description of rehearsing the song 'Surabaya Johnny' with him
after the war:

Right in the middle of it, I stopped for a second and said: "Brecht, you
know your theory of epic theatre – maybe you don't want me just to sing

36

it the way I sang it – as emotional as 'Surabaya Johnny' has to be done?"
. . . He said: "Lenya, darling, whatever you do is epic enough for me."

(*The Listener*, 24.5.79, p.709)

Angelika Hurwicz, who was the first actress to play Grusha in *The Caucasian Chalk Circle*, claims that, during months of rehearsal for that production, she heard Brecht use the term *Verfremdung* only once. This was when they were working on the scene between Grusha, her brother and the sister-in-law, and creating something that struck Brecht as too emotional. Hurwicz remembers that 'he made the actors rehearse with interpolations of "said the man" or "said the woman"' (Hayman, 1983, p.380). This is now, of course, routinely used as a classic Brechtian rehearsal exercise.

When asked about the famous *V-Effekt* by the British actor/director Bernard Miles, Helene Weigel is said to have replied that it simply 'grew out of Brecht's efforts to deal with difficult actors' (*The Times Educational Supplement*, 8.1.82). She confirmed that during the rehearsal process at the Berliner Ensemble there was very little concern with theory. The company's technique was simple, according to Weigel: 'We tell the story'.[16] Most of her comments on performing roles in Brecht's plays were equally direct and matter-of-fact. Nevertheless, she could be scathing about non-Brechtian approaches to performance, declaring that 'the psychology generally used in the theatre is very inferior, old-fashioned and useless'.[17] Yet, like any Stanislavskian actor, she always stressed the importance to the actor of imagination and observation and the interaction of the two:

> Often I observe something and know, for sure, that's a point I can use in a particular role. But mostly you don't know where the ideas come from. Observation and imagination often complement each other.
>
> (Hayman, 1969, p.54)

On the other hand, Weigel made it clear that, like Brecht, she saw a character's action in terms of function, so that when asked, for example, why Coriolanus fought bravely, she answered: 'It was his job' (*The Observer*, 22.8.65). And on the issue of the Brechtian actor's separation from the role, her attitude was equally straightforward:

> How, for example, am I as Courage at the end of the play, when my business dealings have cost me the last of my children, to deliver the sentence: 'I have to get back into business', if I am not personally shattered by the fact that this person I am playing does not possess the capacity to learn?[18]

Schall confirms that Brecht avoided theory when working with his actors, declaring that during rehearsals Brecht was 'only a practitioner. Actually he only gave explanations which helped the actors to present something in a vital manner'.[19] Again, that stress on vitality.

There was, however, one expression derived from his theory that, according to Schall, Brecht did use in rehearsal, 'to epicize' (*episieren*); and that specially invented Brechtian verb places the emphasis in the actor's art on story-telling. As Schall says: 'It's very simple, you just tell the scene, the text and everything that's happening – that's epicizing. He'd say: "Just tell me the scene".' Hurwicz agrees that playing epic theatre quite simply means telling the story clearly in order to show how people behave in certain situations:

> All the work is subordinated to this end. . . . He demonstrates persons as the product of the conditions in which they live, and capable of change through the circumstances which they experience.
>
> (Witt, 1975, p.133)

Hurwicz goes on to stress that on occasion the detailed portrayal of a particular character must be subordinated to the presentation of the more general, social meaning of the play. To her, this pointed to the essential difference between the surface reality of 'naturalism' and the more signif-icant, deeper reality of 'social realism'. Her own understanding of this aspect had grown out of playing Mother Courage's dumb daughter, Kattrin:

> Working on this role I learnt the difference between realism and naturalism. If I'd played the dumbness as the result of an injury done to the tongue . . . my expression could very easily have been rather idiotic. It would have been quite wrong to give an impression of retarded development. What was important was to show that intelligent people, born to happiness, can be crippled by war. Precision in portraying an individual case had to be sacrificed for this general truth.
>
> (Hayman, 1969, p.52)

Schall shares many of Hurwicz's views on the Brechtian actor's approach, but further emphasises the importance of creating a role out of a collection of different social behaviours and actions:

> You can't approach any part with blinkers of moral preconceptions, nor with the preconception of 'character'. You also can't play a certain 'character', rather you've got to play a sum of ways of behaviour in various situations.[20]

Schall does not, however, rule out 'psychology' in the character's make-up altogether but insists that it does not provide the fundamental basis of a role. Moreover, he is very clear about the function of emotions in Brecht's theatre and the way he himself experiences and expresses them as a performer:

> I am not at all a distancing, distanced actor. I am a passionate, very passionate actor. But I'm not an actor who gives out pure emotions: emotions want to impress but not to disturb. To disturb, that's more important to me . . . I don't act emotions, I present them as ways of

behaviour. Brecht's term here would be *Gestus*. And when you fill behaviour with emotion, that's when you get passionate, or intense or vital.[21]

Brecht himself replied, when asked by a visiting actor whether his performance techniques did not lead to an 'inhuman' kind of theatre:

We must have on the stage of a realistic theatre, live, rounded, contradictory people, with all their passions, their direct expressions and actions. The stage is no herbarium or zoological museum with stuffed animals. The actor must know how to create such people (and if you could see our productions, you would really see such people), and they *are* people not despite, but thanks to our principles.

(Ewen, 1970, p.463)

All Brecht's choices of actor and practices in rehearsal discussed here indicate the pre-eminence in his theatre of practice over theory, and his predilection for deploying performers whose make-up included a wide emotional range and power, a strong personality and a vivid stage presence, clarity of physical playing and the ability to make good contact with an audience. In addition, Brecht's actors were required to have a commitment to the common purpose of socio-political change through theatrical art and a liking for a kind of theatre that was fun and that was determined to create via the collaborative working process of an ensemble.

Brecht's last, prophetic message to the members of the Berliner Ensemble was a typed notice placed on the board at the Theater am Schiffbauerdamm, dated 5 August 1956 and headlined 'Our London Season':

For our London season we need to bear two things in mind. First: we shall be offering most of the audience a pure pantomime, a kind of silent film on the stage for they know no German . . . . Second: there is in England a long-standing fear that German art (literature, painting, music) must be terribly heavy, slow, laborious and pedestrian.

So our playing needs to be quick, light, strong. This is not a question of hurry, but of speed, not simply of quick playing, but of quick thinking. We must keep the tempo of a run-through and infect it with quiet strength, with our own fun. In the dialogue the exchanges must not be offered reluctantly, as when offering somebody one's last pair of boots, but must be tossed like so many balls. The audience has to see that here are a number of artists working together as a collective (ensemble) in order to convey stories, ideas, virtuoso feats to the spectator by common effort.

(*B on T*, p.283)

The rest of this book examines the British playing of Brecht.

2

PERFORMING EARLY BRITISH BRECHT
Following the Berliner

Western Europe first saw the work of the Berliner Ensemble in the summer of 1954, when the company performed *Mother Courage* first in Bruges and Amsterdam, and then at the international festival, *Théâtre des Nations*, in Paris. The production was directed jointly by Brecht and Erich Engel and it was a festival first prize winner. When the Berliner Ensemble performed *The Caucasian Chalk Circle* at the next Paris Festival in 1955, they were greatly admired by the influential British theatre critic Kenneth Tynan, who was to remain a Brecht devotee and champion for the rest of his life. In his review of *The Caucasian Chalk Circle*, headlined 'Stars from the East', Tynan wrote:

> I have read a great deal about Brecht's theory of acting. . . . What it boils down to in practice is something extremely simple. The small parts are all generalized . . . we know at a glance what kind of people they are meant to be. . . . We can thus concentrate on the principals, who wear no masks or make-up and play with absolute realism.
>
> (Tynan, 1964, p.239)

The formulation bears all the naïvety of the newly converted and, perhaps significantly in terms of later Western views of Brecht, attempts to see a formalised, structural method, but based on Western assumptions – small parts versus major roles; social stereotypes versus precisely delineated figures; stylised playing versus realism. There was much to learn.

Interestingly, Tynan, in common with many British critics of the time, overlooked the success of another company at the 1955 Paris Festival, the British representative, and the relatively unknown, Theatre Workshop. Under the directorship of the egregious Joan Littlewood, this company had received a storm of praise for its productions of *Arden of Faversham* and *Volpone*. *The Times* carried a review from its Paris correspondent that, unknowingly, showed Theatre Workshop to be operating close to something of the Brechtian manner:

40

Apart from the intrinsic merit of the Company's performances and choice of plays, French audiences and critics seem to derive much satisfaction from the fact that Theatre Workshop is a popular theatre. . . . There is also something attractive about the idea of a theatre group, in which individual performances count for less than does the joint effort.

(Goorney, 1981, p.152)

Theatre Workshop was very soon, in fact, to play its part in bringing Brecht to British audiences, but we shall return to that later. First a look at the preparations for Brecht's reception in Britain.

PREPARING FOR BRECHT

Knowledge of Brecht's work began to filter into Britain in the 1930s. Professional theatre of that time was struggling to retain its audiences in the face of the competition from the cinema, but there was a tremendous upsurge in the development of amateur theatre, drawing for its active personnel on the large numbers of unemployed people. And it was the work of these amateur groups, particularly, of course, ones with a socialist base and overtly political interest, that was to provide a context for the acceptance in Britain of Brecht's plays and of his ideas about the function and ideal form of theatre.

Inspired by the cultural renewal in Russia following the revolution, socialist theatre practitioners in Britain formed the Council for Proletarian Art in 1924. This changed its name to the Workers' Theatre Movement in 1926 and became an 'umbrella' organisation for a number of socialist theatre groups that had sprung up throughout Britain and were to grow to thirty by 1932. Their aim was apparent and straightforward: to provide artistic expression of the views and ambitions of the ordinary worker, and to help 'stiffen the workers' resistance to the evergrowing attacks on their standard of life' (Samuel *et al.*, 1985, p.99).

Since so many of the members of these theatre groups were unemployed, it was possible for a great deal of time, energy and commitment to be devoted to the presentation of their productions, with the result that many of the participants subsequently went on to develop successful professional careers. It was usual for these groups to reject naturalism as a performance mode and to adopt an 'agitprop' style of presentation, borrowed in large part from the work of similar groups in Russia and Germany. Since most of the early performances were presented outside ordinary theatre contexts or in the open air, such as in the street or at factory gates, agitprop, with its reliance on simple, 'cartoon-style' presentation, slogans, songs and stereotyped characters, was singularly appropriate. However, some groups were less enamoured of agitprop, seeing it as 'a type of decadent and pessimistic bourgeois drama' (Samuel *et al.*, 1985, p.167) and, while still wanting to avoid psychological naturalism and the well-made play, sought something essentially realistic (presumably Brecht's notion of 'social realism' would have served, had they known it).This led some in the Workers' Theatre Movement to develop shows within conventional theatres and even to obtain their own performance premises.

The British workers' theatre groups constantly formed and re-formed. In 1935 the Workers' Theatre Movement disbanded and some members joined with others from a group known as Rebel Players to become Unity Theatre. Publicity for the Unity's 'opening' was an invitation for the press to photograph Jocelyn Herbert, the daughter of the MP A.P. Herbert, and subsequently a prominent stage-designer. She wielded a shovel for the cameras and was quoted as claiming that Unity was 'to be a theatre for real, unvarnished plays of everyday life' (Chambers, 1989, p.112).

Unity's first success was with the socialist play *Waiting for Lefty* by the American writer Clifford Odets. It became a favourite with left-wing theatre in both America and Britain in the 1930s. Unity went on to perform this play 300 times during 1936 and 1937, though its realistic form fuelled the vexed debate within the company about the ways in which 'reality' might be portrayed on stage. Options were kept open, however, by Unity's training and education section's offering Unity actors classes both in 'dialectics in art' and in the theories of Stanislavski.

By 1937, Unity's work had developed to such an extent that the company was able to undertake tours to the Midlands and the north-east of England (though this may sound grander than it was in that it amounted to eighteen company members travelling in three London taxis). Within three months there were Unity groups all over the country making socialist theatre, at one time as many as 250. (A small number survives to this day.) The impact of Unity on the development of British theatre in the 1930s and 1940s was significant. This is partly indicated by the fact that in the 1930s Unity's Council, set up to organise and disseminate information to member groups, included amongst its membership such varied luminaries as Sean O'Casey, H.G. Wells and Paul Robeson.

BRECHT SLIPS INTO BRITAIN

While conditions were being created in Britain favourable to an appreciation of a Brechtian kind of theatre, Brecht's own work was simultaneously becoming both known and performed. In 1930 the BBC broadcast a radio version of the Hindemith/Weill opera, *The Lindbergh Flight*, for which Brecht had written the libretto (1928), and in 1933 Hindemith's *The Lesson* was also broadcast on radio, again with a Brecht text. July of 1933 saw the first British stage production of Brecht's one and only ballet, *Anna Anna* (later to be retitled *The Seven Deadly Sins*). This was given three performances at the Savoy Theatre London, performed by *Les Ballets* and choreographed by Balanchine. The piece had been first presented in Paris the month before, but it was a genuinely Brechtian enterprise in that the music was by Kurt Weill, the design by Caspar Neher, and the cast included Lotte Lenya, all of whom had been working closely with Brecht in Berlin for some years. (The earliest and most famous collaboration between the four was on the first production of *The Threepenny Opera* in 1928.)

In 1934, Brecht himself came to London, where, for three months, he sought work in the film industry (unsuccessfully), and tried to promote interest in his plays. All he achieved then was an offer to have *The Threepenny Opera* published in English, but no London theatre producer could be persuaded to present his work. Brecht wrote to his friend (and modernist writer) Alfred Döblin: 'No-one was interested in the culture that was too good for Herr Hitler. . . . Not all that many people are willing to pay for the pleasure of getting indignant' (Brecht, 1990, p.205).

It was partly through the printed word that Brecht's name was now becoming better known in Britain. Sergei Tretyakov's article on Brecht's dramatic theory and some of his early plays, published in Moscow in *International Theatre* (1934), circulated among the membership of the Workers' Theatre Movement; and in 1935/6 Eric Walter White published an article on Brechtian theatre and a translation of Brecht's 'Alienation in Chinese Acting' in *Life and Letters Today*. Other translations of Brecht's own writing becoming available in Britain at this time included his only novel, *The Threepenny Novel*, Christopher Isherwood's versions of some poetry (both in 1937), and the playlet *The Informer* (1939), later to become part of *Fears and Miseries of the Third Reich*. (In America there appeared translations of *The Mother* (1935), *Roundheads and Peakheads* (1937), *Señora Carrar's Rifles* (1938), *Mother Courage and Her Children* (1941), *Fears and Miseries of the Third Reich* (1942), and *The Trial of Lucullus* (1943).)

Despite Brecht's failure to get his plays produced in London in the mid-1930s, some of the small British socialist groups were interested in his work. The Manchester-based company, Theatre of Action, which had been founded in 1934 by Joan Littlewood and Ewan MacColl (subsequently of Theatre Workshop), presented their own translations of scenes from *Mr. Puntila and His Servant Matti* and from *Roundheads and Peakheads* in 1935. The following year the London Choral Union (another amateur socialist group similar to Unity) performed one of Brecht's *Lehrstücke*, *The Expedient*, at the Westminster Hall and subsequently took it on a small tour of other London halls. Then in 1938 Littlewood and MacColl's Theatre of Action mounted a full production of *The Good Soldier Schweik*, acknowledging their debt to Brecht and Piscator as 'the chief sources of our political attitude and theatrical style'.[1] MacColl later noted how innovatory the group had been in trying to master the new language of epic theatre. He describes how they deployed

Piscator's technique of production – except, of course we didn't have his moving platforms and escalators and all that kind of thing. But we did use the mixture of living actors and cartoon figures, which was a big, big jump in the theatre in this country, and we did use back projection for the first time.[2]

The last pre-war production of a Brecht play in Britain was performed in September 1938, when London Unity presented the British première (and first English-language production) of *Señora Carrar's Rifles*, the short piece based on J.M. Synge's *Riders to the Sea*. This production was directed by John Fernald (later to become the principal of the Royal Academy of Dramatic Art), and it was described by *The Times* as being 'well acted' and giving 'a natural and convincing picture of a peasant family waiting in suspense not far behind the front' (Davies, 1987, p.119). Another reviewer (in *Cavalcade*), however, commented on the division he noted in the audience between the upper-class intellectuals (the 'would-be revolutionary sympathisers') and the genuine socialists present who were impatient with the play because 'to them it merely typifies the "petty" bourgeois inaction'.[3] This suggests that Brecht was hitting his mark. This production was subsequently taken on tour 'to raise consciousness, spirits and money for Spain' in its fight against fascism (Chambers, 1989, p.112).

Naturally, Unity membership was substantially depleted during the war and its activity diminished, though some groups managed to stage the occasional performance. In the late 1940s, however, Unity renewed its attempts to promote Brecht's work. For example, Herbert Marshall, one of London Unity's directors, drew up plans for a production of *The Life of Galileo*, bringing Charles Laughton from the States to re-create the leading role. He also had plans to produce *The Caucasian Chalk Circle* with Paul Robeson as Azdak, and *Mother Courage and Her Children*, with the well-known Lancashire singer Gracie Fields as Courage. Nothing, however, came of these plans. Marshall then tried to arrange for the Berliner Ensemble to appear at the Edinburgh Festival in *The Threepenny Opera*, but the Festival Committee rejected this idea because they did not know the play.

The repertoire of British theatre in the late 1940s was dominated by light comedies, crime thrillers and imported American musicals, and, apart from a small flourishing of verse drama (by T.S. Eliot, Christopher Fry and Ronald Duncan), there was very little new on offer by way of content or style. The major development in the period was the founding of a number of new, provincial repertory theatres, which were financially supported by the newly formed Arts Council (1946). Funding was also made available to generate tours to the provinces by London-based companies, but essentially they offered merely old theatrical fare.

Nevertheless, the occasional Brecht play did reach the British stage during the early post-war period. Stretford Civic Theatre, Manchester, presented *The Caucasian Chalk Circle* in 1950, but there are few recorded details of this production other than that it used Eric Bentley's translation and was directed by Frank Millard. Even less is known about the production of *The Good Woman of Setzuan* mounted by the Progress Theatre, Reading, in 1953. The following year London theatregoers were offered a rehearsed reading of *Mother Courage and Her Children* at the Institute for Contemporary Arts.

Then in early 1956, at the initiation of Oscar Lewenstein, who was both the national organiser for Unity and a member of the board of the newly formed English Stage Company based at the Royal Court Theatre, London, plans were drawn up for a production of *The Threepenny Opera* to be performed at an arts festival in Devon. The English Stage Company sought to raise interest in the production by inviting prestigious actors to perform in the production, but Laurence Olivier failed to reply and John Gielgud refused to be involved with a play he considered 'a trifle sordid and a tedious bore' (Browne, 1975, p.8). Eventually, Lewenstein obtained the performing rights for *Mother Courage and Her Children* instead and it was proposed that Joan Littlewood and her company, Theatre Workshop, should mount the production. This company seemed an ideal choice.

THEATRE WORKSHOP AND *MOTHER COURAGE*

Formed in 1945 with the intention of 'taking theatre to the people', Theatre Workshop had toured a mixed repertoire of classical and new plays round Britain and other parts of Europe for eight years before obtaining its own theatre in the East End of London, the Theatre Royal at Stratford East, in 1953. The company manifesto made clear its socio-political intentions and commitment to popular theatre:

> The great theatres of all times have been popular theatres which reflected the dreams and struggles of the people. . . . We want a theatre with a living language, a theatre . . . which will comment as fearlessly on society as did Ben Jonson and Aristophanes.
>
> (Goorney, 1981, p.41)

The company were Brechtian in a number of ways, as the comments of the Paris reviewer on their appearance at the Festival implied (see p.41). It was organised as a collective, believed in long rehearsal periods and drew eclectically on a wide range of sources of materials and production methods. Interested in performers from a variety of backgrounds as well as actors from the legitimate theatre, Littlewood instigated an intensive programme of company training, which comprised a mix of mime and physical exercises, and music hall and cabaret-style performance techniques (which brought them close to Brecht), and also incorporated ideas culled from Stanislavski.

A number of the new plays performed by Theatre Workshop were specially written by Littlewood's co-director, Ewan MacColl. He was an established folk-singer as well as an actor, and in his writing he drew on poetic and song traditions to express his political concerns. Joan Littlewood was a radical thinker. She declared (like Brecht) that theatre, first of all, had to be fun and she claimed that 'Brecht's aesthetic would be much more likely to appeal to the non-theatre going public'. In particular she thought his work would be best presented in non-traditional theatre spaces. However, she was sceptical about Brecht's ideas on theatre being appropriate or fully acceptable in Britain because she thought the values of mainstream British theatre at the time were 'totally lacking in social and artistic dynamic'.[4] But on this the members of Theatre Workshop were enthusiastic to prove Littlewood wrong.

Lewenstein visited Berlin and persuaded Brecht that Joan Littlewood would make an excellent Mother Courage. Brecht in turn offered to send one of his assistant directors, Carl Weber, to help with the production, and work with Littlewood who would also direct. Littlewood herself undertook the adaptation of the text, and arranged it to be played by the fourteen actors the company had available. (Simultaneously, the company was mounting a production of *Richard II* for the same Festival.) In the adaptation, Littlewood cut a number of the songs, largely because she felt she was not up to the singing the Courage part originally called for. During the rehearsal period, it was agreed at a company meeting that Littlewood was finding the double role of acting and directing a great strain, and so she replaced herself with Avis Bunnage as Courage, and concentrated solely on direction. When Carl Weber arrived at the Theatre Royal bearing the photographic record of the Berliner Ensemble production (the *Modellbuch*), Littlewood not only refused to contemplate drawing on that information, because it would compromise her open-ended, exploratory way of working, but, after several arguments with Weber, banned him from rehearsals.

When Brecht heard that Littlewood was not to play Courage, he threatened to take out an injunction against the company. With twenty-four hours to go to the first performance, she took over the part again. It is hardly surprising, therefore, that when the production appeared at the Tor and Torridge Festival in Barnstaple, Devon, in July 1956, it was, as Howard Goorney, one of the actors, admits, 'a bit of a shambles' (Goorney, 1981, p.102). In her autobiography, Littlewood rather dismisses the whole experience by making a jokey reference to the plucking of the chicken in Scene 2 of the play:

> I might have got away with it but for that ****-*** hen. I had to pluck it in the first [*sic*] scene and it was stinking. The smell from its backside turned my stomach. Mother Courage had to stop herself vomiting for wellnigh half the play.
>
> (Littlewood, 1994, p.466)

Reviewers were harshly critical, with Tynan, the new 'Brechtian', describing Littlewood's playing Courage 'in a lifeless mumble, looking over-parted and under-rehearsed' (Tynan, 1964, p.229). She certainly was the latter. Another reviewer criticised the whole company for 'over-acting', while assuming the excesses may have been derived from Brechtian theory. However, he concluded, it was 'a perfect way of disguising the fact that one's actors are not, in fact, very good'.[5] Tynan, furthermore, declared the company to be 'dismally unequal to the strain. The result is a production in which discourtesy to a masterpiece borders on an insult, as if Wagner were to be staged in a school gymnasium' (Tynan, 1964, p.229). The production was not transferred to London. This is a sad and unfitting conclusion to the contribution of Theatre Workshop to British Brecht. In fact, the company's subsequent achievements in making contact with working-class audiences, and in thus exerting a seminal influence on many aspects of British theatre, warrant it a high and honourable place in any history of socially committed art.

ENGLISH STAGE COMPANY AND
THE THREEPENNY OPERA

Shortly after this disappointing British debut of a major Brecht play, plans for an English Stage Company production of *The Threepenny Opera* at the Royal Court Theatre were revived. The American actor/director Sam Wanamaker agreed to take it on. At first glance he was an odd choice: he had been, as he said himself, a well-known Stanislavskian: 'I was an indestructible, unshakeable, immoveable testimonial to the undying truth of *An Actor Prepares*'.[6] And he further admitted that when he saw Charles Laughton as Galileo, he was 'bewildered . . . angry and disturbed. I rejected any further opportunities to investigate the man's [Brecht's] theories'. Then, when he saw the Berliner's *The Caucasian Chalk Circle* in Paris in 1955, he found it

the most overwhelming theatrical experience of my life and yet my doubts and confusions were compounded. It violated to my face all my notions of theatre – and yet it fascinated me.

When Wanamaker was approached to direct *The Threepenny Opera*, his first response was 'to reject any possibility that English audiences could take this'. However, he decided to take the project on and in order to prepare himself thoroughly for the task he went to Berlin to see more performances by the Berliner Ensemble and to discuss his ideas for the production with Brecht himself:

I suggested a method of production which would to my mind have made the play more acceptable to British audiences. I suggested we produce it in a nightclub like a floorshow, in the round, where the audience would be more inclined to accept the lusty and satiric nature of the piece, to get close to the public and make them part of the play. He [Brecht] thought the idea interesting but politely indicated that if the British were inclined to be antagonistic to the material and style, would it not be better to keep them and the actors further apart so that they could thus judge the play objectively?

Wanamaker stayed at the Berliner Ensemble for eight days, watching rehearsals and performances and talking with Brecht and the company. He felt he came away as fully informed on Brecht's ideas as was feasible in the time available and he was impressed by the productions he had seen, which he described as 'brilliantly theatrical and exciting'. Furthermore, Brecht's social and political intentions had been carefully clarified for him:

> Brecht transcends the petty political issues and manoevres in the social struggle of today. . . . He examines MAN as he relates to other men and to his total environment. . . . To deny or fear Brecht's political and social orientation is deliberately to handicap oneself from arriving at an objective evaluation of the theatrical revolution he has set in motion.

He noted that there was a consequent tendency in Brecht admirers in the West to play down his Marxism and his concern to promote Communism, even though that was to protect Brecht from imagined audience hostility:

> They are understandably fearful that the stresses of political antagonism in Britain and America would somehow deny to Brecht the hearing and respectability to his works which it is felt this great artist should have.

Wanamaker's sensitivity to the pressures of political antagonism had been honed in America which he himself had left (for Britain) before his own pronounced liberal sympathies could make him a victim of McCarthyism. However, he had identified shrewdly an aspect of the British unease with Brecht that was already making itself apparent.

For Wanamaker's production of *The Threepenny Opera*, Brecht's designer, Caspar Neher, drew up the designs, which included what Tynan was to describe as 'Neher's brilliant fragmentary scenery and . . . signboards and slides to tell us what is going to happen next' (*The Observer*, 12.2.56). And a special forestage was installed at the Royal Court to facilitate the actor/audience contact (despite Brecht's suggestion above that performers and spectators might best be kept apart).

The cast included Ewan MacColl (of Theatre Workshop) as the *Morität*-Singer, Georgia Brown, like MacColl, well known as a singer as well as actor, in the role of Lucy, and Bill Owen as Macheath. Wanamaker's view was that any British actor would 'find the Epic Theatre not only *not* foreign but distinctly *native* to his temperament and unconscious method of work'. This seems to be in contrast to the British Brecht experience up to that date but an opinion that will be reiterated in the chapters that follow. Wanamaker explained this view by contending that the British actor could not fully utilise the Stanislavski 'System' because 'it demands the complete release of the emotional and psychological self'; and that, he implies, would be much too difficult a task for the characteristic British inhibition to achieve.

Many reviewers of the production, however, were critical of the short-comings of the acting, Ivor Brown suggesting that the cast had 'been instructed to roar and gesticulate at the top of their bent', which resulted in an 'an orgy of boiled ham' (Brown, 1956, p.62). The implicit (and perjorative) contrast between 'natural' and 'ham' was probably a reflection of the current British taste for the understated in acting style, rather than a failure by the actors. Most critics, however, agreed' that Bill Owen was miscast as Macheath. In addition to having a poor singing voice, he had, said *The Observer* critic, played the role as 'a bantamweight swell, whereas what is wanted . . . is a heavyweight grandee who might pass for a banker' (*The Observer*, 12.2.56). This might suggest an expectation of Brecht as something 'heavy' rather than as a writer with a sardonic lightness of touch. Certainly, critics of the production took 'sides' very clearly; no one remained indifferent. Harold Hobson praised the director for the show's 'ingenuity and verve' and described it as 'one of the most exciting things in London for some time' (*The Sunday Times*, 12.2.56). In particular, he expressed admiration for Brecht's dramaturgy: 'It is, of course, in the methods of Brecht that the real excitement lies. Brecht has invented a theatrical technique which is, in a double sense, revolutionary'. Ivor Brown, on the other hand, concluded that the play 'may have been exciting in the Germany of the 1920s. But it is fusty fun in 1956' (Brown, 1956, p.62). Wanamaker remained convinced that a number of the adverse reviews were based on a thinly veiled political antipathy to Brecht:

> The cry 'Communist' or 'Marxist' or 'Left-wing' (as I heard a distin-guished critic of a distinguished newspaper hiss in an angry tone *before* the curtain went up on the first night of *The Threepenny Opera*) is raised before they've had a chance to judge what he *does* have to say.

And this is an issue to which we shall inevitably return.

Critics notwithstanding, the production transferred from the Royal Court to the Aldwych Theatre, making way for the official 'opening' of the newly furbished theatre and the newly formed English Stage Company. The aim of the company was to foster developments in playwriting through a policy of staging new plays. The artistic director, George Devine, and his Assistant Director, Tony Richardson, had in 1952/3, prior to taking up their posts, planned a season of 'neglected authors', including Brecht, but this had not been carried through. The early repertoire at the Royal Court included John Osborne's *Look Back in Anger*, which was in many ways responsible for ushering in a new era of British theatre. Jimmy Porter's irreverent voice served to encourage writers and directors to exchange the genteel drawing-room drama of the pre-war era for a socially relevant, class-conscious theatre that would attempt to address the problems of post-war Britain. This 'revolution' helped to provide a setting in which Brechtian politics could find a congenial home.

With impeccable timing, it now seems, the Berliner Ensemble visited London in September of that same year, 1956 (though Brecht had died two weeks before). The company presented three of the master's plays (in German): *The Caucasian Chalk Circle*, *Trumpets and Drums* (Brecht's adaptation of the Restoration comedy, *The Recruiting Officer*, by George Farquhar), and *Mother Courage and Her Children*. Helene Weigel, of course, played the title role in the last.

Many of the British critics were impressed by the company's acting. Kenneth Tynan drew attention to the difference in their style from that of conventional European companies:

> Brecht's actors do not behave like Western actors; they neither bludgeon us with personality nor woo us with charm; they look shockingly like people, real, potato-faced people such as one might meet in a bus-queue.
>
> (*The Observer*, 2.9.56)

He praised, in particular, the performances of Angelika Hurwicz, who played Grusha and Kattrin, and, predictably, of Helene Weigel, who as Mother Courage was, he said, 'never allowed to become a bawdy, flamboyant old darling; her performance is casual and ascetic'. And he added pertinently, ' we are to observe but not to embrace her'. Harold Hobson agreed that in all the productions the acting was 'of a very high standard. . . . There are performances of deep originality and lofty ambition' (*The Sunday Times*, 2.9.56). However, despite his earlier enthusiasm for *The Threepenny Opera* (above), he took issue with the Brechtian theory of *Verfremdungseffekt*, denying the possibility of the creation of Brecht's rational audience:

> To claim that the theatre, where hundreds of people are crowded together in conditions of more or less discomfort, subject to all the influences of mass suggestion, is a suitable place for clear thinking seems to me childish. I do not believe that, fundamentally, there is any more rational illumination in *Mother Courage* or the other plays of Brecht than there is in *Uncle Tom's Cabin*.

But Tynan, again, drew attention to the extraordinary and powerful visual effects of those Berliner productions:

I defy anyone to forget Brecht's stage pictures. . . . The beauty of Brechtian settings is not the dazzling kind that begs for applause. It is the more durable beauty of *use*.

(*The Observer*, 2.9.56)

Brecht would have been gratified by that last remark. And, as he predicted in his last note to the Ensemble, it was, of course, the visual effects of the productions and the physical aspects of the company's acting that had the greatest initial impact on British audiences, not least, perhaps, because the performances were given in German.

One reviewer of the Berliner's visit, J.W. Lambert, drew significant comparisons between their performances and those of the 1956 production of *The Caucasian Chalk Circle* at the Royal Academy of Dramatic Art, one of the leading British actor-training establishments of the time. The British production, he wrote, contained

all the seeds of all the failings of English players: the softness, the unnecessary grace, the half-heartedness almost. A controlled ferocity is what we need in our actors and what they can most usefully learn from their colleagues in Berlin.

(*Drama*, Winter, 1956, p.18)

The debate on how to perform Brecht was only just beginning.

THE ROYAL COURT AND
THE GOOD WOMAN OF SETZUAN

The month after the Berliner Ensemble's visit to London, the British première of *The Good Woman of Setzuan*, directed by George Devine, with Peggy Ashcroft in the leading role(s), opened at the Royal Court. As director of this prestigious event, Devine was determined to 'get it right', which meant, it seems, adhering closely to the model provided by the Berliner Ensemble. He and Ashcroft had met Brecht and Weigel in Berlin in September 1955 to discuss the Royal Court production. Ashcroft, who was then on tour with a Royal Shakespeare Company production of *Much Ado About Nothing*, remembered Brecht as 'very delightful' and having, to her surprise, 'a terrific sense of fun and humour' (Billington, 1988, p.159). To Devine, Brecht was like 'an intellectual peasant – both shy and shrewd', and although he (Devine) had criticisms of some things he saw at the Berliner Ensemble, he admired the company's clear attitude to its work and the pertinent relationship of that work with East German society: 'Brecht's theatre is above all a theatre of its time, of its place and of its nation. This is its exemplary value' (Wardle, 1978, p.170).

Furthermore, Devine realised that having a social function for its art did not make the company operate in a precious or over-solemn way:

51

The group appears to function in a natural and unneurotic manner, and by West End standards the kind of theatre they believe in seems carefree and dedicated, but without polish.[7]

Devine's efforts to ensure that his own production would be based on all the best advice available led him to employ Teo Otto, one of Brecht's designers, and Paul Dessau, the composer, and to invite Helene Weigel to attend rehearsals. Peggy Ashcroft took advantage of the opportunity this created to discuss acting style with Weigel:

> I asked her what her attitude to alienation was, because it seemed to me, when I had seen a Brecht play in Germany, that it is Brecht himself in the writing of the plays who performs this act of alienation. The actor has, as we say, to realize the character that he plays just as fully as in any other dramatist. But Brecht was not interested in psychological investigations of character, and so the actor has to make his effect with great economy of means, but the realization must be complete. I was rather relieved to find that Helene Weigel agreed with this.
>
> (Burton, 1967, p.95)

Ashcroft demonstrated her understanding of the way an actor can use character to serve theme and story rather than becoming an end in itself through psychological elaboration, by referring to her experience of playing Shakespeare, in particular in the Royal Shakespeare Company's production of the history plays, *The Wars of the Roses*. In these she thought

> it was important that we should all represent and be the characters that were taking part in this story as it unfolded; there was no time for development and ornamentation of character. . . . It was the action of the play which mattered to the spectator, and the impact of the play was from the story and the theme rather than the depth and detail of character.
>
> (Burton, 1967, p.95)

Equally, Ashcroft would find Weigel's views on character accessible because she herself recognised Weigel's Mother Courage as 'totally human. By the end you know all about that woman' (Burton, 1967, p.95).

Ashcroft and Devine developed a good working relationship during the rehearsals for *The Good Woman* and had, according to the theatre critic Michael Billington, 'a wonderful phrase for the business of searching for the truth of a character, which was "digging potatoes"' (*The Guardian*, 15.6.91). Creating the dual role of the prostitute Shen Te and her cousin Shui Ta, Ashcroft encountered 'a good fun problem', and, although she initially tried to persuade Devine that she should play the male part without a mask because she wanted to effect the transformation from Shen Te to Shui Ta without external assistance, she ultimately found the mask very helpful. Perhaps her initial reluctance to use a mask stemmed from a latent resistance to the non-realism of the play itself. However, the Royal Court designer Jocelyn Herbert, who worked on the production, suggests that (despite the 'potato-digging') it was the 'earthiness' of the dual role that caused the problems: 'Peggy doesn't naturally play anyone vulgar and she was better as the man because she found herself liberated by the half-mask' (Billington, 1988, p.168).

There was no question about Ashcroft's political commitment to at least some of the key ideas in *The Good Woman*. This was a commitment to anti-fascist views, as Michael Billington remarks in his obituary following the death of the actress in June 1991, which dated back to 1933 'when she witnessed firsthand the persecution of Jews in Berlin' (*The Guardian*, 15.6.91). This led her to found the Apollo Society (in 1943) which toured poetry and music to military camps, and, later, to be an active member of Amnesty International and the Index on Censorship. For all that, though, Jocelyn Herbert suggests 'there was something in Brecht's message that was alien to her; . . . when things are too overtly political in a doctrinaire way, she withdraws' (Billington, 1988, p.166). Brecht's full-blooded Marxism was certainly a problem for her. Ashcroft's natural tendency for 'ladylike' playing, which Jocelyn Herbert implied above, is further supported by her description of the actress' reaction to Paul Dessau telling her at the dress-rehearsal that she was failing to put across Shen Te's Song of the Defenceless. He said: '"You must get it over." Peggy was so angry that she put it across with real vigour and it was electrifying. It was very funny but she hardly ever did it like that again' (Billington, 1988, p.166).

Furthermore, Ashcroft herself admitted that the whole Royal Court Company found an appropriate style of performance very difficult to achieve and, in her view, it was only towards the end of the run that they began to find how to play their roles. She concluded:

> It's always simplification, and that's what actors are not used to here and why one would probably only find exactly what this simplification had to be if one played Brecht for a very long time.
>
> (Burton, 1967, p.96)

Devine had aimed to achieve a cool way of playing by inviting the cast to limit their general vocal range, but this may merely have hampered the actors in what Peter Thomson and Jan Needle describe as their 'quest of Brecht's supposed anti-emotionalism' (Needle and Thomson, 1981, p.130). Also, at least one critic of the production suggested that, since the company was working in translation, they were not assisted in achieving 'estrangement' by the language itself. (As indicated earlier, Brecht's odd mix of linguistic structures, shifting registers, and slang are very hard to translate into English.) John Elsom writes that this led them to resort to other vocal means to achieve Brechtian 'distance', 'often contorted and unnecessary ones' (Elsom, 1976, p.117).

Ashcroft's performance met with some scathing reviews. Eric Capon, writing in *Encore*, referred to her Shen Te as a 'Roedean whore' (Roedean being an exclusive girls' school redolent of upper-class decorum and refined manners).[8] Tynan thought that her presentation of the dual role was only half successful at best:

> As Shui Ta, flattened by a tight half-mask which helps her to produce a grinding nasal voice, she is superb; nothing tougher has been heard since Montgomery last harangued the troops. Yet her Shen Te won't do. Sexily though she blinks, all hints of whorish earthiness are expunged by those tell-tale Kensingtonian vowels. What remains is a portrait of Aladdin as it might be sketched by Princess Badroulbadour.
>
> (Tynan, 1964, p.232)

But criticism, according to Tynan, had also to be levelled at the direction:

> Honourably bent on directing his cast along cool, detached Brechtian lines, Mr. Devine forgets that the Brechtian method works only with team-actors of great technical maturity. With greener players it looks like casual dawdling.

Other reviewers tended to place most of the blame on Brecht's own dramaturgy. Harold Hobson, again taking an anti-Brecht stance, opined that the story was told 'in a series of straightforward, simplified scenes like those in an infant's school book' (Browne, 1975, p.26). The reviewer in *The Evening Argus* contended that

> the disconcerting aspect of stage Brecht is his direct communion with the audience. One is chided, beseeched and kept in the picture across the footlights and scenically there are [sic] the minimum of concessions to illusion.
>
> (*The Evening Argus*, 16.10.56)

These last comments perhaps indicate the sheer lack of experience of the British critics (and, therefore, audiences) in responding to the new, radical theatrical form of Brecht. However, even 'insiders' at the Royal Court, such as Assistant Director Tony Richardson, admitted the production created 'an academic impression', and one of the actors, Alan Bates, thought, 'the edge was missing' (Wardle, 1978, p.185). Richardson's comment on the 'academic' quality of the production suggests that Devine had tried to follow the Berliner 'model' too closely, perhaps been too reverent towards the outward form of the performance, especially as he was working with actors reared in another tradition. Michael Billington summarises in his biography of Ashcroft: Devine's production was 'too slavishly Brechtian, following the rule-book rather than the natural impulses of the English style' (Billington, 1988, p.167).

Whether as a result of the reviews or because the production coincided with the Hungarian revolution and a consequent rise in anti-Communist feeling in Britain, as John Elsom suggests (Elsom, 1976, p.81), the Royal Court audiences for *The Good Woman* were small. George Devine never mounted another Brecht production, though he did have plans in the 1960s to do *Man is Man* with Tony Hancock, a well-known British comedian, as Galy Gay. He himself appeared as Brecht in a collage programme, *Brecht on Brecht* by George Tabori (in 1962) and in this production (which also brought Lotte Lenya to the London stage for the first time since the production of *Anna Anna* in 1933), Devine came forward at the end to deliver a speech 'on the futility of trying to describe a house by holding up a single brick', a reference, of course, to a Brecht poem (Wardle, 1978, p.238). At that point in the history of British Brecht this might be regarded as an appropriate metaphor for the partial understanding of his work.

Perhaps some British misunderstandings of Brecht's theories and intent were inevitable. Even those setting out to promote and propagate Brecht at this time (such as the magazine *Encore*) frequently based their accounts on secondhand versions of the theory and thus contributed to the problem. But despite all the misgivings with which Brecht's work continued to be viewed, the impact of his work on British theatre in the late 1950s was significant. As Stuart Hall was to write (in 1961) somewhat grudgingly:

> Like Crusoe's Friday he [Brecht] has left his footsteps all over the bloody shop, but of the man himself – or any talent comparable for sheer originality – not a sign. A very skilful critic, reconstructing the dramatic history of the decade from the charred fragments of a nuclear war, might deduce that a composite dramatist lived and worked in Britain in the 1950s whose name was probably Bertolt Brecht – he has been so omnipresent.[9]

BRECHT AND BRITISH PLAYWRIGHTS

While many British theatre critics still failed to appreciate Brecht's plays in performance, either because of his politics, or because of the radical nature of his dramaturgy or because of the inadequacy of British productions, there was no doubt about his growing influence on British theatre practitioners, including playwrights, whose work in turn, it might be argued, helped to ease the acceptance into common practice of Brecht's dramaturgical ideas. Unsurprisingly, the earliest effect of Brechtian theatre seems to have been on some of the writers closely connected with the Royal Court Theatre. At about the time of Osborne's success with *Look Back in Anger*, a Writers' Group had been formed at the Court, at the instigation of George Devine. This included John Arden, Edward Bond and Arnold Wesker. All three were already left-wing, socially committed writers, much absorbed by the class struggle of post-war Britain, and both Arden and Bond were later to acknowledge the direct influence of Brecht on their playwriting. Arden's play *Serjeant Musgrave's Dance* (1959) is Brechtian in its handling of political issues, its use of a kind of pseudo-history, its adoption of an episodic structure and its exploitation of 'popular' music to articulate events and ideas. When Arden was asked in the 1960s if there was any modern play he would like to have written, the answer was *Mother Courage* (Marowitz and Trussler, 1967, p.47). Of all the influences on the writing of the young Edward Bond in the late 1950s, he indicates 'perhaps the most important single event was the visit of the Berliner Ensemble' (Hay and Roberts, 1980, p.16). Later Bond was to place himself in a line of development that began with Brecht:

> I have worked consciously – starting with Brecht but not ending there. Brecht's contribution to the creation of a Marxist theatre is enormous and lasting but the work is not yet finished.[10]

(Bond's contribution to this unfinished work will be discussed in Chapter 6.)

Another playwright who, though not a member of the Royal Court's Writers' Group, also acknowledged Brecht's significance for him at an early stage of his writing career was Robert Bolt. His play *A Man For All Seasons*, highly praised when first produced in 1960 and subsequently made into a successful film, exploits quite consciously the range of dramaturgical techniques, including a particular use of language and direct audience address, to achieve the 'distancing' that the British theatre was learning painfully from Brecht. Bolt saw in Brecht's use of language, a conscious moving away from the fashionable naturalism into a classical 'coolness':

> You may know that Brecht is the writer I would most wish to resemble . . . theatrically I think he was right, particularly when he said about language: 'A noble and dignified prose architecture is the primary alienation effect'. He knew it all instinctively. He knew exactly where we are and how desperately we need the classical.[11]

John Osborne, while never openly acknowledging any Brechtian influence on his writing, drew, maybe unconsciously, on the episodic nature and the direct actor/audience contact of epic theatre in what may be regarded as his best play, *The Entertainer*, about a seedy music hall performer, brought memorably to life by the great 'classical' actor of his age, Laurence Olivier (Billington, 1972, p.200).

However, some British playwrights of the time chose to take issue with Brecht rather than to follow him. John Whiting, for example, doubted whether theatre could be socially and politically useful in the way a committed socialist writer required. In an interview published in *Encore* in 1961 he said:

I think art is a useless instrument of propaganda, that's why I entirely disagree with Brecht. And anyway, I'm right and he's wrong, that's obviously been proved because his plays are not good propaganda.

(Marowitz and Trussler, 1967, p.30)

Whiting also expressed a quite common concern of the time about Brechtian theory, not that it was wrong but that understanding it was too difficult a task for the practitioner. In his book *On Theatre* he wrote: 'Brecht spent many years explaining *Verfremdung* and his disciples are now explaining his explanations. All remains as dark as night' (Whiting, 1966, p.65).

There was at this time another group of British playwrights (many of whom were part of or associated with the Royal Court Theatre) who were working in a very different way to Brecht: the Absurdists, such as N.F. Simpson, Harold Pinter and Samuel Beckett. Their existential view of the world was in many ways in direct opposition to that of Brecht's Marxist view, though it is intriguing to note that in the last few months of his life, Brecht had begun to annotate the text of *Waiting for Godot*, with an adaptation in mind. Pinter, on the other hand, took a distinctly antipathetic stance to Brecht. He wrote on the wall of the director's office at the Royal Court Theatre a quotation from Eugène Ionesco: 'Le théâtre de Brecht est le théâtre de Boy Scout' (Findlater, 1981, p.59). Ironically, his play *The Collector* was among those nominated for the prestigious *Evening Standard* Best Play of the Year Award in 1962 and it lost out to *The Caucasian Chalk Circle*. The other main contender for the award was Arnold Wesker's *Chips With Everything* (a play that itself contains clear elements of Brechtian stagecraft). Despite some initial reluctance on the part of the judges to give this important award posthumously to Brecht, they did so, encouraged by Milton Shulman, *The Evening Standard* theatre critic and one of the judges, who declared: 'That's going to survive'. On the other hand, the Wesker play, he argued, would not. It was, however, agreed that in subsequent years 'living playwrights ought not to have to compete with the dead' (Wintour, 1980, p.18).

WILLIAM GASKILL AND BRITISH BRECHT OF THE 1960s

The production of *The Caucasian Chalk Circle* nominated for the 1962 award was directed by William Gaskill for the Royal Shakespeare Company, whose policy included the presentation of new and modern 'classic' plays. Significantly, Gaskill's professional background included three years at the Royal Court Theatre (1957–60), where his productions for the English Stage Company were almost all of new plays by the Court's Writers' Group (including work by John Osborne, John Arden and N.F. Simpson). The 1956 visit of the Berliner Ensemble, he acknowledged, had had a seminal influence on him, particularly with regard to the writer's political intentions:

For me the visit in '56 was the most striking and influential theatrical experience I shall ever have. *Courage* really shattered me, it was extraordinary. Everything suddenly clarified and came into focus . . . . I don't think we heard much about it [Brecht's dramatic theory] from the political point of view or understood that it was largely political.[12]

Gaskill's approach to directing was also influenced by George Devine. The latter had instituted acting classes as part of the working process at the Royal Court and these included ones on the exploration of the use of improvisation and masks in the *commedia dell'arte* tradition. Gaskill describes in his book *A Sense of Direction* the powerful impression Devine's mask-work made on the classes and how it helped him understand that:

there was another approach to acting which was not analytical, in which the actor does not prepare in the Stanislavsky sense by thinking of the given circumstances, the 'flow of the day' or even his objectivity, but empties his mind to receive the influence, the identity of another being.

(Gaskill, 1988, p.43)

Gaskill himself had trained at the Decroux Mime School in Paris, but it was Devine who encouraged him to believe it was important for a director to create an environment of ensemble working that would provide opportunity for the ongoing development of the actor's skills and open, exploratory approaches to production. He was, therefore, easily drawn to work with Peter Hall at the Royal Shakespeare Company in 1960/1, when the latter was in the process of creating, for the first time with that company, a full-scale ensemble of the continental (German) kind. Gaskill saw it as a 'chance to bring the Court's version of the Epic style into work on Shakespeare' (Gaskill, 1988, p.52), and for the RSC's season at the Aldwych he directed *Richard III* and *Cymbeline*, two Shakespeare plays with strong Brechtian features. A reviewer of the second production observantly described it as 'a resplendent panoramic achievement that would assuredly never have happened had Mr. Gaskill not caught the Brechtian bug' (Tynan, 1964, p.99).

Gaskill then turned his attention to Brecht himself. When he began work on *The Caucasian Chalk Circle*, he tells us, he had only two ideas in mind: one was to work with masks because they were indicated by the text, and the other was to employ Brecht's rehearsal exercise of the actor's relating the action of the scene in the third person. Although he thought that Brecht's symbolic use of masks in this play reflected a 'rather old-fashioned view of good and evil' (Gaskill, 1988, p.47), he adopted their use in the production. The music was a different matter. Gaskill decided to replace Dessau's music written for the original production with songs specially written by the British jazz musician (and comic actor) Dudley Moore. These were to be sung in the show by the disabled performer Michael Flanders, who was well-known as half of a musical duo, Flanders and Swan, that specialised in comic songs performed with piano accompaniment. As Narrator/Singer, Flanders would be permanently seated in his wheelchair at the side of the stage.

As was customary at the RSC, the roles in *The Caucasian Chalk Circle* had been cast before rehearsals began, but Gaskill started the rehearsal process by suggesting that alternative casting might be made on the basis of a series of improvisations by the actors. This, he admits, 'panicked some of the regular members of the ensemble' (Gaskill, 1988, p.53). Susan Engel, one of the company, describes the wholly negative effect of this radical (Brechtian) approach on a company that was clearly less of an ensemble than Gaskill supposed:

> He got us all together and said: 'As we're doing a Brecht, we're not going to start rehearsing with a read-through. Moreover, though I've got you as a cast, all of you in the parts you're cast for, what we're going to do to begin with is to read each other's parts and then we might completely re-cast.' There was pandemonium! All the younger, smaller part actors were thrilled, to have a go at playing the bigger parts – but there was complete turmoil and resistance and fury and suggested walk-outs. It didn't help at all to begin with. Made a kind of atmosphere of total mistrust . . . anti-academic, anti-socialist attitude.[13]

Gaskill underestimated the conservatising strength of the traditional British theatre's hierarchical organisation into stars and bit players. This will be a recurring theme throughout this book. Undeterred by this inauspicious start, however, Gaskill continued to use exploratory improvisation, a novel kind of improvisation which he saw as a means of helping the actors understand and find the *Gestus* for each action in the text:

> In a two-handed scene each actor would narrate the actions as objectively as possible, sometimes in the third person, and this narration was analysed over and over again till both actors would agree on the exact sequence of events; that is, they would tell the same story. So accustomed were the actors to seeing action from the point of view of their character that this often took a long time.
>
> (Gaskill, 1988, p.49)

It is clear from interviews and from his subsequent book (*A Sense of Direction*) that during the process of rehearsing *Chalk Circle* Gaskill came to believe that the director should not tell an actor what to do but should learn to pose the right questions which would clarify for the actor not only his, the actor's, understanding of his role and function but 'his responsibility to his part, to the play and ultimately to society'.[14]

Gaskill's own understanding of Brecht's political intentions led him to see that it was the director's job to 'maintain the objective control of the stage picture and its meaning, [that] it was clear that for this to work there must be no unnecessary clobber on stage' (Gaskill, 1988, p.20). He also came to the conclusion that in producing Brecht, 'one must demonstrate both a physical and an intellectual truth'.[15] By this he meant that the meaning of a production needs to be borne in its physical eloquence and clarity. In retrospect, he was sure that in his work on *Chalk Circle* he had concentrated too much on the intellectual approach at the expense of the physical. He had wanted his actors to understand that so many of the actions of Brecht's characters are 'habitual' and that a contextualization of these actions is crucial to the audience's perception of their social significance. In order to achieve this, significant actions had to be underlined in the performance by the use of pauses, changes in rhythm and the sheer physical panache of the performers:

> Any action, if placed in a certain situation, is significant. To play this, you have to have a tremendously unhurried and spacious feeling, and at the same time you have to have actors of great weight and authority.[16]

In fact, Gaskill appears to have taken this ideal of an 'unhurried' feeling too far. The final run-through of his production ran two hours longer than originally scheduled. Susan Engel explains what followed:

> Peter Hall said to Bill Gaskill: 'This won't do. Either you leave the building and I re-direct it now or you change this, this and that and you cut it. It's got to run at twice the pace.' There was a big row, Bill left the building and Peter Hall 'cleaned' it up. But he wasn't a Brechtian. He was only interested in presenting a show in his theatre which the audience would accept. And Brecht was obviously unpalatable to a West End audience at the time.

Hall increased the running pace so that the final production lasted only (a long) three and a half hours, and he was justified in that, in general, critical response was positive. Naturally, Gaskill's own judgment of his production was coloured by the circumstances of the Peter Hall 'takeover':

> Perhaps he pulled the show together, but he completely misread Brecht's specific instructions – for instance, the manner in which a poor man eats his only crust. The production was a success, but commercial pressures had been brought to bear. The search for a group approach to a new kind of theatre had been blocked.
>
> (Gaskill, 1988, p.53)

John Whiting, who had previously expressed his opposition to Brecht's form of theatre (see p.57), wrote a long and fulsome review of the production in *The London Magazine*, focusing in particular on the acting. He declared that Gaskill had been successful in creating a 'unifying style' that would silence the critics who expressed doubts about British actors' capacity to perform Brecht, though what that style amounted to he did not specify. He did, however, state that he thought Patsy Byrne's Grusha failed to match the stature of Angelika Hurwicz's ('Hurwicz was touched by tragedy, Miss Byrne inclines to pathos'), and that he was impressed by Hugh Griffith as Azdak:

> He is a daring actor, shocking the purists, and then delighting everyone by demonstrating that nothing he does is in the end arbitrary, but a mosaic of meaning.
>
> (Whiting, 1966, p.99)

This suggests that Griffith achieved Brecht's notion of the inventory of a role (discussed in Chapter 1). But predictably, perhaps, in view of the dominance of naturalism at the time, this kind of playing did not please others. Tom Milne (of *Encore*) expressed the view that the play was 'constantly undercut by the inability of the actors to present the reality of their characters',[17] a view supported by the reviewer for *The Evening News*, who suggested that Gaskill, 'thinking he was respecting Brecht's theories, had warned them [the cast] against "character acting"' (*The Evening News*, 30.3.62). However, a fourth reviewer, writing for *The Daily Express*, admired the 'reality' of the performances and seized on that as a stick with which to beat Brechtian theory: 'Here are real people, here is real humour, here are real themes, here is the real urgency of life and of drama. What price the "alienation effect" now?' (*The Daily Express*, 30.3.62). In general, though, the response to Gaskill's production was positive and, despite the rehearsal problems he encountered, he seems to have moved British Brecht a little closer – not merely in the imitative sense – to the Berliner model.

Just over a year later Gaskill was invited by Laurence Olivier to join the newly formed National Theatre Company, which was about to begin its work at the Old Vic Theatre (until its South Bank home was ready). The main attraction for Gaskill was again the possibility of working within an ensemble, an idea which, he claims, 'haunted all our dreams' (Gaskill, 1988, p.55). The example of the Berliner Ensemble was ever-present in the minds of the National directors, so a visit to Berlin was arranged. Gaskill recalls standing

> with Weigel at Brecht's graveside in the cemetery that he used to see from his workroom window. In the evening we went to see *Arturo Ui*. We were unanimous in our admiration for the work, perhaps for different reasons. We believed that it set a standard to be emulated, but we never theorized as to how this was to be achieved.
>
> (Gaskill, 1988, p.55)

Gaskill's admiration, even over-reverence, for Brecht's work with the Berliner Ensemble was candidly admitted in the earnest programme note for his production of *Mother Courage and Her Children*, National Theatre, 1965.

> The Berliner Ensemble production of *Mother Courage* was the best I have ever seen of any play. The present production is largely based upon it. There are three major differences: the play will be played in English, the actors are not the same, and the play is not directed by the author. Apart from these, I see no reason to disregard the author's own detailed notes, not only on the placing of actors and scenery but on how these were arrived at. . . . [Brecht's] main work, which has had little or no influence here, was the training of actors to present the characters in their social situation rather than in terms of their individual psychology. It is this that we attempted to stress.

For his own production, Gaskill had some difficulty in casting the play. To begin with, he decided that there was no ideal actress at the National for the leading role and so cast Madge Ryan as Courage because she was a good ensemble performer. However, he later admitted that he discovered that even in Brecht 'you need stars' (Gaskill, 1988, p.59). In retrospect, Gaskill concluded that both Ryan and Michael Gambon (who played Eilif) had been miscast. Gambon himself agrees on both counts. Of Ryan's performance, Gambon said recently: 'Not strong enough. Not earthy enough. Rather weak vocally. She didn't have a positive enough attitude to it. You didn't feel she was 'there' – she shied away.'[18] About his own performance of Eilif, he commented:

> I don't know why I wasn't right. . . . I wasn't happy with the extrovert side of Eilif – he dances and sings. The song! I never got near that – it was always a terrible strain. . . . Later I met Schall at the Berliner Ensemble. He did Eilif's dance for me. He didn't move his arms. They just hung by his side. It was all so simple.

Gambon recalled Gaskill's bringing the Berliner's *Modellbuch* to rehearsals and drawing the cast's attention to the photographs a great deal, in order, Gambon thought, for the company merely to understand how the stage would be set. When it came to rehearsing the roles, he recalled, there was little reference to 'the inner aspects of character' and most emphasis was placed by Gaskill on 'blocking' and on the creation of physical images. For Gambon, one of the most important (and for that time, bold) decisions was to play Eilif and Swiss Cheese with Cockney accents. This boldness in deploying 'working-class' voices for Brecht may well indicate the influence via Gaskill of the Royal Court and its 'angry young man' of *Look Back in Anger*.

In addition to the miscasting of some major roles in *Mother Courage*, Gaskill judged that the production suffered from the fact that the company failed to achieve the standard of acting in the minor parts that he had hoped for. Crucially, he concluded that this was because 'for the actors the play was just another play in the repertoire of the company; there was no common attitude, political or aesthetic in the work' (Gaskill, 1988, p.59), a view that Michael Gambon would repeat in connection with a later National Theatre production of Brecht (see Chapter 4). The general problem of a lack of common political and aesthetic ground between actors working on Brecht is another recurring theme of British Brecht.

Critical response to Gaskill's production was largely negative. While Penelope Gilliatt (in *The Observer*) thought that 'in a country without a peasant class, I can't think of anyone who would be better' than Madge Ryan as Mother Courage (15.8.65), Harold Hobson (in *The Sunday Times*), again attacking Brecht, dismissed the playwright as 'a gigantic bore', and condemned the production with: 'the tedium of the National Theatre production of *Mother Courage* is beyond description' (16.5.65). Martin Esslin subsequently commented that a 'let's get rid of Brecht' movement had grown up in Britain by this time and that it 'was further strengthened by Gaskill's *Mother Courage*'.[19] While this puts the case a little strongly, it is certainly true that Brecht was more the darling of theatre practitioners than critics.

Shortly after his *Mother Courage*, Gaskill left the National Theatre to return to the Royal Court, taking over the artistic direction of that theatre from George Devine. During his second stint at the Court, Gaskill developed a special working relationship with Edward Bond, the playwright who best earns the *soubriquet* of 'the British Brecht' (see Chapter 6). Gaskill now felt it was easier to do non-Brecht plays in a 'Brechtian style' than to emulate Brecht in productions of his own texts. In fact, Gaskill went on to achieve considerable success with his productions of Bond's *Saved*, *Early Morning* and *The Sea*, and with 'Brechtian' productions of *Macbeth* and *The Recruiting Officer* (the play on which Brecht had based his *Trumpets and Drums*). In 1971, Gaskill directed another Bond play, *Lear*, and the lessons he had learned were well recognised by a review of the production: 'the groupings, the lighting, the colour of the decor and the costumes and the overall visual economy all seemed to derive from the style Brecht evolved at the Berliner Ensemble' (Hayman, 1975, p.209). But in the same year, Gaskill attempted another (and his last) Brecht play, *Man is Man*. Gaskill writes about it that it was 'a not very good production of an unsatisfactory play' (Gaskill, 1988, p.118), and reviewers tended to agree. Harold Hobson, acerbic as ever, described the production as being 'as glum as Mexborough muck' (*The Sunday Times*, 7.3.71).

In the following year (1972), Gaskill again left the Royal Court, though, as a true Brechtian, he 'still nursed dreams of what the Court might have: a permanent group of actors, a studio attached to the theatre exploring new ways of working and a committed but popular audience' (Gaskill, 1988, p.131). (Shades of Joan Littlewood and Theatre Workshop there.)

Some of Gaskill's dreams were fulfilled for a while by his subsequent work with the Joint Stock Company with whom he created the first production of David Hare's play about Chinese communism, *Fanshen*. Of that, Gaskill wrote:

> It was a fulfilment of the process started on *The Caucasian Chalk Circle* and thwarted by the demands of the RSC and Peter Hall, the process in which the actors share an understanding of the political responsibility of the play, they are not just there to serve the writer but, together with the writer, are making a statement.
>
> (Gaskill, 1988, p.136)

We shall return to that in Chapter 3. Since 1971, Gaskill has directed no plays by Brecht.

THE BERLINER ENSEMBLE RETURNS

Immediately after Gaskill's production of *Mother Courage* in 1965, at a time when there appeared to be a growing opposition to Brecht's work (according to Martin Esslin, at least) over the hill came the Berliner Ensemble cavalry with a second visit to London (August, 1965). The company's performances of *The Resistible Rise of Arturo Ui*, *Coriolanus*, *The Threepenny Opera*, *Days of the Commune* and excerpts from *Mahagonny* that summer served to show that in many ways British Brecht had done the master a disservice, for, as Penelope Gilliatt observes in reviewing their programme:

> This is the way Brecht wanted the theatre to be: skimming, speculative, beautiful, fun. I realise that every received idea about him in England teaches the opposite. His plays are expected to be heavy because he was German, shut-minded because he was a Marxist, visually like wartime utility because of his emphasis on use in design and no fun at all.
>
> (*The Observer*, 15.8.65)

This reminds us of Hobson's view of Gaskill's 'glum' *Man is Man*, and she ends her review with the comment that the Berliner 'has an energy and sense of play that hardly anyone but Joan Littlewood in England dreams of'. Of course, it is important to note that this second visit introduced British theatre not only to previously unfamiliar plays in the Brecht canon, but in particular to those, like *Arturo Ui*, that made apparent the more anti-realist and broadly comic aspects of his work.

Harold Hobson, who had expressed very sceptical views on Brecht's theatrical theories when reviewing the 1956 visit of the Berliner, now became an advocate, describing the performances of 1965 as 'Brecht For Grown-Ups'. He went on to make the point that:

English directors seem to misunderstand Brecht. Because he is a progressive writer, they assumed that the reactionary characters in his plays must be absurd. They make them absurd and stop at that. They create no sense of power or conflict. Behind the joke the threat is missing.

(The Sunday Times, 15.9.65)

Hobson identifies succinctly here one way in which British Brecht had been unsuccessful, the failure to see a political dialectic played out amongst the plays' power brokers. There were others. The initial responses to the Berliner Ensemble (in 1956) by enthusiastic British practitioners had sometimes resulted in their placing too much emphasis on the external features of production, lavishing energy on imitating the visual effects of the Berliner staging rather than basing artistic decisions on a real understanding of a production process grounded in a rigorous integration of political and aesthetic ideas. Imitation of the Berliner was, by some directors, too slavishly obsessed with style or too academically obsessed with theory. In the homegrown theatrical context of British subsidised theatre, where for both actors and directors there was no experience of or real opportunity for an ensemble approach to rehearsing, no shared attitude to the political content of the work and limited (often inadequate) rehearsal time, Brecht's production ideas could not be put into practice satisfactorily nor his plays effectively performed. In addition, there was the thorny problem of producing Brecht's plays in translation. The distinctiveness of Brecht's verbal style has been discussed above. Perhaps, though, in that period of the late 1950s and early 1960s, most significant of all the barriers to a successful transplantation of Brecht was the obstacle of the political content of the plays. Brecht's Marxism and the declared socio-political function of his theatre were stumbling blocks for the average, educated theatre-goer in Britain, and many British critics made their ideological opposition quite plain. Such antagonism to the alien politics of the plays may have led some directors to attempt to play them down in their productions. But such a recourse clearly begs a host of questions, both moral and artistic. As Gaskill put it:

There are many people who say, 'Throw away the politics, get rid of the theory, treat Brecht like any other writer, make him theatrical'. In practice this means filling the stage with smoke, rock music and punk hairdos, and the essence of the work is lost.

(Gaskill, 1988, p.58)

In the late 1960s changes in the political climate in Europe and the USA were to create a context much more obviously appropriate to the 'essence' of Brecht; he was about to be taken on – especially in Britain – plays, politics, warts and all.

3

PERFORMING BRECHT
POST-1968

The radical responses

THE 'BOOMING' 1960s

The social changes in the Britain of the 1960s, following in the wake of improved prosperity, included a burgeoning interest in the arts, both in their professional forms and within the education system. This interest stimulated the building of a large number of new civic theatres and of community-based arts centres (with specialised theatre facilities). By 1970, twenty new regional playhouses had been built, many of which broke away from the traditional, proscenium arch architecture to deploy radically shaped stages and auditoria (thrust, in-the-round, etc.) designed to foster a new, dynamic relationship between the actors and the audience. Also, many extant repertory theatres added a 'studio' to their main houses, giving the resident companies greater programming flexibility and the opportunity to experiment with new plays and styles of playing.

Some regional companies also started to provide a 'home' for the new initiative in 'Theatre-in-Education', which was part of the emerging interest in art as education. Drama as a curriculum subject in schools had been given a boost by the governmental investigation that resulted in the Newsome Report of 1963, *Half Our Future*. This report, which expressed strong support for the notion of 'child centred' education and 'learning by doing', recognised the importance of creative drama in the personal and social development of the child. Consequently, during the 1960s many specialist drama teachers were appointed to schools in Britain and the discipline of drama was given a high profile. This in turn provided a receptive context for the new 'mixed' form of Theatre-in-Education, which brought together the learning process fundamental to creative drama and the aesthetic stimulus and dramatic excitement of the theatre experience.

The first Theatre-in-Education company was set up in 1965 as a constituent part of Coventry's (still new) repertory theatre, the Belgrade. This company (or 'team' as such groups are more commonly called) comprised a small group of actor-teachers, who combined the skills of the professional actor and the qualified teacher in their training and function. The team was funded by the local Education Authority and utilised the practical and technical resources of their base in repertory theatre. As a result, they were able to provide a free service to Coventry schools and target their work on specific, often relatively small, groups of pupils. The typical TIE show they created, to be presented in a school, was a short performance piece specifically devised by the team to explore appropriate themes and issues relevant to one class or grade, followed by particpatory workshops for the pupils. Preparatory and/or further classroom work could be conducted before/after the team's visit by the class teacher, who was assisted in this by the provision of a Teacher's Pack containing ideas and suggestions from the TIE team.

Such an operation became the model for the funding, structure and practice of most subsequent Theatre-in-Education teams. By the late 1970s, there were about fifty 'Young People's Theatre' companies throughout Britain, many with a specific Theatre-in-Education programme of work, others with a wider 'community' brief. (At the time of writing, however, many such companies have either closed or are under threat because of financial constraints on schools and local government and because of radical reforms of the school programme, including the implementation of a National Curriculum that in effect 'downgrades' the importance of drama/theatre.)

The relationship between the kind of work created by TIE teams in the 1960s and 1970s and the theatre of Brecht is close in many ways. It was in the spirit of Brecht's theatrical intentions that TIE programmes mostly set out to focus attention on and bring into sharp consciousness specific social issues and to provide an arena in which young people might work out their (sometimes active) responses to them. The work was (and is) seen as educational and innovatory, and, to use a Brechtian term, 'useful'. TIE programmes not only analyse(d) problems but invite(d) the pupil spectators to participate in solving them, both as part of the theatrical event and beyond that in their own social actions and attitudes outside school. All this equates closely with Brecht's aims for his *Lehrstücke*, which were themselves presented in East German schools. Brecht's intention with these pieces was that the children participating should play first one part and then another, thus examining the issues from a series of angles. Only then might they judge what was the right course of action to take. Many TIE teams, at least in the 1960s and 1970s, themselves suscribed to a Marxist view of the social context in which they operated and incorporated into their shows a social reading based on dialectical materialism. They, in turn, contributed to the growing taste and opportunity for new and radical theatre experiences in main house shows.

THE DEVELOPMENT OF ALTERNATIVE THEATRE

A parallel move towards experimentation on the part of the 'mainstream' theatre was in large part stimulated by the rapidly expanding 'fringe' theatre movement of the period. The term 'fringe theatre' was most closely associated in the early 1960s with the Edinburgh Festival, an annual international arts festival founded in 1947, around which grew up the tradition of impromptu and unconventional performances by all kinds of artistic groups. The Edinburgh Fringe, which was given further impetus by the opening in the city of the experimentally orientated Traverse Theatre in 1963, quickly established a reputation for innovative theatrical ideas and thus provided a forum for debate and expression for the growing number of new, radical theatre groups. 'Fringe' theatre groups were soon more commonly known as 'alternative', to denote the idea that instead of clinging to the skirts of mainstream theatre the groups offered something different that in effect provided an alternative kind of theatre experience from that provided by mainstream or established theatre.

Edinburgh's success in promoting alternative theatre was quickly matched by London. One of the most influential of the new, alternative London groups was CAST, which was to play a significant role in the development of Brechtian performance in the UK. CAST is the acronym for Cartoon Archetypical Slogan Theatre. The company, founded in 1965 by Roland and Claire Muldoon, grew out of the work of London's Unity Theatre and, therefore, had a ready-made political heritage. Roland Muldoon foregrounds that one distinctive feature: 'Community Theatre we weren't. Nor were we Agit prop. We were Political Theatre' (Rees, 1992, p.75). Their performances were influenced, he says, by 'the archetypicality of Laurel and Hardy, Charlie Chaplin and the characters in the movie *Les Enfants du Paradis*'. These comic film actors, and Chaplin in particular, link the company directly with Brecht's ideas on performance, and the reference to the nineteenth-century mime artists in the film stresses the company's emphasis on a physical form of acting. Their declared purpose was to hold

> the critical mirror up to those who were saying this is the way forward in the class struggle as well as to those who wouldn't mind something happening but wouldn't follow those who said they knew the way.
>
> (Rees, 1992, pp.69 and 73)

CAST shows characteristically took on a wild, anarchic style, and the company played mostly to worker and student audiences.

The socio-political commitment of a company like CAST was relatively unusual in the mid-1960s, though the contemporary group Ed Berman's Interaction shared some of the same concerns, and the long-lasting People Show developed a similarly anarchic line in audience provocation. But alternative theatre in Britain was given a sudden and dynamic shot in the arm by the political events of 1968: the shock occasioned by the 'Prague Spring' and its overthrow; the anti-Vietnam War movement in the USA and Europe; and the student and worker rising in Paris. All of these things politicised artists and theatre practitioners, and hard upon the heels of these (and part of the movement of protest and emancipation) came the abolition of theatre censorship in Britain, which helped to fuel an explosion of new theatre practice by liberating content and style. This explosion is well documented elsewhere (see Craig 1980 and Itzin 1980), but it is apposite to note here that the stimulus for socially and politically motivated theatre that occurred post-1968 was significant in changing British approaches to Brecht and instrumental in providing contexts in which his work might be not only more favourably received aesthetically but perceived as relevant and useful politically.

In the decade following 1968, the number of alternative theatre groups grew from the handful established in the early/mid-1960s to over 100, performing the work of an estimated 250 playwrights in over 200 small-scale venues. These new companies sought to develop a new concept of theatre, a new aesthetic and new audiences. They assumed a more radical and political function for theatre than had been the norm, and consciously they developed more open styles of performance, aimed at provoking a greater performer/audience interaction than that promoted in conventional theatre. Also they deployed, in the face of the characteristic gentility of British drama, deliberately outspoken language, and they exploited the immediate accessibility of contemporary music as part of a new theatrical language designed to appeal to the young. Many companies, rejecting the traditional primacy of the spoken text, invested imaginatively (if not financially) in the creation of strong visual, staging effects.

A new aesthetic was inevitably developed in that most of the alternative companies had no theatre base of their own and touring required an economy of production means and simple staging. New audiences were found by touring to non-traditional theatre spaces such as clubs, village halls and the upstairs rooms of pubs, and there was a deliberate and strenuous targeting of specific groups, defined by their locality, gender, race or by some other defining feature or shared background.

A large and significant proportion of the immediately post-1968 alternative theatre groups in Britain regarded and described themselves as 'political', and even those not professing a specific ideology were politically different from establishment theatre companies in the sense that they followed a general tendency of the 'alternative' culture to organise and run themselves on collective and/or co-operative lines, and as ensembles. In other words, they offered a direct alternative to the hierarchical power structures of bourgeois, mainstream, British establishment theatre, and their production processes were as radical as their end-products.

Many companies broke away literally, geographically, by touring to towns and venues that did not normally have access to theatre or by taking up residence in a specific, perhaps culturally deprived place. A key alternative company that sought to fill some of Britain's provincial, cultural vacuums in the late 1960s was Welfare State International. Founded in 1968 by John Fox, the company's 'alternative strategy' was to 'fuse fine art, theatre and life-style' (Ansorge, 1975, p.41). This resulted in their characteristic construction of celebratory, carnivalesque, outdoor spectaculars and earned their self-description of 'Engineers of the Imagination', a title that seeks to convey their intended role as facilitators of the development and expression of ordinary people's creative talents. Welfare State have created, and continue to create, shows that draw on and exploit rock music, pagan ritual, large-scale visual imagery and physical constructions, and fireworks. They are often processional in form, and the company consciously plays out what Albert Hunt called 'the role of permanent Lords of Misrule' (*The Times Educational Supplement*, 25.7.75). The socio-political aspect of the company's work resides in part in their commitment to the involvement of the community in the construction and performance of their shows and events. This has led in recent years to their focusing much of their activity on the socially and culturally deprived northern England town of Barrow-in-Furness, where they have instigated a number of celebratory events and created a community film. The ideology of Welfare State continues to reflect, as Baz Kershaw puts it in *The Politics of Performance*, the company's 'sympathy for the underdog inspired by a primitive socialism' (Kershaw, 1992, p.212). There are, of course, dangers of this form of theatre's simply becoming an escapist safety valve for the release of community tension and frustration without resultant political action, a kind of wallpapering over the cracks. The actual programme of reform can be subverted by the creation of a temporary 'feel good' effect. Some would argue, like David Edgar, a socialist playwright, that for theatre to be fully effective politically, it needs to combine the cerebral and the visceral, if it is to avoid 'becoming no more than a radical sideshow to divert the masses' (Edgar, 1988, p.245).

In contrast to Welfare State's emphasis on the visually spectacular, Portable Theatre, founded by David Hare and Tony Bicat, also in 1968, was one of the few genuinely writer-based alternative companies. In its short history (five years), the company provided a breeding ground for some of Britain's best-known socialist writers, most notably David Hare himself and Howard Brenton. Hare, who began his writing career by filling a gap when a play commissioned by Portable failed to arrive, formed a highly productive partnership with Brenton, which one critic, wittily if over-simply, likened to the relationship between Paul McCartney and John Lennon. Hare as McCartney wrote the better tunes, the more sophisticated language; Brenton as Lennon was more outspokenly political.[1]

In Brenton's view, Portable Theatre was political in the simple sense that the company took performances out to audiences that were not accustomed to attending the theatre. The bareness of staging necessitated by small-scale touring had a powerful and stimulating effect on the company's writers. For Brenton, who regards himself as working in the tradition of Brecht, it led to considerable theatrical inventiveness, especially in staging *coups*, such as the giant stomach constructed for his adaptation of Rabelais' *Gargantua*, the use of the Bradford ice-rink for his show *Scott of the Antarctic*, or the playpen filled with newspapers for *Christie in Love*, his play about the double murderer John Christie. In these pieces Brenton put together a skilful, Brechtian juxtaposition of naturalism and the non-real, so that, for example, while Christie was presented as a three-dimensional character, the actor wore a mask, which the writer alled 'an alienation device'.[2] Both Brenton and Hare utilised strong stage images and episodic narrative structures in Brechtian fashion, and created dialogue out of forthright language. They presented a picture of the late 1960s/early 1970s Britain that was often shocking to their audiences. John Bull, in his book *New Political Dramatists*, describes the effect more forcefully as 'a consistent vision of nihilistic disintegration, relying heavily on "uncool" dramatic shock tactics' (Bull, 1984, p.40). Portable Theatre's audiences, while often new to theatre, were predominantly young, and because many were students, they were, therefore, more middle class than those sought by some other politically committed theatre groups of the period.

One alternative theatre company that specifically wanted 'to make theatre of and for the working-class in a socialist way' was 7:84 (McGrath, 1981, p.118). This company's name reflected the socio-economic inequality in Britain at the time of its founding in 1971, that is, that 7 per cent of the population owned 84 per cent of the national capital wealth. It was started by the writer/director John McGrath, and quickly established a reputation for lively, socialist entertainment. While admiring Brecht for the political intentions of his work, McGrath was critical of Brechtian form. He claimed that Brecht created a 'political theatre which is on the side of the workers but expresses itself in the language of high cultural theatre' (McGrath, 1981, p.62). McGrath, consequently, set out to create a new style of socialist theatre, which would directly draw on and exploit those forms of popular performance that would be familiar and accessible to working-class audiences. In his book *A Good Night Out*, McGrath lists what he regards as the necessary ingredients for his style of popular theatre. These include: directness, comedy, music, emotion, variety of effect, immediacy and localism (McGrath, 1981, p.54). And it is worth pointing out that most of these elements could come from a recipe created by Brecht himself. Nevertheless, 7:84 developed its own unique style, one important feature of which was its deployment of contemporary and regional music. The insistence on localism, which requires the show to include material that is relevant and familiar to particular audiences, is also reflected in 7:84's policy of touring to non-traditional theatre venues, including working men's clubs and factories.

The most celebrated example of a successful bringing together of form, content and meaning in the work of 7:84 was the first show McGrath wrote for the Scottish branch of the company, set up in 1973 – *The Cheviot, the Stag and the Black, Black Oil*. In this piece, the local issues relating to the historical changes of ownership of the Scottish Highlands and the impact of the discovery of oil in the twentieth century are dynamically presented and explored by drawing on dramaturgical and performance techniques that ensure both a direct relationship between performers and the audience and the effective satirical and critical embodiment of powerful characters. The whole piece, which is framed by the traditional Gaelic popular music/dance form of the *ceilidh*, in which the audience joins at the end, is blatantly Brechtian in many respects. McGrath claims that his open, accessible and 'popular' form of socialist theatre allows audiences to 'come out knowing that . . . culture is not exclusively in the hands of the children of the rich or the higher-educated: they have culture, too, and this theatre is part of their culture' (McGrath, 1981, p.126).

While McGrath rejected what he saw as the bourgeois nature of the Brechtian form, there is no doubt that 7:84's work was in the spirit of Brecht and certainly the success of their shows both in England and Scotland during the early 1970s helped to nurture a taste for political theatre that was comic yet hard-hitting, contemporary yet set against a historical perspective, and a form of theatre that required individual actors to develop and use a range of personal performance skills while remaining part of an ensemble. The politics and philosophy of 7:84 and of many other alternative theatre groups in Britain at this time made them good examples of the collective ethics of Brechtian theatre and often ideal presenters of his work. And so it is not surprising that some of the best British Brecht (in the view of the present writer) was actually produced by these alternative companies themselves.

BRECHT BY THE RADICAL TOURING COMPANIES

Belt and Braces Roadshow and *The Mother*

Appropriately enough, a company formed by some founder members of 7:84, the Belt and Braces Roadshow, was responsible for an extremely successful production of Brecht's *The Mother* in 1978. The founder/director of Belt and Braces, Gavin Richards, had first worked with John McGrath in 1972, when both were involved in the Everyman Theatre, Liverpool, production of *The Caucasian Chalk Circle*. Richards was an actor in the production and McGrath adapted the script. (More details are given on pp.79–80.) Shortly after this, Richards joined 7:84 as an actor, and late in 1972 he directed for 7:84 a new play by John Arden and Margaretta D'Arcy, *The Ballygombeen Bequest*. This play was a savage indictment of British military treatment of prisoners in Northern Ireland and it was taken off just before the end of its sixteen-week tour because of a threatened libel action. Although the case was settled out of court, the scandal indirectly led to 7:84's growing disfavour with the Arts Council of Great Britain and their loss of subsidy. Consequently, the company ceased working for a time. Phoenix-like, the Belt and Braces company was started at this point, taking with it not only some of the 7:84 actors but a deal of its influence, including a socio-political function and a populist style, including the frequent use of contemporary music.

When Belt and Braces decided to do *The Mother*, Gavin Richards, as director, chose to use a translation by the established playwright Steve Gooch. This version had first been produced (in 1976) at the Half Moon Theatre, a fringe venue in London, and in working on the text, Gooch had, he says, 'looked at the *Modellbuch* and at Brecht's acting precepts, and tried to be as close as possible to the Brecht model'.[3] Richards offered the main role to Maggie Steed, an actress with whom he had been at drama school in the mid-1960s. Steed's strong memory of that drama school experience included two pieces of unhelpful advice she was given there: 'Don't judge the material, you're just an instrument'; 'Don't expect to work until you're 30' (on account of her 'plain' personal appearance).[4] She decided that she wanted to work in Theatre-in-Education – 'it had to make sense, be useful' – and so she became an actor-teacher with the Coventry TIE team and worked with them for several years.

Steed was 30 when Gavin Richards offered her the part of Vlassova in *The Mother*. Still literally too young for the role, she was aided by her tall, bony figure, strong face and flaming red hair effectively to suggest the charismatic and tough character of Vlassova. Steed had had no previous experience of performing Brecht but, because of her TIE background, she 'took it for granted that you had to look for political objectives'. In working on the production, the Belt and Braces company members saw that a commitment to the political ideas of the play was fundamental to the rehearsal process, but that did not bind them to an over-fidelity to the text. Gooch himself records the fact that he advised them to approach Brecht as they would any other text, and Steed remembers:

> We were deliberately irreverent but we were passionate about the ideas. We knew it had to be entertaining yet not seduce the audience by its comedy. It was true to Brecht. We couldn't help following the process but not by rote – it was in our bones. Nobody was ever in doubt about what the particular political point of a scene was.

During the rehearsal period company members also participated in real political action and confrontation, in connection with the miners' strike that was being conducted at that time. The experiences of the actors with the strikers, as they faced hostile employers and government, were then fed into the rehearsals. Despite this relevant background for performing the play, the results, according to the director, were not always felicitous. Richards recalls there were disagreements over when and how emotion should be shown by the actors and he felt that they undercut the impact of the ending of the play by playing it 'dead-pan' (Banks, 1984, p.164). However, in the view of the present writer, the production presented both the narrative and the characters clearly to the audience, and succeeded in expressing emotion while remaining 'cool'. The company conveyed a strong sense of the ensemble and of their own enjoyment in performing, and the humour of the text was brought out without any loss of the element of menace that is an important feature of the piece. Maggie Steed's Vlassova was bold but played with a lightness of touch, with the result that she was moving and ironically satirical by turns. The actress's view of the kind of acting appropriate for Brecht is now (as then) refreshingly straightforward:

> I believe it was a mistake for Brecht to talk about alienation. You can't bring your own objective reality onto stage as an actor. But I do understand what Brecht meant. The idea of presentation – it's me saying these lines. Brecht is much more to do with Music Hall. In that sense you are naked as an actor. You have to make the story work.

Steed stayed with Belt and Braces for eighteen months, though it was, she says, a lifetime's experience.

There is a postscript to the company's success with Brecht. In 1979 their interest in European socialist theatre led them to mount a production of Dario Fo's *Accidental Death of an Anarchist*. The tour of the show was a huge success and led to the offer of a run in a West End theatre. While recognising the paradox of a socialist, alternative company playing in the heart of bourgeois theatreland, Belt and Braces could not refuse the financial opportunity (and perhaps might expect to salve their consciences by regarding the project as 'strategic penetration'). The West End run made the company ineligible for their current Arts Council grant, and so they gave their remaining three months' grant to CAST. Thus two socialist companies benefited from the success of the production, albeit in different ways.

Foco Novo and Brecht

Another 'alternative' British company of the period that successfully produced Brecht was Foco Novo. It was founded in 1973 by director Roland Rees, writer Bernard Pomerance and administrator David Aukin. Rees had been a student in New York, during which time he directed some Brecht. After his return to England, he joined CAST as an actor for their production of *How Muggins Was a Martyr* (1968), an experience of considerable importance in his subsequent work as a director with Foco Novo. Brecht's influence, however, was paramount. 'He was one of our heroes,' claimed Rees,[5] and David Aukin provides detailed substantiation:

The first serious impact on me were two performances which I saw on successive nights at the Old Vic in 1965 – the Berliner Ensemble doing *Arturo Ui* and *Coriolanus* by Bertolt Brecht. . . . The whole thing was extraordinary. That was the sort of theatre I was so lucky to be exposed to. It was not that it was intellectual, it was so exciting.

(Rees, 1992, p.48)

Rees and Aukin were the only permanent members of Foco Novo, the rest of the company being hired for particular productions. But the presence of four playwrights on the company's Board of Directors was evidence of the company's commitment to new writing. Foco Novo's policy was to encourage and nurture very new playwrights, usually through a collaborative working process. And this kind of approach penetrated all aspects of production, for, as Rees puts it, the company:

wanted to change the conception of hierarchy in the rehearsal room. People did have their specialisations . . . but there was an attitude and openness to receiving opinions whatever position you held.

(Rees, 1992, p.44)

In style, they eschewed the social realism for which the Royal Court was becoming known and saw the way forward (literally 'Foco Novo') as being a form of theatre that achieved a more significant integration of aesthetics and political commitment. This, in Rees' view, was what Brecht strove for and it was, therefore, logical for his company both to acknowledge his influence and to take on his plays. In his book *Fringe First*, Rees writes:

Brecht gathered a variety of political and artistic tendencies and cohered them into a philosophy and an aesthetic. In the juxtaposition of image against image, the singular use of objects, and the emphasis he placed on the inter-disciplinary and collaborative nature of theatre, he continues to be a covert influence on many of the most adventurous in contemporary theatre.

(Rees, 1992, p.78)

In directing Brecht's play-texts, Rees responded to them in much the same way as when he was collaborating with a new, live writer. He embraced the plays' politics, respected the language, and recognised the importance of their comedic and musical elements, but he avoided a reverential approach and consistently 'intervened'. Brecht's texts were usually adapted, therefore, rather than 'performed in a faithful translation', and thus were 'made to work' for Foco Novo and for their audiences. Rees was of the opinion that British productions of Brecht tended to be 'grey, dull, monolithic, lacking in spirit, fun and vitality'. He stressed the theatrical importance of telling a story clearly – in all theatre, not just in Brecht – and asserted that the key to clarity is getting the rhythm right. (As a jazz drummer, albeit a 'bad' one by his own admission, Rees was/is ever sensitive to the theatrical impact of the performance rhythm.)

As a clue to directing Brecht, Rees considers Brechtian theory useful, provided it is assessed in the light of its original context. Moreover, in common with Sam Wanamaker (see previous chapter), he sees British actors, despite the dominance of the Stanislavski tradition in drama schools, as instinctively Brechtian because they have a natural inclination towards the ironic. Consequently, he asserts that 'the Brechtian "double frame" is very much part of British acting'. However, he sets against this natural advantage for the British actor the disadvantage of the lack of opportunity in Britain for continuous acting experience in a single company, which leads, in Rees's view, to 'a tendency [in the actor] to exploit personality, to show the self too much' at the expense of developing the intention and meaning of the play.

In Foco Novo's first year of existence (1973) Rees directed *Drums in the Night*. The adaptation was by a young playwright, C.P. Taylor, destined for a considerable, though sadly short, playwriting career. The production first appeared at the Traverse Theatre as part of the Edinburgh Festival and then transferred to the Hampstead Theatre Club, London. In fact, a year before, Rees had directed the play for another alternative company, Freehold. In his second attempt, he set out to improve his first in three ways: by making the visual effects more surreal, by placing more emphasis on the play's humour and by attempting to 'sharpen the political references' (Rees, 1992, p.67). In order to fulfil these aims, Rees drew on features he admired in the work of CAST: the cartoon-style of playing, the underscoring of the performance tempo by music, and hence the creation of an exaggerated, grotesque, form of comedy. The lead role of Kragler was played by the same performer in both Rees productions, the Irish actor Stephen Rea. He wanted to play the part a second time 'because I thought there was a way into it that had not happened the first time . . . of being more clownish' (Rees, 1992, p.41). Rea was also very interested in the politics of the play and agreed with Rees that the characters had to be very sharply drawn, in order to highlight the social attitudes in the piece. He recalls the production as having 'a lusciousness . . . with its colourful blinds and Grosz cartoons' (Rees, 1992, p.41). Rees managed to achieve a rare blend (in British Brecht) of politics and entertainment, and reviewers of the production were full of praise. Michael Billington wrote in *The Guardian* (12.9.73):

> Roland Rees' production has the clarity, lightness and speed of good Brecht. . . . It's the kind of production even congenital Brecht haters (and the backwoods are full of them) should enjoy.

The second Foco Novo Brecht was *Man's a Man* (1975), which toured nationally before going into London. Again the text was adapted, this time by Bernard Pomerance. (The latter is probably best known for his play,

then film, *The Elephant Man*, about the Victorian 'freak' John Merrick.)
Pomerance saw Brecht as

> a mountain you had to climb, at least to see what the view looked like
> . . . it was like a college you went to, where you studied approaches
> which had not been tried out in English-speaking theatre.
>
> (Rees, 1992, p.59)

Man's a Man has a colonial setting and Pomerance and Rees agreed that
in presenting the play in the mid-1970s, they would incorporate the recent
'colonial' history of the Vietnam War. Pomerance's adaptation was thus 'like
demolishing a house, except for the facade. I completely re-built the inside'
(Rees, 1992, p.58). Galy Gay, the main role, was played by an actor of
Indian origin, Stefan Kalipha, which, Rees says, was 'in some sense a
political statement but more about taking on the contemporary world view
and situation'. A number of critics appreciated both the adaptation and the
production, but the liberties taken were not universally admired, one critic
admonishing that 'Brecht should be allowed to be Brecht' (*New Statesman*,
14.11.75).

The other Brecht productions mounted by Foco Novo all belong to the
early 1980s (and, therefore, not to the immediately post-1968 focus of this
chapter), but can usefully be considered here. For the company's 1982
production of *Edward II*, Rees told the show's designer, Adrian Vaux, to
utilise whatever he felt would be useful in the body of Brechtian theory.
Rees has since commented that in designing for Brecht simplicity is the key:
'You only need what you need; the rest is irrelevant. The way you deal with
the rest is by making the unity through the use of colour and material.' For
his production of *Edward II*, Rees, taking a leaf from Brecht's own book on
Marlowe, as it were, decided to update Brecht's text. He also made an
expansive use of music to represent the battles and 'the eerie sounds of
Edward's inner life' (Rees, 1992, p.173).

The last Foco Novo Brecht production was of *Puntila and His Servant*,
in 1983. Howard Brenton, the playwright, who had joined Foco Novo to
work on another project, has a vivid memory of the show:

> I remember the physical sensation of it – a very bright, hard-edged
> set, uncompromising Brechtian light, gleaming out into this Saturday
> matinée . . . with our very young first son, Sam. He has never
> forgotten it. Sam can still tell you the story of *Puntila*.
>
> (Rees, 1992, p.208)

Rees corrects Brenton's recollection of the lighting by explaining that in fact
there was full colour lighting but adds that he used a 'rock-rig', lighting
appropriate to a rock music concert, and this, presumably, is what created
Brenton's visual memory. By using a 'rock-rig', Rees was updating Brecht's use
of open, white light in order to remind the spectators they were in a theatre.

In 1988 Foco Novo ceased to exist when the company lost its Arts Council subsidy. In *The Politics of Performance*, Baz Kershaw claims that they were victims of an act of political censorship (Kershaw, 1992, p.147). However, Rees himself does not adopt the 'conspiracy theory': 'They [Arts Council] wanted to fund other companies and had a limited amount of money. . . . We just fell out of favour. We'd been there long enough.' The issue of the subsidisation of political work is one to which we shall return in subsequent chapters.

BRECHT AT THE RADICAL REPERTORY THEATRES

Touring alternative companies were not alone in finding Brecht's plays both challenging and in themselves appropriate to a more radical view of producing theatre than was common in the mainstream. Some building-based, regional companies were also creating programmes and ways of working in which productions of Brecht's plays would take a key place and have a major impact. The Everyman Theatre in Liverpool was one.

Brecht at the Everyman Theatre, Liverpool

Founded in 1964, the Everyman had quickly established, under Peter James and Terry Hands (subsequently to direct the Royal Shakespeare Company) a reputation for

> a firm local commitment and involvement with Liverpool issues both present and past; an abundant use of music; the encouragement of local writers and actors; an irreverent approach to the classics; an informal and lively style of production.[6]

All of these features would suggest a favourable climate for playing Brecht. In 1969 the artistic direction of the Everyman passed to Alan Dossor. In common with many British theatre directors he had a degree (in Drama from Bristol University), but unlike most he had also trained as an actor (at the Bristol Old Vic Theatre School). His first professional job was as assistant director at the Nottingham Playhouse, where his first full-scale production in the late 1960s was a 'Sunday night' *Mother Courage*. Dossor admits that 'it was a copy of a copy: it was Bill Gaskill's version of the Berliner'.[7] The production incorporated a large number of slides of the Vietnam War, lasted three and a half hours and was, the director now thinks, 'probably deeply boring'. In preparing the production, Dossor had 'read all the stuff', but he later came to the conclusion that, despite all his theorising, Brecht 'was just trying to cut through some very dusty old acting styles and was extremely long-winded about it'.

Dossor was an admirer of the work of Theatre Workshop under Joan Littlewood and considered that their style, energy and way of working were appropriate to the kind of company he was attempting to create at the Everyman. Importantly, they were appropriate for attracting the kinds of audience he sought: 'We were trying to get a young, articulate, working-class audience. . . . We were targeting people who would be running their unions and community centres in fifteen years' time'. John McGrath (of 7:84), in Liverpool in this period, recalls the success of the company:

> In 1972 I was in the Fisher-Bendix factory while it was being occupied by the workforce. Almost every worker there that I spoke to had been to the Everyman and was going to keep on going. And the work at the Everyman was getting better, livelier and more like real theatre than anything I had seen at the Royal Court.
>
> (McGrath, 1981, p.53)

McGrath offered his services to Dossor and together they worked on the Everyman production of *The Caucasian Chalk Circle* (1972). Dossor explains: 'I wanted to have a go at *The Caucasian Chalk Circle*, exploring the relationship between the company, the play and the country we were living in.' Consequently he sub-titled the show as 'a Play for Liverpool'. The original framing device of the group of peasants who open the play was changed to a small company of actors who were looking for an audience. They arrive at a Liverpool building site and ask the workers if they, the actors, can return in three weeks' time with the play they have in rehearsal. The workers 'occupy' the site (when one of them falls from scaffolding) in protest at the prevailing working conditions, and they ask the actors to perform their play immediately. The story of Grusha and Azdak then ensues.

Dossor's approach to the acting style for this production was clear:

> I wanted the politics to be there but also 'high definition acting'. . . .
> We tried to combine the jokes of Morecambe and Wise [comic double act] with the skills that enable an actor to play Hamlet.

He had a very strong group of young actors in the cast, most of whom have since become nationally or internationally known. The Singer, for example, was played by Jonathan Pryce, who much later claimed that he had been 'politicised' by taking part in that production.[8] The politics of the text, however, were not discussed during rehearsal but simply understood, that is, taken for granted. The focus of the rehearsal process was on how the company could make the story work for its audience. In effect, the contemporary setting of the run-down city that was Liverpool provided a dialectic with the 'magic' of the story of love and war, and the staging stressed this. The bridge that the actor of Grusha crossed in Scene 3, for example, was the planking from which the worker had fallen at the beginning; and her baptising of the child (Scene 10) was done with water from a builder's bucket. This fusion of contemporary reference with the timeless narrative reached a peak for Dossor when 'at the end a copy of the

Industrial Relations Act was burnt in a cement-mixer, and the audience stood up because they wanted to see it burn'. The director's commitment and purpose in presenting *The Caucasian Chalk Circle* was clarified in the production's programme note by a quotation from the modern German playwright Martin Walser:

> One can now, with Brecht's help, adopt a social or socialist attitude without being against the capitalism of today, which does not exist in Brecht. One thus borrows the spittle of history, spits at a historical corpse and nevertheless has the satisfying feeling of having today spat in the right direction.

Billington in *The Guardian* praised the production in terms that endorsed Dossor's intentions by recognising the appropriate influence: 'Joan Littlewood's Theatre Workshop at its best would be proud of the production' (*The Guardian*, 3.6.72).

Two years later Dossor directed his second Brecht at the Everyman, *The Good Woman of Setzuan*. This time he enlisted the help of poet/playwright Adrian Mitchell, and they adapted the text by setting it in the foyer of the Setzuan 'Imperial Hotel', as though the district (and hotel) had been part of the British Empire. However, Dossor later judged that he had failed to find the proper contemporary reference: 'It was terrible. I was trying to repeat something that I'd achieved with *The Caucasian Chalk Circle*. You should never repeat.' He was also less than enthusiastic about the original play, concluding that it is 'one idea stretched out'. But Antony Sher, who played Wang, thought the production succeeded in that it made good contact with its audience through its humour.[9] And McGrath adds his praise, too, claiming that Dossor 'found ways to present Brecht that kept faith with that audience's expectations' (McGrath, 1981, p.53). In both Everyman productions, Dossor's bold approach to the text, his creation of an ensemble company, and his pursuit of a direct way of communicating with the audience all contributed to making Brecht acceptable to and enjoyable for ordinary young spectators in Liverpool.

Brecht at Contact Theatre, Manchester

Another regional company that has achieved a reputation for staging Brecht for young audiences is the Contact Theatre Company, Manchester. The company was set up in 1973 and based originally in a small industrial building (known as the 'Brickhouse') adjacent to the Manchester University Theatre. Subsequently the company took over the University Theatre, where they remain to this day. The company, with a policy of work for and with young people, developed a programme of in-house productions, tours in the Manchester area to non-traditional venues, and special school workshops and 'Playdays' on set texts. Their performances were frequently described as radical or irreverent, and an attitude of irreverence was brought to bear on their first Brecht: *The Caucasian Chalk Circle* (1973). This was directed by Paul Clements, and Bernard Hill played a wily and very funny Azdak, contributing humour to a production notable for its overall lightness of playing and its highly developed sense of fun. However, not every critic was in favour, Billington, in *The Guardian*, maintaining: 'Here the jokes are indulged but the pain evaded' (12.9.73). Clements' second Brecht production, *The Resistible Rise of Arturo Ui* (1975), was criticised in a similar vein: 'The disquieting menace which should shadow every line in the play was often missing', reported Stephen Dixon in *The Guardian* (29.3.75). But the audiences for both productions were enthusiastic and large.

In 1975, direction of the company was taken over by Caroline Smith, and, in 1976, she mounted the company's third Brecht, *Mother Courage and Her Children*. Smith's innovation was the addition of a narrator, and, though the production was praised for its clarity and 'exemplary lightness and speed' (*The Guardian*, 29.10.77), David Mayer, in *Plays and Players* (May, 1976), thought the narrator unnecessary, betraying on the production's part a lack of trust in Brecht's text.

The artistic direction of Contact was taken over in 1977 by Richard Williams, who had previously worked as an actor at the Everyman, Liverpool, appearing in a number of small roles in Dossor's *Chalk Circle* (1972). He had then worked as assistant director to Richard Eyre on a production of Brecht's *Trumpets and Drums* at Nottingham Playhouse (1976). Williams opened his own Brecht account at Contact by directing a production of *Schweyk in the Second World War* (1979). The director himself was a committed Brechtian but was of the opinion that there was no need for the actors in the production to resort to Brecht's theory. When questions on theory were raised during rehearsal, Williams simply showed them his photograph of Brecht at the *Lachekeller*, Karl Valentin's cabaret, and said that the picture told them all they needed to know about Brecht's view of acting; 'everything else was in the writing of the play'.[10] In Williams's view the already established ethos of the company, especially their focus on 'making contact' with their young audiences, meant that the socio-political intentions of the piece and the ways of making them clear to the spectator would be second nature. The reviewer for *The Manchester Evening News* summarised things succinctly: 'a fine piece of Brechtian theatre from a company renowned for their Brecht' (8.3.79).

Williams's next three productions of Brecht, in the early 1980s, properly fall outside the compass of this chapter, but demonstrate the continuation of the radical, irreverent approach that he had already instituted. In 1980 he directed *The Threepenny Opera*, setting it in 1953 in order to refer to the occasion of the Festival of Britain, and exploiting in the production style a period of post-war drabness and black-market nylons. In the same year he also mounted a production of *Man is Man*, which, influenced by the director's visit the previous summer to China, featured huge Chinese masks. The following year (1981) the company presented a Brecht double bill: *The Breadshop* and *The Respectable Wedding*. Reviewing these, Robin Thornber of *The Guardian* (8.10.81) ambivalently acknowledged Williams's success in a doubtful enterprise:

> If the audience, mostly teenagers in stripey socks, yawned at first they were grabbed by the revolutionary bun fight at the end. The credit for this conquest has to be divided equally. Brecht may have had a quirky, even crass dramatic sense but he knew how to write lucidly. And Richard Williams' direction of a spirited company in both plays showed even-handed respect for the demands of academic authenticity and actually entertaining the audience.

Both one-acters were given theatrically exciting and politically clear productions, in which Contact Theatre remained faithful to the spirit of Brecht while avoiding the trap of being tied to an over-faithful or reverential treatment of the plays as 'sacred' texts.

There is an additional postscript to the Contact Theatre's Brecht story. In the spring season of 1994 the company mounted another production of *The Threepenny Opera*, this time directed by Annie Castledine. This rated, in the opinion of the present writer, as one of the very few, fully successful British productions of a Brecht play. It was a relatively faithful version (textually) that was both theatrically stunning and acutely powerful in its political engagement. The set design (by Simon Banham) was eloquent in its simplicity. It provided an open space in which the actors could make direct contact with the audience and it assisted skilfully in the telling of the story. Almost the entire stage and wing area was exposed and the theatre walls were painted blue/grey. A spiral staircase rose from the up right stage level to the catwalks. There was a set of glass revolving doors (stage left) and, centre stage, a grand piano (which provided the only musical accompaniment). The production lighting, reminiscent of *film noir*, contributed rhythmically as well as visually to the witty, choreographed entrances and exits of the actors. The political thrust of the production was based on the director's *aperçu* that the Peachum organisation is, in effect, a bourgeois operation and that the Peachums are representative of the *nouveaux riches*. The production thus avoided the more traditional, and usually embarrassing, reading of the play, in which the main characters seem to have stepped out of Fagin's gang in the musical *Oliver*.

Crucial to the success of the production was the fact that the Brechtian politics of the piece had been carried through into the rehearsal process. Castledine, a freelance director whose background includes teaching and Theatre-in-Education, strove to make her actors feel responsible for the work, by requiring them to research background material on Brecht and on the social period of the play, and by creating an open, exploratory approach to the text. For example, she encouraged actors to run rehearsals of each other's scenes.[11] The pay-off was evident. Although the cast of actors did not constitute an ensemble as such, the impact of this way of working was to create a performance of considerable detail, intelligence, commitment and – equally to the (Brechtian) point – fun. In the process, Contact Theatre lived up to both its reputation and its name.

Brecht at the Citizens Theatre, Glasgow

Theatricality and an open approach to text can also be said to characterise the Brecht productions of another regional company with a radical agenda, the Citizens Theatre, Glasgow. The Cits, as it is widely and popularly known, has among other distinctions that of being the repertory theatre company that has presented the greatest number of Brecht plays in Britain; in the last thirty years (up to 1994) it has staged seventeen. (The only other British company to have reached double figures is the Royal Shakespeare Company with ten.) The first two Brechts at the Cits were staged during the management of Iain Cuthbertson, who initiated a clear policy of establishing an ensemble company that would explore 'drama with a message'. Cuthbertson's *The Good Woman of Setzuan* (1962) was the first production of a Brecht play mounted in Scotland and it was acknowledged by *The Scotsman* reviewer as 'an absorbing experience' (23.10.62). In response to the company's second Brecht production, *The Caucasian Chalk Circle* (1964), *The Glasgow Herald* acknowledged that 'tremendous efforts have been made by the Citizens, both to do their best for Brecht and . . . to make him acceptable to an audience still uncertain what to make of him' (9.9.64). These reviews remind us of the slow development of Brecht's accessibility for British theatre audiences referred to in the previous chapter.

The third Cits' Brecht was produced when the theatre was under the management of two co-directors, Michael Meacham and Michael Blakemore. The latter was the Brecht enthusiast in the team and in 1967 he directed the first British professional production of *The Visions of Simone Machard*. The critical response to this was generally not positive, but the director achieved a notable success later in the same year with his production of *The Resistible Rise of Arturo Ui*. This opened at the Edinburgh Festival and then went to London via Nottingham. The title role was played by a then relatively unknown actor, Leonard Rossiter, whose portrayal blazed a remarkable trail for subsequent, would-be Brechtian performers to follow. In his book *The Modern Actor*, Michael Billington describes Rossiter as giving a 'superb Chaplinesque performance', the essence of which was contained in the actor's first entrance:

Ui sprang dramatically through a paper screen like a clown at the start of a circus. . . . Physically he was grotesque: the vast-brimmed, top-heavy felt hat made him look like a walking advertisement for Spanish sherry; the wide, board-stiff shoulders suggested a coat from which the hanger had, uncharitably, not been removed. . . . A great performance. Partly because of its sheer mimetic vitality; partly because it left behind an ineradicable physical image as of an animated Grosz cartoon; partly because of its truth to the Brechtian ideal in that it revealed the abject cowardice and fear behind the character's public mask of brutality.

(Billington, 1972, pp.72–4)

The young assistant director on the production, Keith Hack (who later became a full-time director at the Cits – see below), claimed that Rossiter did not like or understand Brecht, but that he had a natural, driving energy, an obsessional quality that suited the role.[12] (See Chapter 5 for further discussion of Rossiter's Ui.)

In 1969 a new regime began at the Cits under director Giles Havergal and designer/director Philip Prowse. They were joined in 1972 by writer/director Robert David MacDonald. This management has been responsible for generating thirteen Glasgow productions of Brecht plays (to date). Appropriately, from the beginning the company comprised an ensemble of young actors, all employed at the same rate of pay and all engaged on the condition that they would 'carry the play one month and carry the tray the next'.[13]

Since 1969, the artistic policy of the company has been based on a diet of British and foreign classics, including a high proportion of German plays (many specially translated by Robert David MacDonald). The typical production has tended to place 'emphasis on visual style at the expense of verbal clarity' and to reject 'the Anglo-Saxon tradition of psychological realism in acting' (*The Guardian*, 7.5.90). Also the company has been deeply committed to making its work as socially and intellectually accessible as possible. To this end the theatre offers relatively low seat prices (plus concessions for the young, the unemployed and the old), and a special programme of performances, workshops and other activities for young people. Furthermore, Giles Havergal instituted in the season of 1970/71 the practice of employing young, local 'extras' to fill out the casts, which was still being done at the time of writing.

The first Brecht production under this new regime was *Mother Courage* in 1970, directed by a young protégé director, Rob Walker. He had joined the company the year before to take charge of the 'studio' theatre, The Close, and he was, by his own admission, a politically motivated director who believed in a collaborative and democratic approach with the actors in the rehearsal room. He had begun working in the theatre backstage at

Joan Littlewood's Theatre Workshop and this experience had had an enormous influence on him:

> Working there transformed my life. The whole approach, the attitude to theatre had a tremendous impact on me. I've been trying to do it ever since. I wanted theatre to be as joyful, as life-enhancing as hers – as unpretentious, as buccolic as she could make it.[14]

At the instigation of his designer, Philip Prowse, Walker made what seemed at the time a radical decision in setting *Mother Courage* in the Second World War, with Courage's canteen wagon made from the battered shell of a motor-truck and pulled on skis. The cast was young and eager, and Walker wanted them to avoid being burdened with Brechtian theory. Instead, and with instinctive insight, he advised them to draw on a certain kind of comic performance: 'I read the theory, I took it on board, but I talked to the actors about how stand-up comics work. . . . Think of Frankie Howerd [a stand-up comedian], I would say, and try to get them to discover the act of acting in that moment.' Challengingly, a male actor (John Duttine) was cast in the part of the prostitute, Yvette, but without incurring any adverse criticism from the reviewers. However, Ann Mitchell as Mother Courage was described in *The Scotsman* as 'too young and jaunty for the part' (26.10.70).

The next Glasgow Brecht was *The Life of Galileo* (1971), and the actor cast as Galileo, Ian McDiarmid, was also, technically, too youthful for his part. The young director Keith Hack was responsible for this production. He had begun his theatrical career by working for a year as a *Mitarbeiter* at the Berliner Ensemble (which meant he was present at rehearsals but had to put any suggestions he wished to make in writing to the directors). Hack watched carefully and learned a great deal. Later he said: 'The Berliner Ensemble worked on a very gestic kind of theatre – working from moment to moment and building up an amazing jigsaw puzzle on stage, piece by piece'.[15]

In 1971 Hack joined the Cits as a trainee director, working mostly in the studio theatre, The Close. His mainstage production of *The Life of Galileo* was set in a 'dissection academy', with Galileo presented as a 'Faustian scientist'. The Prince was played by a ventriloquist's dummy. Hack, disarmingly, claims that the main purpose in his directing was to tell the story clearly and to remain sensitive to Brecht's liking for jokes. Ian McDiarmid, whose slight stature made a Laughtonesque playing of the role out of the question, is said to have given a very intellectual yet sensual reading of the part. Hack compares it to the idea of Brecht himself playing the role. *The Glasgow Herald* reviewer thought McDiarmid's performance 'a brilliantly inventive and adventurous realization' and reported that it was 'constantly absorbing to watch and hear' (20.9.71).

The following year (1972) at the Cits, Hack directed *In the Jungle of the Cities*, providing his own translation/adaptation for the production. He cut the text heavily and described the play in the programme as 'a play with music'. The auditorium was stripped of its normal end-stage seating and effectively turned into a boxing-ring with seats on four sides. The set was created out of 'the detritus of an American city', incorporating structures made of corrugated iron and neon lighting. The characters that Brecht intends to satirise were presented on *kothurni* to express their inner grotesqueness; and the mother was played by a male actor because Hack wanted to emphasise her brutality. Many reviewers admired the boldness of the production which, the reviewer for BBC Radio 4 concluded, allowed 'the complete realisation of the several levels on which the play works . . . the serious concern of Brecht comes through and holds the ring' (18.4.72). Shortly after this Hack left the Cits, and the production transferred to London where it played a short season at The Place (March 1973).

Meanwhile at the Cits, Robert David MacDonald had arrived to complete the triumvirate of directors and to carry on the company's Brecht tradition. In his first year (1972/3) he directed *Happy End* with Philip Prowse as designer. In fact, it was the set – with its vast, chequered revolving stage that enabled swift and ingenious changes from beer-hall to Salvation Army Hostel – that drew particular notice. But Cordelia Oliver, the Glasgow critic and writer, recalls the production as being memorable for both the set and the music.[16]

The same team of MacDonald and Prowse directed and designed the next Cits Brecht, *St Joan of the Stockyards*, in 1974. Di Trevis, later an enthusiastic director herself of Brecht (see Chapter 5), played Joan. Michael Coveney's review of the production noted, perhaps ironically, that 'Joan's simple, blazing speech about the truth of all political systems . . . met with a little spontaneous applause even at Friday night's official opening for the city's fathers and betters' (*Financial Times*, 9.9.74).

For his next Brecht, *The Threepenny Opera* (1978), Prowse took responsibility for both the direction and the design. This was the Cits' second production of the play. It was set in a *fin-de-siècle* drawing-room furnished in grey and featuring a grand piano, and the director/designer framed the set by swathing the proscenium arch in white chiffon. As the play opened, thieves and beggars took over the drawing-room in a sequence that Prowse described as 'a kind of bourgeois rape'.[17] Reviewers found the production provocative but were divided in opinion as to its success. However, Ned Chaillet of *The Times* thought the liberties taken by the director paradoxically made the production closer to Brecht 'than many a more dutiful performance' (2.10.78).

The next four productions at the Cits effectively come outside the period under review in this chapter, but they are worthy of brief mention because they underscore the notion that a more open and radical approach to Brecht's plays (as opposed to a reverential treatment of the text or an imitation of the external features of the Berliner Ensemble) continued to lead to lively and accessible British productions. The Cits' Brecht of the early 1980s – *Fears and Miseries of the Third Reich* and *The Caucasian Chalk Circle* (both 1980), *Puntila and His Servant Matti* and *The Mother* (both 1982) – were all directed by Giles Havergal.

Havergal has admitted since that he had originally considered that Brecht was not a congenial playwright for him. He had assumed that directors of Brecht were obliged to assimilate 'all the philosophy and the surrounding data'.[18] However, he later came to realise that this was untrue and that others at the Cits had undertaken Brecht productions without paying any close attention to Brechtian theory.

Nevertheless, Havergal remained acutely conscious of the political demands of the texts and the need to realise them in performance. For his production of *The Caucasian Chalk Circle*, for example, in order to heighten the audience's awareness of the political dynamic of the play, he re-framed the first scene (as McGrath had done before him), opening with a group of 'actors', rather than the original peasants, who:

> all sat round a huge table and made remarks about poverty. . . . [The device] was used as consciousness-raising for a new *politique* as it might be in a country newly behind the Iron Curtain after the war and they were trying to tell people what it was like to be a communist.

Reviews sympathetically recognised that this production had a 'real fidelity to the spirit of the play', a fidelity that was developed, rather than hindered, by the avoidance of what Havergal called 'po-faced Brechtian stances'.

In Havergal's view *Puntila* was his most successful Brecht production and certainly the one he most enjoyed directing. The whole piece was presented as a play-reading done for an on-stage figure of Brecht himself. This device not only enabled the actors easily to adopt a Brechtian demonstration of character but served also to enhance the comic potential of the play through the juxtaposition of the 'reality' of the original scenes and the 'theatricality' of the author's witty comments.

Havergal took even greater liberties with *The Mother*, produced later in that same season. He not only incorporated some of the Gorki text which was Brecht's original source, but, more importantly, radically changed the ending by having the Mother killed by the state police. (In Brecht's script, of course, she simply marches on at the front of the revolutionary protest.) The director explained the changes:

> The optimism, the sense of her marching in triumph, I felt utterly inappropriate. Alas the wages of revolution are not victory. In our version she was beaten up while handing out leaflets.

What is quite extraordinary is that no reviewer noted, perhaps noticed, this significant departure from the original text.

The richness and variety of the Cits' productions of Brecht are a clear indication of not only the company's enthusiasm for the playwright's work but their commitment to making the plays appropriate for the productions' own context. While not neglecting the political demands of the script, the Cits directors have applied fully their characteristic theatrical and visual flair to the Brecht productions. Perhaps most significantly, they have shown a 'healthy disrespect' that has led to some imaginative adaptations and interpretations. The boldness of their approach is explained simply by Havergal:

> We treat Brecht in the way we treat Shakespeare, which is not very reverently, but we do a lot of his work. Most people treat him extremely reverently and do very little of his work.

The story of Brecht at the Cits will be resumed in Chapter 5. The impact of working with that company on young directors such as Rob Walker and Keith Hack was lasting and significant. Walker went on to direct Brecht plays at several other theatres, most notably *Arturo Ui* at the Half Moon, a Fringe venue in London. Still trying to emulate the pioneering work of Joan Littlewood, and building on his experience at the Cits, Walker sought at the Half Moon to create an ensemble: 'Everyone was on equal pay all the time I was there. This gave the whole company a sense of authority.' Maggie Steed (previously of the Belt and Braces Roadshow) went to the Half Moon for its production of *Arturo Ui* in 1978. She comments:

> Rob's a showman, so he didn't want anything reverent. He was very passionate about it as well. . . . It was very Expressionist and we had white make-up, sculpted faces and the pictures [created by the physical placing of actors] were wonderful.

The lead role was played by Simon Callow, and he recalls in his book, *Being An Actor*, that the director had conceived the production 'as a Fritz Lang *film noir*' (Callow, 1984, p.96). Accordingly the set comprised a metal jungle of underground garages and boiler-rooms. Callow also remembers Walker's open and collaborative approach to the rehearsal process: 'Everything that went on in the theatre concerned us all equally and we were all free to be involved in decisions' (Callow, 1984, p.47). His own views on playing Ui were very precise. Appropriately, he saw the character not as a coherently unified human being but as a figure put together out of spare parts, 'sub-human, a Frankenstein's monster' (Callow, 1984, p.93). This approach to the performance was, therefore, boldly non-Stanislavskian:

> One thing I was absolutely certain of was that there should be no vestige of psychological truth in the performance. It was to be a series of disconnected impulses, as if his nervous system and his brain had likewise been made up of scraps from the laboratory dustbin.
>
> (Callow, 1984, p.96)

To realise this, Callow bravely played Ui, in Walker's words, 'as a sham-
bling clown, wearing a wig he had found in a dustbin behind the Royal
Opera House'. And Walker adds, significantly drawing attention to the
essential amalgam needed both of menace and comic power in the role,
that Callow's playing of Ui made one 'understand how he attained his
position by sheer will. He showed how mean-minded he was. And he was
really funny.'

Keith Hack's most significant contribution to British Brecht after leaving
the Cits was a production of *The Good Person of Setzuan* in Newcastle-
upon-Tyne (1977), which transferred to the Royal Court Theatre, London
(same year). Hack's textual adaptations included the creation of a 'framing'
device of a play-within-a-play, which involved the poor people of Setzuan's
staging the main play. This served the director's intention of highlighting
what he saw as the play's key issue, that of poverty, in place of Brecht's
main focus on the 'good' receiving their just desserts.[19] The overall image
conveyed by the production was of a grey, overcrowded, grindingly poor
society. The set comprised vast numbers of old tyres (replaced by oil drums
when the production transferred to London), and the whole cast was
dressed in dark rags. Shen Te/Shui Ta was played by the South African
actress Janet Suzman. Hack cast her because he felt she had a considerable
range as an actor, and, in particular, she could play a 'woman' (as opposed
to a 'lady'). British actors, in his view, are often limited to portraying 'polite
behaviour' (through background and training), a limitation that, as has
been noted, evidently affected the first enactment of this dual role by Peggy
Ashcroft (see p.53).

The company prepared for the style and stance of the production by
working together on a programme of Brecht songs and 'platform' readings
of short Brecht texts. This was performed at the Newcastle theatre during
the main play's rehearsal period. There were long discussions during
rehearsal of the politics of the play but none about Brechtian theory.
Instead, it was assumed that the information needed for performance was
inscribed in the text itself. Suzman felt very strongly that in playing Brecht
the politics of the piece had to be at the centre of the work. Her own,
left-wing political commitment was strong and she was herself a Brecht
enthusiast. As someone brought up in South Africa, however, unlike many
of her British counterparts, she had no preconceived ideas or anxieties
about playing Brecht.

In personal preparation for the role of Shen Te, Suzman decided it was
important to discover what drives women to become prostitutes. The cast,
she felt, needed to understand the social reality of the poor people in the
play in order to present them as credible and human, warts and all: 'They
[the characters] must not be patronized or guyed; we have to help the
audience understand their need and their behaviour'.[20] (We will return to
this issue in Chapter 5.) The company agreed also on the importance to the

production of the elements of music and comedy. Suzman particularly enjoyed the opportunity for comic playing that the Shui Ta half-figure afforded her. She and Hack agreed that she should not use a mask (as the text suggests); instead Suzman developed her whole costume (a scruffy white suit and panama hat) as a mask and attempted to make Shui Ta 'vulpine' by revealing her teeth as much as possible. This male side of the dual role was, Suzman says, 'great fun to play because you can go all out to show a man'. Equally, she was constantly aware that the actor of Brecht must be respectful of the spareness and directness of the text and resist embellishing it with psychological extras:

> Like all apparently simple texts, it's very difficult. You are naked out there, you have nothing to lean on somehow. It requires a strong inner sense of what you are doing as an actor.

Both Hack and Suzman felt the production worked better in Newcastle, where it 'made real contact' with the audience, than in London. For the present writer, who saw the London version, the production had a fierce energy and vitality that generated great excitement, and the swift juxtaposition of the comic and tragic brought out the socio-political significance of the play. Most reviewers, however, favoured Suzman's performance over the interpretation as a whole. Barber, of *The Daily Telegraph*, thought the production lacked 'the invention to achieve the bitterly comic effect intended' (10.10.77) and Esslin commented that in

> a thoroughly misguided production . . . Janet Suzman is a wonderful Shen Te. She has strength as well as goodness and both her strength and her goodness are clearly seen to emerge from an earthy sensuality and a lusty enjoyment of life.[21]

SUMMARY

In the decade or so after the social and political upheavals of 1968, the changes and developments in British theatre provided an appropriate cultural context for Brecht's plays, and there followed a series of strong and radical productions. Thanks to that second visit by the Berliner Ensemble, the British Brecht repertoire had been widened, particularly for the alternative companies. The common threads running through and connecting up the work of the radical companies considered here include, crucially, a willingness and ability to 'take on' Brecht in every sense – politically and theatrically. The productions did not merely imitate what was perceived as the Brechtian 'style'. Rather they were concerned to engage intellectually and artistically with the full implications of the plays as socially significant theatre pieces.

The practitioners accepted and exploited the notion that Brecht can be at once fun, artistic and politically purposeful. Their work often involved other shared features that lent themselves to a proper realisation of British Brecht: collaborative organisation, company structure and ways of working; openness to experimentation with performance style (drawing on cabaret, comic technique and contemporary music); the pursuit of new (often young) audiences; and a broad, sometimes irreverent response to the texts themselves, adapting and re-framing them so that productions might be relevant and accessible to the particular audiences for which they were made.

In a sense Brecht was only truly discovered and recognised in Britain when British theatre practitioners re-discovered his own ways and purpose of working. The next stage, inevitably, is for the new ideas to be absorbed by the mainstream theatre that had provided in some ways the impulse of opposition and confrontation. The next chapter looks at the way in which Brecht becomes a 'classic' writer, adopted and admired, but simultaneously de-politicised.

4

PERFORMING 'CLASSICAL' BRECHT

Making the strange familiar

In 1978, in an article entitled 'Brecht, Bond, Gaskill and the Practice of Political Theatre', Peter Holland wrote:

> The history of the reception of Brecht in Britain is an embarrassing one. A series of imbalances, of half-aware ideas about the purposes of Brecht's practical dramaturgy, were made worse by a far more influential misconception about his politics and the significance of his politics for his drama. It is to a large extent through a refusal to accept the fundamentally political basis of Brecht's theatre practice that critics have created the illusory split of Brecht into a good playwright and a bad politician.[1]

And it was not only British critics who created that split between the perceived quality of the plays and a deploring of their socio-political purpose. Many theatre practitioners either deliberately ignored the political commitment of Brecht's writing or failed to find a way of integrating it not only into their interpretations of his plays but, just as importantly, into their methods of work. Unlike the alternative theatre companies considered in the previous chapter, many establishment companies lacked any kind of corporate, political commitment and their members did not share a common aesthetic stance from which might be created a sense of collective endeavour and purpose for their work. And this was, of course, especially significant when they chose to mount productions of Brecht.

That Brecht had been 'adopted' by British theatre on a wide scale by the late 1970s there can be no doubt. His plays, already an important feature of alternative theatre, had become prominent (in number at least) in the repertoire also of mainstream, repertory theatre. During the 1970s there were over eighty productions of Brecht put on by provincial British repertories. But the price of Brecht's popularity was his frequent assimilation into a politically bland and bourgeois context, and his de-politicisation in order to make his work conform to the social and artistic perceptions and taste of the mainstream theatreworld.

As has been suggested in previous chapters, it is inevitable that the context for any form of theatre has an impact on its presentation, or is part of its theatrical interpretation. Repertory theatre companies in the 1970s and 1980s (as, indeed, today) were state-subsidised, building-based operations that presented a programme of half a dozen or so plays in two- or three-weekly production runs from September to the following early summer. Actors were employed on contracts of various lengths, some for the whole season, others for one or two productions. Artistic directors often tried to 'through-cast' for the whole season whenever possible, mostly for financial reasons (because an actor could then be in rehearsal for the next play while performing the current one). Thus an actor might be required to perform in a mix of plays that included, say, a Shakespeare, a traditional Christmas pantomime, a British comedy (Coward, Wilde, etc.) and, maybe, a modern classic such as Brecht. British actors had, and still have, a wide range of professional backgrounds and experiences, and although most drama schools focus in their actor training on the Stanislavski System, or at least on a naturalistic, psychologically motivated approach to performance, company members in a provincial repertory theatre were/are unlikely implicitly to share many views with each other on the appropriate approaches to production for a particular play. The likelihood of their sharing a common theatrical purpose, let alone a political ideology, was/is extremely remote. These factors, combined with the short rehearsal periods customary in this kind of theatre, the insecurity of employment, and the hierarchical structure and power relationship between director and actor (with the right of 'hire and fire' resting firmly in the hands of the artistic director) were, and are, hardly conducive to the creation of a democratic work process or to the development of a shared view of what constitutes good theatre practice. The notion of creating an ensemble in the British mainstream theatre of the 1970s and 1980s, though frequently mooted, was generally found to be over-idealistic and remained largely unrealised because of the constraints of time and money and because of the traditional tendency towards hierarchical management in British theatre.

More opportunities for ensemble playing for actors and companies than were possible in the regional repertory companies – because of longer contracts, greater stability of work practices, more rehearsal time, and a repertoire system that ensured an extended life for a production – existed (and still exist) in the two national theatres of Britain: the (now Royal) National Theatre and the Royal Shakespeare Company. The overall management and organisation of each of these companies were at times similar. Each operated for a period a system of small 'companies' within the whole, giving individual directors not only responsibility for the artistic direction of productions but also a say in the choice of product and overall planning strategy for a season or programme of plays in one of the company's theatre spaces. Both also had (and have) a complex system of 'guest' directors and 'associated artists' (in the areas of direction, design and performance), which enabled them to call on the skills of a wider range of practitioners than they could afford to keep permanently 'on the books'. Actors in both organisations were/are on longer contracts than is customary or possible in most other British theatres and were/are often offered two- or even three-year contracts with renewal clauses and release clauses to enable them to do other work during the period of the contract.

However, neither the National Theatre nor the RSC had or has an overall policy on 'practice' in terms of the ways of working on any particular production. That would be left very much in the hands of the individual directors. While these two companies offer the performer a greater sense of job security, there is no real opportunity to develop an ensemble, as actors are frequently cast in productions with different directors. Further- more, in the case of the National Theatre, and the RSC's London base at the Barbican Centre, the theatre buildings themselves are unconducive to the kind of pleasant and purposeful atmosphere typical of the best of ensemble theatre practice, being 'warrens' of similar underground rehearsal rooms that resemble concrete bunkers. The stories are legion of actors at both theatres getting lost backstage during a performance, or of workers on a production discovering colleagues working on the same production only at the final rehearsals. The effects of these and other chronic information problems in the large theatre organisations will emerge in the accounts of particular productions that follow.

BRECHT AT THE ROYAL SHAKESPEARE COMPANY

The RSC, as noted in Chapter 3, is the only British company apart from the Citizens Theatre, Glasgow, that has produced a substantial number of Brecht plays. Alongside their extensive programme of Shakespeare and his contemporaries in their main Stratford and London theatres, the company mounts new plays and revives what are described as 'modern classics' in their smaller venues (in Stratford and London). Brecht's plays came into the RSC's definition of modern classics during the 1970s. And one director in particular became associated with RSC Brecht – Howard Davies.

Howard Davies and Brecht

Davies did an English degree at Durham University and followed this with a one-year course in directing at Bristol University. But there he discovered that 'no-one knew what a director was',[2] so he decided, unusually for a British director (*pace* Deborah Warner, see Chapter 5), that he should learn about backstage craft by being a stage manager. His subsequent four years at Birmingham Repertory Theatre meant that he came to directing, as he says, 'with an appreciation of the difficulties of the actor's job – the amount

94

of graft and craft'. He then began his directing career proper with a small, alternative theatre company, Avon Touring, whose programme included agitprop, street theatre, and, later (that is, post-Davies) Brecht. After that an interest in new play-writing led Davies to set up and run (for five years) an important London fringe venue, the Donmar Warehouse. He claims that the experience in this period of working on new plays, the exploration of texts in open fashion with both the actors and sometimes their authors, confirmed his antipathy to 'directing through concept', that is to the idea of a director's imposing his interpretation of a text in an authoritarian way not only on the play but on the company. Davies's formative experience, training background and natural inclination thus provided him with the appropriate credentials for tackling Brecht.

Davies's first production of a Brecht play was *Fears and Miseries of the Third Reich* for the Bristol Old Vic Theatre (1972). He claims to have been particularly attracted to this fragmentary piece because of its songs: 'I liked the idea of drama arising from song rather than the other way round.' His approach and design for the production drew on his agitprop touring experience, in that it was simple and bold, focusing on the need to make direct contact between the performer and the audience. His next Brecht, *The Threepenny Opera* at the Theatre Royal, York (1973), made him 'aware of the need to stay within some sense of social reality. I realised that the story needs to emerge out of the gutter not just out of style.' He was, in fact, moving away from the external, 'out front' playing of agitprop and attempting to create a theatre form that was closer to 'social realism'.

His next Brecht production was *The Caucasian Chalk Circle* at the Birmingham Repertory Theatre (1974), and in this Davies enlisted the help of playwright Steve Gooch, in order to 're-frame' the play by providing an updated setting for the opening, as had been done for the production of this play at the Everyman Theatre, Liverpool (1972). Gooch placed the first scene in an urban context, which was intended to highlight the contemporary issue of homelessness, so that, as Davies says, 'the play spiralled out of the Prologue'. The production was very well received, and the critic of *The Birmingham Post* (17.5.74) remarked:

> Howard Davies has persuaded his company to adopt a taut, understated manner of playing and to do without caricature and the trappings of pantomime or music-hall . . . rather than hiding behind the characters they play, they are more like advocates on their behalf.

Clearly the agitprop style of his early Brecht ventures had been superseded by a more serious treatment of character and situation as Davies moved towards the new goal of social realism, though he insists that he continued to emphasise the comic aspects of Brecht's text.

It is, therefore, ironic, and certainly indicative of the RSC's notion of legitimate ways of playing Brecht, that Davies claims when he joined the company in 1975 that 'at the RSC no-one ever trusted me with comedy. They said I could do Brecht and Bond. I was type-cast like an actor.' Clearly, the old perception of Brecht as 'serious', even heavy (and certainly not comic) still persisted in Britain's largest theatre company. Davies' first Brecht production for the RSC was *Man is Man* (1975) performed at the Other Place, the company's small venue in Stratford. The director again enlisted Steve Gooch to do the translation/adaptation and he invited the RSC's resident composer, Guy Wolfenden, to compose new music. The contributions of both were admired by reviewers, who recognised the point of re-working the material rather than simply purveying it straight, as the reviewer in *The Daily Telegraph* (30.9.75) made plain:

> Steve Gooch's adaptation with songs and music by Guy Wolfenden drives the old ambiguous morality along with such a zest that it seems more theatrically effective than ever before.

Davies was intent on finding new ways of tackling Brecht and he claims that in these productions he felt he 'found a style in which to present the politics of the piece . . . ironically rather than head-on, on the nose . . . I saw the soldiers as a gang of squaddies in a panic, not monsters. In that sense they were seen as real, not cruel or vicious.' It is evident, again, that he sought (and found) a kind of realism in the piece, and his achievement is underlined by the judgment of one critic who expressed pleasure that the production 'was not "textbook" Brecht, but rather a compromise that does not threaten the British actor's general reliance on internal motive'.[3] Many reviewers noted Davies's efforts to be a little more adventurous than was currently common with British Brecht. One commented approvingly (in *The Sunday Telegraph*): 'at last those reverential winding sheets are being stripped off the Brechtian image' (28.9.75). And *The Guardian* critic (24.9.75) summed up the implications of the production for the British approach to Brecht at large:

> it symbolises our growing realisation that Brecht is best approached not in a mood of dogged cultural piety but with a lively awareness of his pungent humour, delight in theatre and profound moral ambivalence.

The success of the *Man is Man* production spurred Davies on to tackle *Schweyk in the Second World War* a year later (1976), also at the Other Place. This time the translation was provided by Susan Davies (the director's wife), who is a German speaker, and the lead role was taken by Michael Williams, an experienced Shakespearean actor, well known for playing comic roles. In particular he had shown an especial adroitness at depicting the 'little man', a talent appropriate for the title role of *Schweyk*. Davies thought that in playing Schweyk 'the trick was to find that line so that you didn't know if he was being disingenuous or ingenuous', and, obeying his own instincts and thanks to the appropriate casting of his lead actor, the director focused on the comedy in the piece. He also wanted to 'scale it down': 'I firmly resisted the epic proportions of the piece . . . it's to do with people in rooms, it's not a war movie.'

Williams's gentle, almost Chaplinesque style of playing, his relaxed and casual way of telling distracting stories to his adversaries and his talent for comic improvisation meant, Davies says, that 'people almost had cardiac arrests in the audience. We couldn't stop them laughing.' But professional critical opinion was more divided on this production than on Davies's previous Brechts. Reviewers were uncertain about the overall impact of the production. For example, one wrote that Davies was

> one of the few directors in Britain who can sense the appropriate temperature for Brecht. This isn't a matter of underplaying so much as restricting a natural temptation to flaunt.[4]

But on the other hand, the same reviewer found the production 'timid and unadventurous . . . more faithful to the script as written than to the spirit of Brecht the imperturbable changer and adaptor'. Again, as with previous British Brecht, we encounter the issue of fidelity to the text, and the possibility of an over-reverence, not to Brecht's practice, but to preconceptions about the stylistic conventions demanded by authentic Brechtian theatre.

By now Davies was well established as the 'Brecht director' at the RSC and in 1977 he undertook *Days of the Commune*. This, he knew, was in some ways a more difficult Brecht play than any he had tackled hitherto.

> I saw it like *Danton's Death* – a sprawling mass of people trying to learn how to conduct themselves. They have created a revolution which they do not know how to conduct. You have to revise your game-plan once you're in power.

He has acknowledged since that this reading of the play could equally have been applied to the rehearsals for the production. He had at his disposal a large company of experienced and prestigious actors but it quickly became apparent that many of them were not enamoured of the play itself and that there was certainly no sense of an ensemble spirit throughout the cast:

> Nobody was prepared to conform to a consensus view of the play. There were too many individualistic voices, too many very strong personalities and I wasn't mature enough as a director to handle that. I hid behind my own fear of dealing with a company of that size.

Furthermore, during rehearsals the director was so bombarded by the actors with questions about Brechtian style and 'alienation' that, he admits, he

> retreated behind theory in order to try and answer their questions and that compounded the problems. As a last resort, the production became an attempt at style but ended up as a morass of acting techniques.

In the circumstances, such was the pressure that Davies was under in attempting to create a working process that he became ill and rehearsals had to be taken over by another director. One of the actors in the company, Richard Griffiths, recalls the whole experience from a performer's point of view:

> The play felt very unwieldy. Howard hadn't placed the 'importances' in each scene, he hadn't found how to orchestrate it. What's more, the company didn't want to play a crowd.[5]

No collective sense of purpose was generated, and no commitment to the socio-political meaning of the piece via a mutually supportive approach operating through the company in rehearsal and performance. Consequently, by the time the production opened, cast morale was very low. Griffiths was sharing a dressing-room with eight or so other actors. He remembers that each night, as the play opened, the offstage actors were already playing cards backstage. When the first line of the play, 'A terrible thing has happened', came over the tannoy, those in his dressing-room regularly chorused: 'Not yet, mate, but it soon will!' Ian McKellen, another cast member, recalls that he thought Howard Davies 'didn't have a clue' and adds that *Days of the Commune* was the only production he has ever regretted being in.[6] Even allowing for the usual tendency among actors to blame the director for all the faults of a production, there clearly were problems in the whole approach to this show, which Davies himself readily admits. During the early part of the run of *Days of the Commune*, the company held internal, post-show discussions. Davies now calls them 'post-mortems' and remarks:

> The company wanted to punish me. About half of them wanted to persist with it and try to make it work, the others wanted to cancel the show. I just felt I had got it all wrong, lost my touch. It was a failure.

However, the failure was the whole company's, the RSC's, insofar as the production problems directly stemmed from the fact that the implications of the decision to mount a Brecht play had not been fully thought through at a management level. Instead, it would seem that an assumption had been made that *Days of the Commune* was just another 'classic', requiring no special kind of approach, or preparation, or, indeed, casting of the actors.

Reviewers generally agreed with Davies's and the actors' own verdict. While several admired the production's clarity of story-telling, the overall view was unfavourable. Irving Wardle in *The Times* drew attention to the actors' unease in their roles, remarking that he had never seen 'such grey performances from Bob Peck, Marie Kean and Ian McKellen' (7.11.77). Peter Lewis of *The Daily Mail* was unsure where the criticism should fall: 'The only thing to be decided about this dismal evening is whom to blame for it most: Brecht or the Royal Shakespeare Company? About 50/50 I should say' (8.11.77). And Bernard Levin wrote off the play itself with rumbustuous derision:

> It has the depth of a cracker-motto, the drama of a dial-a-recipe and the eloquence of a conversation between a speak-your-weight machine and a whoopee cushion.
>
> (*The Sunday Times*, 6.11.77)

The larger significance was that the British approach to Brecht had again made the playwright seem both dull and superficial.

Unsurprisingly, Howard Davies abandoned directing Brecht for a while, in fact for seven years. In the meantime, two more productions of Brecht plays were undertaken at the RSC. The first of these, in 1979, was of his first piece, *Baal*, directed by David Jones with Ben Kingsley in the title role (and the latter was also responsible for the music). This played to very good houses at the Other Place in Stratford, and at the Donmar Warehouse, then used as the RSC's 'alternative' venue in London. It was a very clear, sharply etched production, bold and appropriately expressionistic. *The Guardian*'s critic thought it 'precisely catches the mood of this tough, gritty, biliously fascinating play' (26.8.79).

In the same year, John Caird directed a touring production of *The Caucasian Chalk Circle* with a relatively small company of actors, which, therefore, necessitated a good deal of doubling of roles. The RSC Press Office's announcement that the company 'chose *Caucasian Chalk Circle* because it is a popular, funny, sentimental play and is part of our policy of reviving modern classics' drew attention both to the RSC's misconception about the nature of the play itself and to their motives in mounting the production. Nevertheless, one regional reviewer (for *The North Western Evening Mail*) described the text as a 'risky choice for a provincial tour' (19.9.79) and assumed that it would not attract audiences. Two problems emerge here: Brecht is seen as a modern classic writer of a 'sentimental' play, and he is likely to do poor business in the regions.

The resulting production, according to most reviews, was given particular strength by the playing. Azdak by Alun Armstrong, who was 'outrageous and irreverent', contrived to steal the show (*The North Western Evening Mail*, 19.9.79). Armstrong's strengths as a comic actor, in particular his *penchant* for almost grotesque, out-front playing, made him an ideal choice for the role of the judge. He revealed, however, that he had received little guidance in how to play him:

> I had heard that there was a special way of acting Brecht roles but since no-one seemed to be able to explain what this was, I assumed it was the usual hype and promptly forgot about it.[7]

But he did admit that he found performing a Brecht play more difficult than many others he had done, noting that Brecht is 'deceptive'.

99

In 1984 Howard Davies resumed his work on Brecht and began preparations for a production of *Mother Courage and Her Children* with Judi Dench in the lead. Unfortunately, performing rights for this play had been simultaneously granted by the Brecht estate to Oxford Playhouse for a production featuring Glenda Jackson. After a somewhat bitter campaign Oxford Playhouse (and Glenda Jackson) agreed to cancel their production when it transpired that rights for *Mother Courage* had also been granted to the Citizens Theatre, Glasgow, for a later production and they, too, were interested to cast Jackson (see Chapter 5).

The painful memory of *Days of the Commune* still lingered for Howard Davies, and so he undertook his preparation for *Mother Courage* with particular seriousness. He even insisted that the audience should be made aware of this by printing in the production programme the list of books on Brecht he had consulted. In his directing, he states he was especially concerned to find a balance between the psychological reality of the individual character and the socio-political content of the play as a whole:

> I'd gone away from 'personalised' Brecht (like in *Caucasian Chalk Circle*) towards productions on a more epic scale, but I'd failed to mix and match the personal and the public successfully.

The text was created by commissioning the socialist playwright Hanif Kureishi to write a version by working from a literal translation provided by Susan Davies. Kureishi admired Howard Brenton's version of *The Life of Galileo*, presented at the National Theatre in 1980 (see p.105), for its wit and cleverness and wanted to emulate those qualities. He intended also to reveal *Mother Courage* as warm and funny, and not 'a long, tedious, stodgy anti-war play'.[8] With that in mind, he trimmed the text of some of its more complicated sequences, such as when the audience is confronted by dialectically structured passages of action. An example of this is the scene in which Kattrin tries on Yvette's boots, while her mother discusses the politics of war. Courage's lines were greatly reduced by Kureishi while Kattrin's action was foregrounded. Thus, the ironic, contradictory effect of the scene was carefully eschewed.

A similar decision was made by the director in the second scene of the play, in which the focus in Brecht's text is again divided into two: on the Cook and Mother Courage in the camp kitchen on one side and on the General and Eilif in the General's tent on the other. In Davies's production the Cook simply repeated over and again the action of wiping his table as though not to distract from the action in the tent. Again, this prevented each half of the scene being presented as a dialectical counterpoint to the other.

Kureishi claimed in an interview with Ria Julian that in his view there was nothing 'left of the alienation concept in *Mother Courage*. I think that in a way the character goes against some of the things Brecht believed about alienation'.[9] He was prepared to remove himself some of Brecht's 'distancing', as suggested above. As adaptor, Kureishi then reduced it still further by firmly integrating the songs into the stage fiction, making them a seamless part of the action. The ways in which the music, specially composed by George Fenton, was deployed in this production are roundly criticised by Maarten van Dijk in his punningly titled article 'Blocking Brecht':

> it drowned the words, upstaged the action, aimed for atmosphere instead of meaning (gypsy-style violins and tunes were much in evidence), and in the case of Yvette's song, accompanied by a banjo, descended to pop-song banalities.
>
> (Kleber and Visser, 1990, p.121)

Kureishi and Davies agreed that they wanted to emphasise and highlight qualities in Mother Courage of warmth and affection and in so doing they intended the audience to empathise with the character more than might be expected in a Brecht play. Davies looked for a playing of Courage as 'warm, youngish and randy. In a way that Helene Weigel wouldn't have been.' Judi Dench, an actor whom he knew contradicted 'conventional expectations' of how to cast Courage, was his ideal choice. Thus the director and the translator set out to turn on its head Brecht's idea of Mother Courage as a 'social construct', as a woman created primarily by her circumstances. They were to adopt a psychological rather than sociological approach to the character, and this approach inevitably affected their view of characterisation in the whole production. Davies demanded that all the actors find as much psychological 'reality' in their portrayals as possible. He had for some years been working closely with Trevor Nunn, the Artistic Director of the RSC, and was a great admirer of his work, and he wanted to direct *Mother Courage* in the manner in which Nunn approached Shakespeare:

> Nunn humanizes every character. . . . You meet all these characters and feel that the play could have been about any of them. I didn't want to treat Mother Courage as an epic, brave figure on a canvas of wore-torn Europe but as somebody in a bit of a bloody fix who was going to damn well survive by cheating and looting.

Davies found Dench easy to work with as an 'instinctive' actor who appears to follow no particular analytical system when developing a role. Richard Eyre, now director of the National Theatre, supports this view of her:

> Judi Dench is an actress who works almost entirely on her instincts . . . Judi has technique to burn – she can turn a line on a fragment of a syllable, a scene on the twist of a finger. She doesn't *study* a part but works through a process of osmosis, soaking up the details with a sometimes disconcerting randomness.
>
> (Eyre, 1993, p.100)

Shortly before tackling Mother Courage, Dench had had considerable success with a television comedy series, *A Fine Romance*, teamed with her actor-husband, Michael Williams (incidentally, the RSC Schweyk). This had confirmed with the public her comic lightness of touch and had shown off to perfection her impeccable timing in the handling of comic material. Her studiedly 'non-intellectual' approach to performance is borne out by her claim to have avoided all pre-rehearsal preparation for the Brecht production: – 'I didn't read *Mother Courage* until the day before rehearsals' – and she was pleased to share virginal naïvety about the play with the production team: 'director, designer and translator all gratefully acknowledged they had never seen a production of the play'.[10]

Dench's visual appearance contributed towards the creation of empathy with the character. She appeared as a diminutive, chirpy figure with a startling shock of red hair, striding about in heavy boots and a huge, oversize greatcoat. She used a gritty, Cockney-accented voice and she delivered the songs with considerable assertiveness. This caused her to have some problems with her voice during the first few weeks of performances and she had to rest several hours a day in order to overcome vocal strain, as the part made more demands of her than she had anticipated. Physically, though, Dench managed to convey a relaxed strength in Courage, planting her feet firmly apart and deploying frequent shrugs of the shoulders. But the toughness was only physical, not emotional. This Courage was a warm and amusing human being, lacking the temperamental toughness, even harshness, usually associated with her.

According to Davies, Dench enjoyed finding practical rather than intellectual solutions to theatrical problems encountered in rehearsal. This was just as well, since the set-design for the production certainly provided a number of physical problems. Instead of the usual Courage wagon, the designer, John Napier, provided a 'Heath Robinson' war-machine construction. It comprised a lengthy truck, with the cart at one end and a tent and flag at the other, and the whole structure turned on a central pivot, which was topped by a weathervane. This evidently was intended to represent the cyclical processes of war, and it had to be turned, in the centre of an otherwise bare stage, by Dench as Mother Courage. In fact, Napier's non-realistic device was strangely at odds with Davies's concern to portray the characters and the situations of the play in a naturalistic manner. It also had the knock-on effect that props were necessarily reduced to a bare minimum, because there was virtually nowhere to put Courage's stock. Consequently, objects were often mimed by the actors, and this further undermined not only the sense of the 'reality' of the action but also the meaning of certain key episodes in the play. For example, the absence of all the items referred to in Courage's stock-taking of the cart (Scene 6) substantially reduced the clarity in Brecht's text of the fundamental idea that Courage is trading off the war in a morally indefensible way. Furthermore, this unwieldy and strange cart caused regular hitches in the performance, sometimes breaking down completely, so that the stage-crew had to come onstage and help Dench get the thing moving. The director claims that it was poorly constructed and admits that, inevitably, 'the actors lost all confidence in what we had achieved in rehearsal because they became preoccupied with the fear of the set going wrong'.

Most reviewers, however, were positive about the production, and Davies was praised by Michael Billington for attempting to jettison 'the museum-piece approach to Brecht' (*The Guardian*, 9.11.84). However, the central design feature of the cart and its pivoting machinery came in for much criticism. One reviewer (in *Drama*) talked of Judi Dench's suffering 'death by scenery' (Spring, 1985), but more fundamentally, Michael Ratcliffe of *The Observer* saw the stage problems with the machine as a metaphor for a more serious flaw in the whole production, the lack of a political centre: 'Brecht's marvellous concept . . . is consumed in the spectacular visual rhetoric. . . . There is a hollowness at the heart' (11.11.84).

Dench's unusual emphasis on the warmth in Courage's make-up provoked controversy. John Peter in *The Sunday Times*, in describing Dench's performance as one of the finest in Brecht he had seen, thought her acting 'dry but gripping, pitiless and unsympathetic but eloquent' (11.11.84), and, therefore, not warm at all. On the other hand, others thought her portrayal too 'chirpy', too plucky and too encouraging of the audience's empathy. John Barber (of *The Daily Telegraph*) remarked shrewdly (and with unknowing irony): 'Judi Dench is altogether too warm and homely a personality. It is a role for Glenda Jackson' (9.11.84). (More of that in the next chapter.)

Perhaps the actor herself was anxious about her warm portrayal, too, for Howard Davies reveals that in late rehearsal, in the second run-through, Dench played the part without the humour she had been developing and instead made Courage brutal and savage. Davies concluded that:

> somebody had talked to her after the first run-through. I took her on one side and said: 'what you've been working on for the last six weeks is fantastic and you've thrown it away today.' . . . We've never discussed why she did that. Maybe she thought we hadn't explored that aspect of the character and this was a way of exploring the parameters of the role. I suppose I limited her.

However, Davies defended his demand for a 'warm' Mother Courage by implying that, in any case, the audience would remain objective and still be able to judge her:

> I can't imagine that anyone would have identified with Mother Courage as played by Judi Dench. I don't think they would empathize with her in such a way that they would lose their judgment. They

might be bemused at the end as to why this figure hasn't gained in heroic stature. They come out of the theatre thinking: 'I quite liked her really but her bravura wasn't getting her anywhere'.

Significantly, the account of Dench's performance in the biography of her by Gerald Jacobs, reads: 'Judi strode the stage – joking here, cajoling there, . . . and *pace* Brecht, she expressed her character . . . in basic human terms with which audiences can identify' (Jacobs, 1986, p.142). Indeed, *pace* Brecht. Maarten van Dijk, again, sums up accurately the way in which Davies's pursuit of Courage's warmth defeated Brecht's purpose:

> The so-called warmth, therefore, that the translator and director wanted to put into the play (and about which they might have been more wary had they consulted *Theaterarbeit*) amounted, as usual, to nothing more than a pandering sentimentalism.
>
> (Kleber and Visser, 1990, p.120)

And Christopher McCullough, in a chapter entitled 'From Brecht to Brechtian: Estrangement and Appropriation', describes the Davies/Kureishi production of *Mother Courage* as 'an intriguing case of cultural appropriation', in which 'the work and example of the historical materialist theorist and playwright is accommodated into a humanist concept of unchanging human nature' (Holderness, 1992, pp.120 and 123). This RSC production was thus part of that British tradition that separated Brecht the artist from Brecht the socialist, or failed to understand the socialist dramaturgy of the text itself.

BRECHT AT THE NATIONAL THEATRE

By 1979 the National Theatre Company had presented only one original Brecht play, *Mother Courage and Her Children* (1965), since its establishment in 1963. The National's Literary Adviser, the theatre critic Kenneth Tynan, had initiated in 1964 an audience questionnaire, by means of which he enquired which playwrights the patrons would most like to see represented in the National Theatre's repertoire. In order of preference, Brecht came third (after Ibsen and Shaw). The following year, the National presented *Mother Courage*, directed by William Gaskill (and discussed in Chapter 2). Under the artistic direction of Laurence Olivier the company had also mounted two Brecht adaptations, *Edward II* (1968) and *Coriolanus* (1971). For the latter, two directors from the Berliner Ensemble had been drafted in to assist.

Peter Hall took over from Olivier as Artistic Director in 1973 and remained in charge when the company moved into its specially built complex on the South Bank in 1979. Hall and the new Literary Adviser, John Russell Brown, agreed that a Brecht play should be produced at the National, and opted for *The Life of Galileo*. The reason for the choice, Brown admitted, was that 'it's more like other people's plays than the rest of the canon' (Hiley, 1981, p.2), which points to a certain lack of confidence in things Brechtian. Rather Brecht was being regarded as a 'modern classical' writer whose work ought to be represented in the National's programme, providing his work could be made to appear like that of other playwrights.

Hall judged that Brecht's British reputation had suffered from the 'inept and fustian' translations that were customarily performed, and so he and Russell Brown decided to commission a new version. They agreed what would best serve as a translator would be a dramatist 'who would respond to Brecht's concise yet open style, who was used to pitching scene against scene and voice against voice' (Hiley, 1981, p.6). This obviously indicates a greater sensitivity to Brecht than Brown's words quoted above might have suggested. The choice of translator was the Marxist playwright Howard Brenton, who had been a co-founder of Portable Theatre in the 1960s (see Chapter 3). Only one year previously he had been the first contemporary playwright to receive a commission for a new play from the National. He now accepted the task of translating *Galileo*.

Although Brenton was not a German speaker/writer, he was a Brecht enthusiast and felt he understood the way that Brecht used language in the plays:

> Brecht admired English writing. We have an informal tradition which he was trying to inject into his own German text. The result is great formal language with a dirty underbelly. All the notes of cynicism, all the ironies come out in a very un-Schiller-like German.
>
> (Hiley, 1981, p.7)

Brenton worked with a literal translation and relied largely on his own instincts with regard to the subtleties of the original: 'It was like water-divining. I hit a rhythm which is apparently very Brechtian' (Hiley, 1981, p.7). Furthermore, through working on *Galileo*, Brenton came to appreciate the impact of Brecht's episodic dramaturgy:

> Each scene is a play in itself that you could almost lift out and play as lunch-time theatre. . . . All his great big epic plays have this odd quality, which means that while the scene is playing, it's actually very intense, or very funny, but the general sweep is quite cool because the scenes . . . have a sort of beginning, middle and end.
>
> (Reinelt, 1994, p.32)

Peter Hall was reluctant to direct *Galileo* himself because he felt cramped or outfaced by the Berliner Ensemble:

> God knows I admire Brecht, but I'm not sure I'm competent to direct him. I saw the Berliner Ensemble in the 1950s and they were so breathtaking it incapacitated me.
>
> (Hiley, 1981, p.10)

Brecht's Marxism was also a stumbling block for Hall. In his *Diaries*, he gives an account of a production of *The Caucasian Chalk Circle* by the Rustaveli Company which he saw at the Edinburgh Festival (1979). He notes that it was particularly enjoyable because 'ideology and politics were out of the window' (Hall, 1983, p.460). In a speech made to mark the opening of the National's *Galileo*, Hall was, however, careful not to reveal his hand too openly with regard to Brecht's politics:

> On the one hand, he asserted that the play was nothing like as subversive as Brecht's disciples thought, and that it 'did the reverse' of making him want to be a Marxist. On the other hand, he said: 'It could be the mark of a mature society that it will pay to be criticised or challenged'.

> (Hiley, 1981, p.4)

Hall persuaded John Dexter, who had been an Associate Director with the National Theatre since 1963, to take on the direction.

John Dexter and Brecht

Dexter's theatre 'pedigree' for the task appeared excellent. His directing career had begun at the Royal Court, where he had been Associate Director to George Devine. There he had directed a number of new plays, including Arnold Wesker's trilogy, and, in more Brechtian vein, his *Chips With Everything*, which had competed with *The Caucasian Chalk Circle* for the 1962 Best Play Award (see Chapter 2). Dexter had seen the Berliner Ensemble production of *Galileo* (featuring Ernst Busch) in 1957, and had been 'knocked out by it' (Hiley, 1981, p.13). Unlike Hall, he had not been made nervous by the experience of tackling Brecht, and *Galileo* had been on his list of dramatic work that he was determined to direct from that time.

Dexter had long discussions with Brenton, the translator, about the last scene in the play (in which Andrea smuggles Galileo's *Discoursi* across the border). This had been cut in the Berliner production Dexter had seen and he also wanted to cut it. Brenton, however, argued that the scene should be performed because it served to erase the otherwise final image of Galileo as a sensual man, at table eating his goose. What Brenton understood by Brecht's last scene was that 'the play should be about what Galileo did, not a personal tragedy' (Hiley, 1981, p.53). Dexter was persuaded to try out the scene in rehearsal, and for the production he not only retained it but utilised in it almost the entire cast to create a crowd of people waiting with Andrea (and the *Discoursi*) to cross at the border-post.

While at the Royal Court, Dexter had also established a strong working relationship with the designer Jocelyn Herbert, whom he now invited to design the set and costumes for the production. (She had also designed the set for Gaskill's *Mother Courage* in 1965.) According to Herbert, she and Dexter shared, in typical Royal Court fashion,

> the same feelings about the kind of theatre we were interested in, where the text was the organic centre of the production and not just a coat-hanger for director and designer.
>
> *(The Independent*, 26.3.90)

Since 1974 Dexter had been Director of the Metropolitan Opera House in New York, and so he now relished the opportunity to direct *Galileo* on a physical scale of the size afforded him by the National's Olivier Theatre. He had at his disposal a large, open, arena stage with a 'bowl-like' auditorium seating over one thousand spectators. Since its opening, however, there had been technical problems with this theatre (with its scene-shifting equipment, for example) and some performers had felt daunted by its sheer size and the demands it made on actors' vocal skills. (These are still issues for actors today.) Herbert was aware of these problems and proposed a re-design for the stage area (for permanent use), including a 'platform' stage that would bring the actors closer to the audience. This new stage would provide the basis for her design for *The Life of Galileo*, which comprised a huge central stage 'disc' (on top of the square platform stage), approached by ramps and surrounded by a semi-circular 'back wall' of metal shutters. Herbert notes in her book, *A Theatre Workbook*, that Dexter was keen, in Brechtian fashion, on using slide-projections for the production, so the metal framework around the acting area was utilised to provide a frame for a projection screen (Herbert, 1993, p.112). The interior scenes in the play were to be staged on a truck that moved from upstage onto the central disc. After protracted discussions, the National Theatre management decided that Herbert's new permanent stage for the Olivier was too expensive. This meant that the disc stage for *Galileo* had to have its own supporting structure, and this, when built, was to prove a major source of technical problems and escalating costs for the production. (In fact, the original structure had to be replaced after the previews; see Hiley, 1981.)

Herbert's working relationship with Dexter bore some similarities to that between Brecht and Neher. As did Neher for Brecht, she supplied rehearsal drawings 'to help plot getting actors from one place to another and from scene to scene' (Herbert, 1993, p.112). However, Dexter's directing imperatives, it transpired, were often more of a technical nature than concerned with making the socio-political intentions of the play clear. As Herbert points out, Dexter in fact had the play blocked in his script at the start of rehearsals so that he could give actors precise moves (*The Independent*, 26.3.90). Brecht and Neher, on the other hand, worked together with the actors in the rehearsal room to evolve the 'stage pictures' that would carry the political meanings of the production.

The casting of Michael Gambon as Galileo caused some initial surprise at the National Theatre because at the time he was best known as a comic actor who had made a fine reputation in the social comedies of Alan Ayckbourn. Few saw him as having the necessary 'weight', in terms of seriousness, for this 'heavy' Brechtian role. Again, as with the RSC and Howard Davies, experience of and commitment to comedy were not deemed appropriate by many British theatre practitioners for interpreting Brecht, because the satirical and comic elements in his plays were often either underestimated or overlooked by actors and directors alike.

Gambon had had no formal training as an actor but first appeared on stage as a teenager in 'semi-professional' productions by the London Unity Theatre, the left-wing workers' theatre that started in the 1930s (see p.42). He claims that he did not realise Unity was political; rather his main concern at that time was how much make-up to put on.[11] He quickly graduated via the Gate Theatre, Dublin, to the National Theatre company where, in 1965, he played Eilif in the Gaskill production of *Mother Courage* (discussed in Chapter 2).

The casting of the large number of roles in *Galileo* had caused some concern at the National because many of them have only one or two 'major' scenes. Dexter had written to the company's Casting Director, Gillian Diamond, about his plans:

> I am suggesting to some leading members of the company that when we cast them we will be asking them to play a role and do at least one mute scene. . . . The reasons for this tactic are . . . to create an appearance of an ensemble.
>
> (Dexter, 1993, p.229)

And to Peter Hall, he elaborated on this:

> I think it appropriate that we can begin to build an interior life for the company on *Galileo* and let the actors develop a responsibility for each other and to each other.
>
> (Dexter, 1993, p.235)

Dexter's plan was to create the sense of an ensemble operation for the production of *Galileo* and to encourage that to spill over into the general ethos and working of the company at large. Predictably, however, some of the actors were not pleased with the roles offered. Simon Callow (previously Arturo Ui at the Half Moon), for example, wanted to play Andrea but was given the Little Monk. To rub salt in the wound, he received a letter from the director on how to play the role: 'You can play the scene two ways: sitting down or standing up. Never let it be said that I'm not a flexible director' (Dexter, 1993, p.237). And Callow maintains that this was not intended as a joke, adding that by the time he came to rehearse the scene, Dexter had decided that he should sit down, and so that was that (Callow, 1984, p.114). Even allowing for some exaggeration on the part of the actor, the director appears here to adopt an autocratic approach.

Michael Gambon also received a letter from Dexter (in August 1979, a year before the production opened) that was intended to assist in his preparation for the role of Galileo. The director asked:

> Can you draw the epicyclic orbit of Venus according to Ptolemaic assumptions? I think you had better learn to do that before you learn the words, and I had better do it before I start to think about the moves.
>
> (Dexter, 1993, p.228)

Evidently, this was part of Dexter's careful planning of actors' positions and moves on stage, which he based to some extent on the spatial relationships between stars and planets and their orbits (rather than on human social relationships). His leading actor, meanwhile, was worried not only by the sheer size of the role and what Dexter expected of him, but Gambon also feared that Brecht would not appeal to a British audience: 'When we first started rehearsals, I thought: "Is this interesting for an audience? Will they come?"'

There was clearly a general nervousness at the National about taking on Brecht, and this affected Dexter to the extent that, as Brenton recalls, the director avoided the traditional start to rehearsals of a read-through of the play:

> The reason was that he knew the anti-Brecht feeling and he knew that he'd probably get a bad reading and then the bitching would start about teutonic heaviness.
>
> (Banks, 1984, p.105)

In rehearsal, Gambon (like Callow) found Dexter 'a very autocratic man' who demanded a high level of technical accuracy in the actors' blocking:

> You had to be accurate. So much so that if a door was marked on the floor with tape, if you didn't mime using the door, he would shout at you, which was very annoying.

It was not, however, the demand for technical precision that annoyed Gambon. Indeed, he had admired that feature in the directing of Alan Ayckbourn. What he objected to was Dexter's often dictatorial and abrasive manner of handling actors. Despite the suggestion to Hall that working on *Galileo* would be an opportunity to create an ensemble, Dexter was often less than democratic. This was not just a matter of telling actors how to play their roles physically in terms of stage moves, but also of not allowing them to contribute to the overall interpretation of the text. Simon Callow recalls the first rehearsal when the director

> declared that we were going to get rid of all the Marxist rubbish in the play; moreover, he said, this wasn't a play about the church or even science, but about Brecht himself, who knew he'd sold out. John may

have been right or wrong, but how could we not discuss such a fundamental proposition?

(Callow, 1984, p.114)

Gambon's recollections of the early rehearsals support Callow's view that there was little discussion in the company of the meaning of the play, but offer a more sympathetic account of Dexter's way of working with the cast:

John didn't touch on the politics much – there was no real talk of the 'meat' of the play, but he would make us read Brecht poems in the mornings. Sit round in a circle. That was simply to do with getting actors relaxed together.

Gambon develops this in remembering that Dexter told the company that all they needed to know about Brecht's ideas on performance was contained in his theatre poems, which may well be a useful and perceptive piece of guidance. Furthermore, during the rehearsals the actors were shown reproductions of Brueghel paintings which Dexter drew on in particular to help actors create make-up for the Carnival scene, thus making the connection that Brecht had himself made (*B on T*, p.159). These accounts of Dexter's approach to rehearsing *Galileo* suggest the director understood a good deal about both Brecht's theory and dramaturgy. However, he chose for the most part to set aside the implications of that knowledge with regard to the actor/director relationship and the development of a collaborative working method.

Gambon's own approach to acting, like that of Judi Dench, is largely instinctive rather than theoretical or intellectual. He declares he has no 'method' and is rather suspicious of actors who talk about their processes: 'There's really nothing in it, is there? Fundamentally it's the sheer and utter arrogance of wanting to get on stage – and people wrap it in flowers!' Clear, physical expression is basic to Gambon's portrayal of character. Once he has read the script, he begins to construct the character externally, often by finding a physical outline or shape, or a way of walking: 'I look back and see this person standing there.' Jim Hiley, in the account of the *Galileo* production in his book *Theatre at Work*, confirms this by reporting that during rehearsal Gambon constantly experimented with the physical aspects of conveying Galileo – 'trying a stoop here, thickening the voice there'. And Hiley goes on with a detail that harks back to Brecht's own influences, 'and employing . . . silent film comedy business' (Hiley, 1981, p.94).

Gambon was also concerned to convey clearly the way Galileo ages during the play (which covers a twenty-year period), so he experimented with 'instant ageing', by means of wig, beard and costume changes often carried out onstage with his back to the audience. This reflects an interest in make-up technique developed during the actor's time with Unity

Theatre. For Gambon, Galileo's ageing as part of the journeying in the play, both literal and metaphorical, was an important aspect of the play's action and narrative, but it was achieved by very simple means. As he said in an interview: 'I turn my back in order to age by twenty years. I did one or two things to my face, turned round and there it was.' And the interviewer added: 'When he turned, he seemed to have been ravaged by time, disgrace and self-disgust' (*The Sunday Times*, 9.2.80).

Whereas some company members were anxious about the size of the Olivier Theatre and its implications for their vocal projection, Gambon enjoyed the opportunity the role afforded him for changes in and ranges of voice: 'I've got a big voice. I relish all that in a massive, epic play.' As indicated by the Hiley reference to his drawing on silent films, he utilised his experience as a comic actor in developing his role for *Galileo* and was convinced that comedy was crucial to the impact that Brecht intended his work to have on the audience:

I think it's the actor's responsibility to find the comedy . . . not silly comedy but that within the confines of the play . . . especially in Brecht. It enriches the audience's experience if in the same evening they can laugh and also be hammered by the message.

Gambon considered the main challenges in rehearsal were practical, technical ones and that the text itself was straightforward:

The scenes are all quite simple; it's very clear what happens. And I liked all the mechanical things . . . visual aids, rolling balls down slopes, demonstrations. All that really helped the clarity.

But there were problems in the company; some actors were still unhappy at the limitations of their roles (Dexter's plan for an ensemble had already crumbled), and the problems with the set (the costly re-making of the support structure) led to the sacking of the Production Manager. Even the leading actor was struggling for confidence, and then Dexter became ill and necessarily took time off. Intriguingly, the absence of the director improved matters. Gambon explains:

The rehearsal process rocked in the middle. It started well and then John got ill. I hadn't got any confidence. He was away for four days and I was able to relax and we were really able to achieve things . . . things he'd set but we hadn't had time, or been given time, to explore. When he came back the last week was joyous. I *knew* we had some good stuff.

When Dexter returned to rehearsals he was pleased to find that Gambon had solved what the director viewed as a major problem: 'He finally found a way of sustaining each scene as a separate entity, kicking the habit of referring mentally to action past or to come' (Hiley, 1981, p.154). Thus

111

Dexter makes clear his own understanding of one aspect of role-playing by the Brechtian actor, that is, the avoidance of a psychologically-based 'through-line' by which the actor charts a cause/effect process from scene to scene.

Gambon's Galileo won him several 'Best Actor of 1980' awards and it remains one of his three favourite roles (with Eddie Carbone in Miller's *A View From the Bridge*, and Philip Marlow in Dennis Potter's *The Singing Detective*, which in themselves indicate Gambon's impressive range). Jim Hiley writes that Gambon's Galileo was not Brechtian 'in the received sense of being austere. Rather it was Brechtian in its relish. Gambon seized the part with both hands and, like Galileo at his goose, devoured it greedily' (Hiley, 1981, p.210). (And the notion of 'relish' might remind us of Gambon's physical as well as emotional similarity to Charles Laughton, Brecht's own choice for Galileo.)

The production's set design was not universally admired. One reviewer wrote (in *The Times Literary Supplement*) that Herbert had paid too much attention to Brechtian theory in creating such an 'open' design (her attempt to exploit the full stage of the Olivier Theatre). More importantly, it was suggested that the large, often undefined spaces deployed in the production were wrong for *Galileo*, which is 'above all a play of interiors' (22.8.80). A related criticism (by the reviewer in *Drama*) was that of Dexter's handling of the crowd scenes, in which characters were observed 'standing around in detached, statuesque groupings' (October 1980), as opposed, presumably, to presenting a vibrant and energetic sense of interaction. One critic concluded, however, that 'Dexter's great *Galileo* took the curse off Brecht in Britain' (*The Guardian*, 17.9.81). And we note that the perception of an anti-Brecht prejudice in Britain persisted until 1980.

Dexter declared himself 'totally satisfied' with his production: 'I felt we hit the style dead centre' (Dexter, 1993, p.239). Despite his own success in and enjoyment of the role, Michael Gambon recognised that the 'approach' at the National Theatre was not collaborative, nor were participants even informed about company policy or the purposes of the work: 'The actors didn't know about the politics upstairs, about why the play was chosen. There was no real engagement with the company there.' It is sad to relate that the leading actor was acutely conscious of his own lack of power and status within the organisation. This became evident to him when the management failed to protect him (by re-scheduling) from the pressure of performing in another production during the evenings of the final week of *Galileo* rehearsals. His view was that the 'top people' thought of him as 'sweaty and smelly and working class' (Hiley, 1981, p.191). Again allowing for an actor's high degree of sensitivity to others' perception of him, this is a further indication of the National Theatre's inability or unwillingness to ensure a collective creative process and a sense of collaborative responsibility for the work from the company as a whole.

It is probably a truism that the success in developing an ensemble approach for a particular production is dependent first and foremost on the attitude and working method of the director. When John Dexter subsequently directed *The Threepenny Opera* (1989) in New York, his Macheath, pop singer/actor Sting, anticipated: 'John is going to interpret the play and I am going to do what he says' (Dexter, 1993, p.290). That may be an appropriate strategy for a pop star; it is not the kind of context in which actors working in the National Theatre are inevitably going to produce their most effective and responsible work.

Richard Eyre and Brecht

In 1982, the National tackled two Brecht plays in the same year. The first production was of *Schweyk in the Second World War* in the Olivier Theatre. A brief analysis of this example of 'National Brecht' serves to place in context some of the problems encountered by the company in the staging of *The Life of Galileo*. This time the directing was the responsibility of Richard Eyre, who had just become an Associate Director at the theatre and had been given his own 'company' to work with. Eyre was undoubtedly a 'rising star', (and would take over as Artistic Director of the National Theatre when Peter Hall left in 1988). His qualifications for directing Brecht were strong. In the early part of his theatre career in Scotland, he had directed productions of *Trumpets and Drums* (Brecht's version of *The Recruiting Officer*) and *Schweyk in the Second World War*, and he had also worked with John McGrath's socialist company, 7:84 (see Chapter 3). As Artistic Director of Nottingham Playhouse (1973–8), Eyre had mounted another production of *Trumpets and Drums* (1976) and, perhaps as importantly, he had directed a number of new plays by young socialist playwrights, including Howard Brenton and Trevor Griffiths. Eyre writes in his autobiography, *Utopia and Other Places*:

> I was lucky enough to work with several of a new generation of playwrights who were young, ambitious, cocky and keen to repudiate the old avant-garde and establish a new one. They embraced new forms, new kinds of staging, vivid use of language, of music, of design. . . . There was a new directness about political issues.
>
> (Eyre, 1993, p.97)

Some of that directness had been learned from Brecht (see p.70)

When Eyre left Nottingham Playhouse and became a producer and director for BBC television, his interest in and commitment to new and especially political work continued (with, for example, productions of Griffiths's *Comedians* and of Wood's *Tumbledown*, a controversial drama-documentary about the Falklands War). His appointment to the National Theatre was, therefore, seen by many as a welcome development in the

113

profile of politically committed art within the establishment theatre. And he joined at the National a number of other socialist practitioners, including Howard Brenton, David Hare and Howard Davies.

In the 1982 (Eyre's second) production of *Schweyk in the Second World War*, the lead role was taken by the Scottish actor Bill Paterson, who had seen the director's first production and whose own theatrical background made him ideal casting for Brecht. While still a drama student, Paterson had taken part in Michael Blakemore's production of *Arturo Ui* at the Citizens Theatre, Glasgow, in 1968 (see Chapter 3). Paterson had been very impressed by Leonard Rossiter's *Ui*, and the whole experience of watching Rossiter work and of the production at large had had a significant impact on him:

> For me it was staggering. He [Rossiter] would come to rehearsals with everything just 'there'. He always looked on top of it. He had this tremendous energy. . . . That taste of Brecht was electrifying for me. To be doing something about politics on stage, I just loved that.[12]

After drama school, Paterson joined and ran the Theatre-in-Education team at the Cits. In 1973, the company took an agitprop style show about the Upper Clyde Shipbuilders to the Edinburgh Festival, where it was seen by John McGrath. Paterson was invited to join 7:84 for their legendary and very successful production of *The Cheviot, the Stag and the Black, Black Oil* and stayed with the company for over two years. The experience of working with 7:84 confirmed Paterson's approach and attitudes to theatre and defined his favourite mode of performance. For him, the company's work was

> the perfect combination of collaboration, political commitment, and up-front acting that made total sense. [It] was so important to me I can't shake it off.

The female lead (Mrs Kopecka) in the National's *Schweyk* was taken by Julia McKenzie, whose background was very different to Bill Paterson's but nonetheless was appropriate for playing Brecht. She had developed a reputation as a musical comedy performer and had appeared, immediately prior to *Schweyk*, as Adelaide in the National's much acclaimed production of *Guys and Dolls*, also directed by Richard Eyre. Having never performed in Brecht before, however, she was concerned in rehearsal about her ignorance of Brechtian theatre. 'What about Brecht's style?' she asked the director. 'Forget about the style', said Eyre, 'just do it'.[13] There are echoes here of Brecht talking to Lotte Lenya (see pp.36–7).

This, in fact, was Eyre's general approach. In rehearsal he avoided discussions about Brechtian theory and about politics, preferring to focus on the physicalisation of scenes in the way of Brecht's own idea of *Gestus*. Bill Paterson puts it simply:

Richard was strong about the pictures that he wanted. He knew what he could do with the play. He just kind of turned up the volume on what we were doing.

Eyre's directing manner is generally gentle and encouraging but firm. He adopts a much more democratic strategy than Dexter. Derived from his own brief and (by his account) totally unsuccessful attempts as a professional actor, Eyre has respect for the performer. He understands the paradoxes involved in all good acting but of special significance for the production of Brechtian 'distance':

> actors must be conscious of themselves, but not be self-conscious; they must know themselves, but they must also, on stage, forget themselves; they must be self-less, but will undeniably be selfish; and they must find the balance, while acting, between the heart and the head.
>
> (Eyre, 1993, p.97)

Bill Paterson's work on the character of Schweyk was influenced, perhaps predictably, by the Grosz cartoons that were part of the design for Piscator's version of the play (1928). Paterson commented: 'they seem to capture that little chap so well, intelligent but innocent', but the actor was reluctant to 'get hung up on theories' and felt that he knew instinctively, when playing Brecht, whether what he achieved/intended was right or wrong. In his own judgment, his particular skill lay, and lies, in making contact with an audience; and he relates this directly to the demands of Brechtian ('distance') playing:

> I don't find any problem in talking to the audience at the same time as talking to someone on the stage. I'm not perhaps as careful in the minutiae of character-building as I should be. I think letting the audience know that you are actually listening as actively as they are is important. Not the character listening but you, the actor, listening. If that's Brechtian then I do that more naturally than disguising myself as a character.

In Paterson's view, Ekkehard Schall, the Berliner Ensemble actor whom he had seen perform several times, was the epitome of a Brechtian actor for this very quality of audience contact: 'He spends a great deal of his time playing to the gallery. He's like a variety turn.' And Paterson also acknowledged that his own experience in Theatre-in-Education was crucially important to an understanding of how to play Brecht, both for that form's typical emphasis on socio-political commitment and for the characteristic mode of performance developed for it that 'feeds off' the audience and encourages its active role.

In a general way, Paterson is an admirer of Brecht's plays, but during rehearsals of *Schweyk*, he began to feel uneasy about Brecht's re-setting the Hašek story in the Hitler period. His concern was with how the audience would read the play 'politically', particularly as the Nazi figures are presented as gross caricatures or buffoons. In effect, he thought Brecht's use of Nazism distorted his own intentions:

> I don't think it really translates into the Second World War. I think somehow Schweyk was better, more telling, left in the context of his own period. The scale of the Gestapo sort of evil was far beyond the sort of bureaucracy – the petty, narrow-mindedness of Hašek's Austro-Hungarian Empire. Confronted with that I think Schweyk was out of his depth and I felt that when I was playing it.

Gradually Richard Eyre allayed actor anxiety in the rehearsal room and the production developed a lightness of touch, a deft sense of irony and a narrative clarity. In the transition from rehearsal room to the Olivier stage, however, some of these qualities were mislaid or perhaps overlaid. The simple and direct playing of the actors became overwhelmed by an overall busy-ness in the production of the set and of flying props and of a distracting lighting design. This busy style may have been an attempt on Eyre's part to make more explicit the comedy or perhaps it indicates a lack of trust in the text to 'fill' the vast stage of the Olivier Theatre. In retrospect Bill Paterson thought:

> The production became over-fussy, it got lost in the Olivier. Afer a few days of rehearsal someone comes along with a modelbox of the set and you think 'Do we need it?' I know Brecht didn't want his plays done by six people in a pub, but most of those done on a grand scale in this country, don't work.

Most reviewers of the production agreed with his comments on this production. Paterson's Schweyk was much praised, however, Michael Billington writing: 'I'm reminded of W.C. Fields' surly, envious comment on Charlie Chaplin: "The guy's a goddamned ballet-dancer!"' (*The Guardian*, 25.9.82). But the staging was much criticised. John Barber of *The Daily Telegraph* (24.9.82) put it most strongly:

> Richard Eyre's busy production buries Brecht's peculiarly elusive humour under spectacular stage effects as ponderous as the Nazis he's satirizing. . . . This overblown interpretation seems to leave the master race in possession of the field.

Howard Davies, who had resisted the temptations of epic staging for his own production of *Schweyk* in 1976, remarked: 'You've got to see the sheer buffoonery of the piece.' Despite the fact, therefore, that the production process had been collaborative and the text had been carefully and openly explored by the actors and director, in the final stages, in the move from rehearsal room to stage, visual effects and stage spectacle had been allowed to spoil the clarity of the story-telling.

THE NATIONAL THEATRE ON TOUR

By way of direct contrast, during that same year (1982), another group of National Theatre actors, under the direction of Michael Bogdanov, took out on tour what was described as 'a workshop presentation' of *The Caucasian Chalk Circle*. This production was specially mounted by the National's Education Department for schools and colleges and toured to eighteen venues before giving six performances in the National's 'studio' space, the Cottesloe Theatre. The company comprised only eight actors and they performed without costumes or set. Props were 'found' and so 'the production is therefore improvised with materials immediately to hand and by taking advantage of the physical surroundings'.[14] The production had clearly defined, didactic intentions, as was made evident in the programme:

> The National Theatre presentation is a basis for discussion on the theme of land usage and current disputes over environmental development.

There was an accompanying 'educational pack', which included a chronology of Brecht's life, notes on *Lehrstücke*, *The Caucasian Chalk Circle*, and Brecht's music, some of his poems, and a list of 'Contemporary Connections' and issues for debate. This was, of course, very much a Theatre-in-Education project in style, targeted at a very specific audience, and it is perhaps a little unfair to make direct comparisons with other productions on main stages. However, with this *Chalk Circle* the National Theatre was openly acknowledging the socio-political and didactic purpose of Brecht's work, and finding a way of allowing an ensemble of actors to make direct contact with an audience. In contrast, the conditions and purposes of their in-house productions of Brecht made such contact difficult, if not impossible, to achieve.

SUMMARY

During the late 1970s and early 1980s in Britain, Brecht's work became familiar on the major, national stages, but in order to fit the playwright into such a bourgeois context, to make him acceptable and undisturbing, and less strange, less challenging, it became the fashion to adopt what was perceived as a Brechtian 'style' and to ignore the fundamental principles and intentions of his working method. This perception of style may well have led to so many British productions of Brecht at the national theatres being overwhelmed by their scenery. Furthermore, the companies in mainstream theatres that produced Brecht during this period were often more concerned with ends than with means, with results and not processes, and with an aesthetic of theatre art that was divorced from, even antithetical to, the socio-political intentions of the play. The very organisation of mainstream British theatre, its lack of real ensembles, the hierarchical

117

structure that allows directors autonomous power over actors, the lack of job security and continuity for the performers, all contributed to this way of producing Brecht. To all intents and purposes Brecht's plays had been widely accepted into British theatre, but his explosive, theatrical power and stimulus to social action were largely de-fused.

5

PERFORMING BRECHT IN THE 1990s

Three approaches to post-wall Brecht

THE LEGACY OF THE LATE 1980s

The social and political changes in Europe in the late 1980s – including the advent of *glasnost* and *perestroika* in Russia, the dismantling of the Berlin Wall and the reunification of East and West Germany, the toppling of President Ceaucescu in Romania, and the widespread discreditation or abandonment of Marxist political thinking and practice – provided an exciting and challenging new context for 'committed art'. The West, of course, was eager to step into the political breach with its tried and tested capitalism, and to claim credit for predicting that communism would never work. And if Marx was well and truly 'dead', and history's own demise reported if not validated, presumably Brecht, too, was an artist whose day was done.

This was an issue that Michael Billington, theatre critic of *The Guardian*, explored in an article of April 1990, 'Brecht to the Wall?'. He quoted Brecht's view (via Eric Bentley) that if world socialism did not come about, he, Brecht, did not expect his work to have a future. And then, like so many before him, Billington entertained the notion that one can still enjoy Brecht's plays while rejecting his ideology. Marxism had become irrelevant, it was assumed, but since Brecht was politically ambivalent anyway, we need not let the politics in his plays worry us. He then made comparisons with Shakespeare and explained that just as we perform *his* plays without reference to his world view, so we can with Brecht.

The article then examined Brecht's influence on contemporary British theatre, claiming that while he is still an important dramatist, his influence on theatrical style (note this recurring theme) is 'minimal'. It went on: 'Brecht's dramatic greatness will survive the Marxist twilight even if his theatre techniques don't' (*The Guardian*, 24.4.90). Billington concluded that 'Brechtianism may be dead' but that Brecht lives on through his poetry, and 'his unquenchable vitality, his dark irony'. Much of this serves to demonstrate a continued misunderstanding or undervaluing of Brecht's significance and lasting influence as an advocator of a method, a careful theatrical process contrived to explore and debate as a means of demonstrating socio-political ideas – not merely as the creator of an externalised, visual style. Seemingly little had changed by 1990 in the British view of Brecht.

There had, however, been significant changes in the British theatrical context for the performance of his plays. The 1980s had seen a major funding crisis in the arts in Britain: in 1981 the Arts Council of Great Britain announced that forty-one theatre clients were to lose their subsidy. These ultimately included several important alternative theatre groups, known for their left-wing political commitment: 7:84 (England), CAST, Foco Novo and Joint Stock. Then, in 1984, the Arts Council published its report, *The Glory of the Garden: The Development of the Arts in England – A Strategy For a Decade*, which caused considerable consternation, thanks to its implicit funding cuts, disguised as 'regional rationalisation'. In the end no dramatic losses of building-based companies actually ensued from this. The national companies (National Theatre, RSC) were in fact rewarded with additional funding, not least because of their important contribution to the 'heritage' and tourist industries. However, the Arts Council, responding to pressure from a powerful Tory government, insisted that theatre companies should more actively seek business sponsorship for their work. This business ethic, of course, was already a viable idea for the large companies who produced 'middlebrow' art that would be attractive to sponsors, but was virtually impossible for smaller theatre organisations, and anathema to alternative, political groups. As Baz Kershaw puts it in his account of these issues in his book *The Politics of Performance*:

> Now the nationals not only were setting 'artistic standards', they were also the model for a new consumer-oriented attitude to cultural production in the subsidised theatre.
>
> (Kershaw, 1992, p.174)

Nonetheless, during the first half of the 1980s, alternative theatre did continue to expand at a considerable rate, assisted by the increasing number of small, 'studio' venues available for performance, and, ironically, often supported by special government 'Enterprise' allowances for 'new businesses'. Thus groups of theatre practitioners gained some, albeit usually short-term, benefit from state funds made available (cynically, many would say) to reduce generally the numbers of unemployed. However, the contemporaneous cuts in funding for other theatre groups, particularly those with a political basis, seem likely to have been cautionary. In any case, during the 1980s, the oppositional stance of alternative theatre was largely channelled into targeting specific issues and audiences, resulting in the growth of the number of feminist, gay and ethnic companies. Radicalism in British theatre mostly retreated from open political confrontation into being expressed primarily through the collective and collaborative devising

120

of shows. Increasingly the focus of alternative theatre in the 1980s was on aesthetic experimentation, drawing on postmodern theories that foregrounded the insecurities of verbal communication, arguing that art should offer a multiplicity of meanings and that the authoritative 'reading' lay with the individual consumer. The emphasis was shifted to the deconstruction of the written text, the substitution of physical expression for the word, and the high profile of music and visual effects in a performance that was increasingly multi-media. The influence of such innovators as Pina Bausch and Robert Wilson and (latterly) Robert Lepage was everywhere.

It can be argued (and has most convincingly by Elizabeth Wright in her book *Postmodern Brecht*) that such postmodern performance is, ironically, closely related to Brechtian notions of dialectical theatre. But it has to be said that most British alternative – or more properly avant-garde – companies of the 1980s, unlike Brecht, did not have a socio-political purpose in their work. They were often more concerned with form than content, sometimes interested to exploit popular forms and styles of communication (such as film, television and pop video), not to offer criticism as such of the capitalist society that has developed a symbiotic relationship with these media. These issues will be discussed more fully in Chapter 6.

There is one other part of the contextual jigsaw of the British theatre scene in the 1980s to put in place before moving on to examine the three key examples of British Brecht that provide the focus of this chapter. The theatrical pattern of that decade would not be complete without reference to the changes in community art that happened then. As discussed in Chapter 3, community theatre companies had been effectively serving local and regional arts' needs since the 1960s. The work of such companies was complemented in some ways by small groups known as Community Arts teams, whose prime function was to teach and share their arts skills within a specific (normally urban) community. Teams comprising four or five artists, each with different specialist skills (in the visual arts, music, drama, and so on), would run workshops aimed at helping members of a community to discover their artistic potential. This often resulted in, for example, painting murals in the locality, or making unusual kinds of music or developing drama and theatre skills for local performance. The teams were funded by local councils, regional arts associations and sometimes education authorities. Their mixed funding reflected their varied and multiple function but also made them vulnerable to cuts, on the grounds that often one funder would withdraw support on the erroneous assumption that one of the other agencies might pick up a larger slice of the bill. Like Theatre-in-Education work, that of the Community Arts Teams, because of its amateur clientele and participatory approach, bears a close resemblance to Brecht's ideas for his *Lehrstücke*. However, along with many forms of alternative arts, this kind of community-based work also suffered funding cuts during the 1980s.

121

Yet that same period also saw the establishment of a new concept of community theatre, the Community Play. This is a term used to describe a play, created within and performed mostly by and for a specific community (village or town), normally with the aid of professional theatre practitioners commissioned to lead the activity. Such plays usually dramatise a local event, issue or historical episode as a way of celebrating the community itself. The 'inventor' of this kind of Community Play was playwright/director Ann Jellicoe, who had been a member of the Royal Court Theatre Writers' Group in the 1950s and who achieved wide fame with her play, later a film, *The Knack*. In 1978 she invited the community theatre company Medium Fair to work with her on a play she had written for a school in Lyme Regis (south-west England), where she then lived. This play was based on a seventeenth-century actual event in the town, had a cast of one hundred amateur performers and was presented in promenade form – and it provided the model for many subsequent community plays by both Jellicoe and other writer/directors.

In 1980 Jellicoe set up the Colway Theatre Trust to manage these projects, and a number of contemporary socialist playwrights were invited to develop scripts. Despite, however, the open courting of politically committed writers, Jellicoe's emphasis in the Community Play has always been on the celebratory, even the aesthetic aspects of the work. When, for example, she solicited a text from Howard Barker in 1981, she was anxious lest his left-wing views might disturb the conservative Dorset context in which it would be performed. But the ensuing play, *The Poor Man's Friend*, steered a skilful course between honouring local concerns and being, as Baz Kershaw puts it, 'worthy of Brecht at his best' (Kershaw, 1992, p.198). The politics of mounting community plays have been hotly debated in some quarters. Some critics have argued that to bring professional practitioners (writers, directors, designers) into a community in order to create a piece of theatre is patronising and smacks of an élitist attitude, insofar as the incomer becomes the arbiter of taste, the repository of a universal (not local) culture. Others suggest that the kinds of artistic and social negotiation involved in these events should be seen as a form of 'barter', similar to that advocated by Eugenio Barba and his Teatret Odin (see Chapter 6 for more details). Kershaw mounts a stout defence of the form in general and of Ann Jellicoe in particular:

> Ann Jellicoe perhaps has done more than her critics allow to solve some of the creative and ideological problems posed for radical practitioners by conservative communities, and perhaps even by eras as reactionary as the 1980s. Within a broadly liberal practice she has pioneered a model of performance which is both popular, and, in its use of contextuality to sometimes insinuate oppositional readings, potentially socio-political or critical.
>
> (Kershaw, 1992, p.205)

Against this mixed backdrop of political exhilaration at the ending of the Cold War, and the gloom about artistic difficulties brought on by rampant recession and entrenched conservatism, we now set three major British productions of Brecht in the 1990s. The issues of the vexed relationships between method and performance style, between working process and end-result, between politics and aesthetics, and between fidelity to text and contemporary adaptation that have been considered in earlier chapters are here explored in greater depth by means of detailed reference to rehearsals, interviews with directors and actors, and critical responses to the performances, in three case studies.

THE GOOD PERSON OF SICHUAN AT THE NATIONAL THEATRE, 1989

This production, which opened at the National Theatre on 28 November 1989, was directed by a then new Associate Director of the company, Deborah Warner. She was one of a new breed of young British theatre directors who came to the fore in the 1980s. She had already gained recognition for her bold productions of classical plays, especially Shakespeare, but would later gain especial prominence by becoming one of the few female directors to work within the male bastions of both national companies in Britain (National and RSC).

Warner originally trained as a stage-manager. Then, after working for one company in that capacity, and another (Steven Berkoff's London Theatre Company) as administrator, she formed her own company, Kick Theatre, in 1980. The specific aim of the company was 'to make sense of Shakespeare through an experimental, exploratory process with a small nucleus of actors'.[1] In her work with Kick Theatre, Warner effectively trained herself as a director: 'I evolved my working methods by simply watching actors act.' In particular, she developed a process of play rehearsal in which, she claims, the actors play a fully collaborative and creative part, determining with the director the line that the production will take. From a Brechtian point of view this looks very promising, and, indeed, one of her first productions with her own company was *The Good Person of Setzuan* (1980). Furthermore, Kick Theatre's productions of Shakespeare were remarkable for their narrative clarity and audience accessibility, for their trademark use of bare staging, for their exploitation of simple theatrical effects and music, and for their reliance on the overt skills of a small ensemble of actors, striving, as Warner puts it, 'to find out what theatre is'. Inevitably, perhaps, Warner's work drew comparisons with that of the young Peter Brook. For example, in praising Warner's very successful production of the challenging play *Titus Andronicus* for the RSC (1987), the critic Robert Hewison referred to 'her love of Brookian space' (*The Sunday Times*, 29.7.90).

123

The production of *Titus Andronicus* was immediately followed by a widely acclaimed *Electra* with Fiona Shaw in the leading role. Shaw had had a small part in an early Kick Theatre production but had not worked with Warner since then. Rehearsing the Greek tragedy, the two of them experienced a shared enjoyment in an 'open, experimental process'. Shaw had already made her name playing Shakespeare and was known particularly for her considerable emotional range and depth of characterisation. Casting Shaw as Shen Te/Shui Ta in the National's *The Good Person of Sichuan*, Warner planned to build on their excellent working relationship. She explained: 'We don't work together in order to be comfortable, but because we will push each other further than anyone else' (*The Sunday Times*, 1.9.91). The rest of the cast was also strong. Bill Paterson, who had played Schweyk for Richard Eyre (discussed in Chapter 4), was to play Wang the Water-Seller, and Yang Sun, the pilot and lover of Shen Te, was to be played by the experienced actor Pete Postlethwaite (nominated in 1994 for an Oscar for his role in the film *In the Name of the Father*). Postlethwaite's career had started at the Everyman Theatre, Liverpool, and by the time of the production of *The Good Person*, his considerable experience included appearances in nine Shakespeares and Edward Bond's *Lear* (all for the RSC). The role of Widow Shin was to be played by an equally experienced performer, Susan Engel, whose career had included appearances in two other major British productions of Brecht: Gaskill's *The Caucasian Chalk Circle* (1962, see Chapter 2) and *Herr Puntila and His Servant Matti* (directed by Michel St Denis, 1965). The omens for this National production were good.

Warner believed that the time was right for a large-scale, British production of *The Good Person*, which was an 'important play' for the late 1980s/early 1990s. She was anxious to acquire an 'accessible' version of the text. Early discussion about a new translation was held with the playwright (and German speaker) Edward Bond, but, Warner explained, 'We both knew at the same moment we couldn't do it together and I didn't want him in rehearsals.' It was agreed that Michael Hofmann, a Cambridge-educated German whose translation work included books by Joseph Roth and Wim Wenders, would provide a script based on Brecht's second version of the play, written when he was in exile in the United States and known as the 'Santa Monica' text. Warner thought this 'Americanised' version of 1943 was 'harder, punchier' than the previous one. It was, however, left unfinished by Brecht, so Warner and Hofmann inserted scenes from the other version (such as the Wedding Scene), but excluded the Epilogue (of the original text) because Warner deemed it 'unnecessary'. One of Brecht's significant changes in the Santa Monica text was the substitution of an opium business owned by the wicked cousin Shui Ta for the tobacco business of the original version. This has the effect (as was argued in the National Theatre programme for the production) that Shen Te's willingness to allow her cousin to become involved in a more heinous trade than tobacco for the sake of her child raises a question mark about her moral sensibility, and thus strengthens the ethical dialectic of the play. It is thought that Brecht's late introduction of the drug issue was made, in fact, in reference to his actor-friend Peter Lorre, who was having serious problems with morphine addiction at that time. Warner's view was that the drug motif gave the play 'more contemporary relevance'.

Contemporaneity of reference was also important to the director in the setting for the production. The designer was Sue Blane, who had begun her career as a trainee designer at the Citizens Theatre, Glasgow, working on the 1971 production of *The Life of Galileo*, directed by Keith Hack (see Chapter 3). In order to 'research ideas', Warner and Blane paid a visit to Hong Kong. The consequent set design for *The Good Person*, which, following *Galileo* (1980) and *Schweyk* (1982), was to be presented on the vast stage of the Olivier Theatre, was conceived as an open, bleak and urban wasteland of grey concrete, made up of square concrete beams and broken blocks and backed by a huge black wall. Even the trees (for the park scene) were concrete 'pillars' with reinforcing wires protruding from the top. The whole effect was that of a dreary city building site. As one of the actors, Bill Paterson, wryly remarked, highlighting a general concern about production costs and the waste of resources at the National Theatre: 'You don't need to go to Hong Kong to see that. The whole of the South Bank looks like a building site!'[2] (The National Theatre, a concrete complex itself, is situated on London's South Bank.) Additions to the main set, in the form of flown-in scenic flats, provided the shop and other interiors, and a sunken, half-revolve provided a prison-like opium den. The 'Chinese' ambience was created by the random placing of a number of black-painted bicycles around the set, while the audience was given fleeting glimpses of figures in coolie hats and pyjama-style trousers cycling across the stage. The lighting was almost entirely in (Brechtian) open white.

Warner's already established reputation as a democratic director was very evident in the early stages of rehearsal, as the cast confirmed. Paterson said: 'Deborah is very group orientated. She lets the group come up with the ideas. She's very accepting.' The director spent the first two weeks of rehearsal leading the cast in theatre games, an experience which might initially have been helpful. Susan Engel points out, however:

> Deborah tried to make us into a company through game playing and cycling around but, ironically, it didn't have an effect when we started to perform. Somehow it didn't carry over. It took quite a time in performance for us to work together. You can't force that.[3]

Again we encounter the problem at the National of the lack of mutual trust and hence creative working habits of a ready-made ensemble. But additional issues relating to the working process in this production also affected the interaction of the company members. First, Warner had already decided on her own, and therefore the production's, approach to the play as a Brecht text. She told the actors they could learn about Brechtian theory if they wished but that they 'weren't applying a Brechtian working method – even if we knew what that was. We were treating it as a "classic of sorts".' It seems to be a corollary that she also declared that no discussion of the internal politics of the play was necessary. So much for a collaborative approach in which actors contributed to the working process.

Second, despite rehearsing with the whole company as a unit at the beginning, Warner often kept subsequent work 'private', with actors who were not actually appearing in the particular scene being explored finding themselves excluded from the rehearsal room. This practice smacks more of a defensive anxiety about process than a trusting open exploration. Indeed, Warner spent a considerable period rehearsing the leading actor, Fiona Shaw, on her own, until, that is, other cast members complained. The director explained the complaints: 'You pay the price for 'over-casting' – very good actors in small and unsatisfying parts.' This is an echo, of course, of the problems (discussed in Chapter 5) in casting *Galileo* and *Days of the Commune*. As before, it says a great deal about not only the ensemble issue but about prevalent attitudes to performing Brecht.

The third issue, as Warner later admitted, was that she and the company spent a large part of the rehearsal period 'going in the wrong direction', in effect looking for psychological motivation of character and for opportunities to express real and deep emotion. As Paterson bluntly puts it: 'We spent several weeks trying to turn Brecht into Ibsen. That's the major problem with the production.' By the time this was seen to be an inappropriate approach, a number of the cast felt they were floundering and simply began to seek their own solutions.

While the expression of emotion by the character, as in all Brecht, is an essential element of *The Good Person*, the wrongheadedness of Warner's approach is evident in her further admission that she and Fiona Shaw spent considerable time trying to 'justify' from the character's point of view transformations from Shen Te to Shui Ta. They were thus attempting to deploy a Stanislavskian technique for a theatrical demonstration of a 'split-personality' or the physical presentation of a moral dialectic. In any case, the mechanism of the mask promotes a different approach. But both the director and the leading actor declare a passionate interest in the kind of theatre that displays 'large emotions', a capacity they exploited fully in *Electra*. As Warner says: 'The size of emotion, that's what theatre's about for me. There is a huge hole in English theatre – the full expression of feelings.'

Shaw supplements this by saying that what she most admires about Warner's way of directing is that 'she helps you to get directly to the emotional root of the character'. Consequently, both of them were disappointed with Brecht. Warner found 'the heart of *Good Person* is cold', and Shaw thought Brecht 'harder than Shakespeare because he doesn't help the actor. He is "bald".'[4] In common with a number of other British performers, Shaw did not enjoy Brecht's re-location of the actor's focus from role to narrative, and preferred a (naturalistic) continuous engagement with character rather than a collective contribution to story-telling. There were, of course, key moments in her performance of Shen Te/Shui Ta when the actor's ability to tap into her emotions and express them clearly, and her natural warmth as a performer proved very effective. For example, the reality of her relationship with Yang Sun – in particular in the first park scene – provided a good springboard for the rest of the story. But too often the performance seemed that of an actor trying too hard, and, as Brecht says, 'If you want to master something difficult, take it easy' (*B on T*, p.243).

In contrast to Shaw, Paterson felt that he had no problem with the fact that Brecht 'doesn't allow the actor the "emotional release" of naturalistic theatre'. He recounts an anecdote in which he reinforces this point:

> I met Ian McKellen the other day in the theatre canteen, and I was telling him about a close friend of mine dying. He said: 'Can you use it in the play?' 'Not really,' I said, 'It's Brecht, you know'.

As reported in the analysis of the actor's Schweyk (see p.114) Paterson enjoys the contact with an audience, and so that aspect of the role of Wang, in which the character operates as a kind of narrator, came naturally to him. And, as with Schweyk, Paterson's approach to the part was direct and simple. He explained: 'Wang's an outsider. He engineers the plot. I just play every scene at full-tilt for its contradictions and let the audience worry about them.' He also knew instinctively how to play the comedy boldly without separating it from the socio-economic reality of the character. This was evident in his suggestion that for Wang's water-selling business he should have a customised bicycle and carry two buckets on a shoulder-yoke made from a car-exhaust system. This was an effective, visual way of presenting the city setting and Wang's business practice and combining that with opportunities for comic stage-business. But Paterson intended more:

> I had this idea about the bicycle. If it's your living and it's a semi-urban place, at least technology ought to be tuned up a bit. So that grew into this half-jokey machine – that produces Holy Water for the gods – I think Brecht would like that! – which is also about this poor water-seller trying to earn both an honest and dishonest living.

In performance, Paterson's Wang was both honest and cunning, poor yet wily, comic yet poignant. Overall, as *The Times* reviewer put it, he gave 'a marvellous comic study in moral compromise' (30.11.89).

The differences in approach to performing Brecht between Shaw and Paterson are clear enough. Susan Engel, playing Widow Shin, thought (like others before her) that part of the problem of performing the play lay in the formidable challenge of the huge Olivier Theatre:

> You can't play small and realistically on the Olivier stage, so you have to find another style. I think the actors were in a complete quandary as to how the hell to play their lines.

She decided to play her character 'very pantomimic', by which she meant she adopted an 'up front', physical style of performance. She would, she admitted, have preferred to 'play it for real' (i.e. with some approximation to realism), or at least to build some of the 'inner' aspects of the role (which, of course, begs the question of whether Brecht inscribed such aspects). She was critical of the fact that the actors playing the poor people who invade Shen Te's shop caricatured them in pursuit of humour. There was no attempt to find any kind of real, social basis for their behaviour, and this Engel considered to be the product of a patronising attitude. To exacerbate the problem, the production programme contained photographs of real, homeless people living under London's Waterloo Bridge (just a few hundred yards from the National Theatre), and adjacent to these photographs were Shen Te's lines:

> They are poor
> They are homeless
> They are friendless
> They need someone
> Who could turn them away?

The artistic integrity of this would be questionable even if the production had tried to foreground the politics of poverty, but given that such issues were never discussed in rehearsal and that the poor in the play were portrayed, as *The Daily Telegraph* reviewer said, agreeing with Engel, 'as ridiculous grotesques' (30.11.89), locating such tendentious material in the programme risks appearing merely offensive. Irving Wardle wrote in his review of the production:

> The theatre's management might take to heart that scene in the play where Shen Te holds up a child and invites the audience to take care of it instead of shedding aesthetic tears; if they are so concerned about the homeless on their own doorstep, they might do something more useful than taking photographs of them.
>
> (*The Sunday Times*, 1.12.89)

As if these photographs were not enough, the programme also included pictures of dead bodies lying in Bejing's Tiananmen Square, following the crushing of the student protest in June 1989. Again, the reference seemed to have little connection with the production (except that one picture contained a heap of bicycles). Both sets of photographs appeared, therefore, a tasteless gesture towards the politics of a piece that the director never properly entertained. Curiously, she said with unintended irony: 'I wanted ten weeks of rehearsal so I had time to explore but I don't think Brecht needs a long rehearsal period. We could have done it in two weeks.'

Warner also regretted that Brecht had not written a much more interesting play about a woman as a prostitute, declaring, 'He doesn't take on the issues.' *He* doesn't take on the issues? The leading actor shared these views and declared that she would not perform in another Brecht; she preferred the classics, 'which are great expressions of the human heart'. Paradoxically, she received the 1989 Best Actress of the Year Award from both *The Evening Standard* and the Society of West End Theatres for her performance in this production.

The premise on which the production was based was clearly misconceived, as was evident in a series of unclear stage pictures, a general muddling of the narrative, a poor (vocal) delivery of the songs (despite the assistance of radio-microphones), and an inconsistency of performance styles. The actors were not an ensemble to begin with and no amount of game-playing will substitute for a shared exploration of the issues of the play and its purpose and an agreed process of working together to minutely examine, dissect and reassemble the text in order to communicate collectively its essence with the audience. The production was, as Warner admitted, 'a difficult experience with an unhappy company'. There were touches of high quality in the performances of the main actors, but these fragments could never make a whole, meaningful interpretation of the role or the play. As Susan Engel pertinently remarked: 'When Shen Te says, "Help!" at the end, the audience should be shattered, not laugh.'

MOTHER COURAGE AT THE CITIZENS THEATRE, GLASGOW, 1990

This production, which opened at the Citizens Theatre, Glasgow, on 4 May 1990, was directed by one of the theatre's three resident directors, Philip Prowse, and featured Glenda Jackson in the title role. This was, in fact, the long-awaited interpretation of the part that had been suggested by the Brecht estate but postponed because of the RSC production with Judi Dench (discussed in Chapter 4). Glenda Jackson is regarded as one of the most accomplished performers of her generation, having achieved international recognition in theatre, television and film, and all despite being warned, when she left the Royal Academy of Dramatic Art, not to expect to work much before she was forty, because she was essentially a 'character actress'. (This, as Maggie Steed of Belts and Braces Roadshow also knew, was drama-school-speak for 'plain' in looks.) Jackson was, in fact, rejected early in her career by the RSC, when the director, Peter Hall, wrote in his notes: 'Interesting but a bit rich for our blood' (Nathan, 1984, p.19). She did, however, catch the eye of Peter Brook, who cast her in his Brechtian/ Artaudian productions of Peter Weiss's *Marat/Sade* and the devised piece, *US*. These featured in the 1964 Theatre of Cruelty season in London, generated by Brook and Charles Marowitz and could be said to have had considerable influence on British attitudes to and understanding of Brecht at that time. This experience was also crucial to the development of Jackson's notion of the function of an actor. She recalls:

> These two productions crystallised my attitudes and ideas about what is best in a theatrical sense and that, in turn, extends into what I regard as being best in a social context. I'm not interested in theatre that is merely a spectator sport. The most exciting and, to me, the only valid reason for having a theatre is that, upon occasions, you can create a microcosm of an ideal society.
>
> (Nathan, 1984, p.29)

With this seminal experience behind her and drawing on her strong and interesting, if unconventional, looks, Jackson quickly developed a highly successful career. In many of her roles she has displayed a love of and skill in handling complex text, which she attributes to a childhood spent listening to the radio: 'I grew up with radio as a strong influence. . . . It's the most perfect medium, the purest . . . because the imagination is liberated'.[5] But she resists the notion that there is anything mysterious about performing. For her, it is the practical, no-nonsense, concentrated hard work in rehearsal that allows acting to 'look easy' in performance. She is scathing about actors who show the audience how hard they are working in order to win applause. She has earned a reputation in the profession for toughness and a number of colleagues regard her as a 'workaholic'. Michael Billington, the theatre critic, praises her for being 'completely free from that cursed English vice of genteel and ladylike restraint' (Billington, 1972, p.235). (One might compare here similar comments on Janet Suzman, p.89).

Except when absolutely required, such as when playing Queen Elizabeth I, who aged from 16 to 69,[6] Jackson makes little effort to change herself physically for a role. Instead she tends to draw the character towards herself, knowing clearly what of her own characteristics she should deploy to portray the role. She does have an extraordinary charisma, which she prefers to call energy:

> It's energy that makes all the difference between a live and a dead performance. . . . Acting is absolute freedom with absolute control. That paradox produces something else – the performance.
>
> (Nathan, 1984, p.46)

Her emphasis on the actor's need for energy chimes, of course, with Brecht's comments on actors he admired, as discussed in Chapter 1. Jackson declares that one of the greatest actors she has ever seen, appropriately, is Ekkehard Schall, and she recognises the importance in his work of its social context:

> It is clear that part of the quality of his work stems from the reality of his living in a society where what he does is regarded highly – not only on its own level as theatre, but where it is used as a tool to create the kind of society that these people want.
>
> (Marowitz, 1986, p.167)

When beginning to work on a part, Jackson looks for 'a fact about the role which releases the imagination',[7] and, although she states that for her 'acting isn't being', she searches in true Stanislavskian style for the sub-text of the role and talks of her personal need for that 'fourth wall' that separates her from the audience. She stresses her enjoyment of working closely with other actors, of being part of an ensemble rather than playing prominent leads: 'I have never been interested in "great" parts, the one diamond in the garbage' (*The Independent*, 25.4.90). But that is perhaps easy to say when you have already played characters such as Elizabeth I, Hedda Gabler, Sarah Bernhardt and Phedra.

This last role, Phedra, was played by Jackson in 1984, when she was denied Mother Courage. The production was directed by Philip Prowse and, although it seemed to her he found the actor's art somewhat mystifying – 'He didn't understand that actors have to find the bridges between the images. They have to make it all up' – she enjoyed the freedom she was given in rehearsal and agreed enthusiastically when he proposed she should play Mother Courage at the Citizens Theatre. There was an added attraction in that the production was to feature as part of the 1990 Mayfest and it would also coincide with Glasgow's year as European City of Culture.

As discussed in Chapter 3, Philip Prowse had been involved in four previous productions of Brecht at the Citizens, three as designer and one as designer/director. His taste, however, lies predominantly in Elizabethan and Jacobean drama and in foreign (non-modern) classics, such as plays by Goldoni, Schiller and Molière. He has a reputation for flamboyant designs with a marked theatricality, yet, paradoxically, he claims that one of the main influences on his design work is black and white films. This accounts for Prowse's extravagant use of theatrical space and a tendency to avoid colour in his designs: 'I'm not a colourist. I can only use colour in a schematic sort of way. I just use tone.'[8] Yet for all his flamboyance Prowse is very pragmatic and sensitive to the need to keep within the Citizens' budgets. As Michael Coveney writes in his book about the Citizens Theatre, Prowse's philosophy of theatre design

> extends only to the belief that there is not a play in the world that cannot be done on one set; [he] will have nothing to do with trucks, painted cloths, mobile flats and furniture removals between scenes.
>
> (Coveney, 1990, p.30)

131

This belief in the single, eloquent set and the ability to integrate all aspects of a production into a unified vision was to characterise the design for *Mother Courage*. Jackson, too, notes this:

> He always starts from the visual. Then that means that the production as a whole *is* a whole – the way it looks, the way it moves, the area that it goes into emotionally are interwoven.

As a director, Prowse has, in fact, a considerable skill in creating quasi-cinematic stage pictures, and like many film directors, he directs scenes rather than actors. His account of the key concept for his set design for *Mother Courage* illustrates the value placed on the stage picture:

> A cornfield idyll being destroyed . . . European peasant farmers living close to the land, leading boring, reduced lives but not doing harm to anyone. Then being ripped apart for reasons which they would be totally unaware of. So I wanted the production to open on a realistic, sunlit cornfield that was being gleaned by a group of quietly moving peasants. A plane passes overhead, an enormous explosion and the field disappears, leaving a huge area of blackened walls that look like bombed buildings.

In addition the whole stage was a dark grey, scattered with burnt bricks and quite steeply raked. This last feature was to prove a significant problem for Courage's wagon, which had to be chocked when stationary, and substantially stripped down for the final sequence of the play, so that Jackson would be able to pull it on her own. (This stripping-down unfortunately not only marred that last image but worked against the idea in the play that little has changed for Mother Courage.) In keeping with the 'filmic' design, Prowse also wanted the lighting and sound to be atmospheric, including strong cross lighting through stage smoke and an extensive use of background sounds (birds, gunfire, church bells, babies crying). Costumes were designed predominantly in grey, the main splashes of colour being reserved for Courage's dark red jacket and (of course) Yvette's red boots. The soldiers' uniforms, also grey, were intended to suggest those of Nazis, complete with large peaked caps and jack-boots.

Prowse regards any play-text as ripe for adaptation and radical alteration, and so in the new version of *Mother Courage* (*and Her Children* was dropped from the title) provided for this production by his colleague, Robert David MacDonald, substantial cuts were made. These included the excision of all references to the opposing armies in the Thirty Years' War (allowing the same soldiers to be used throughout), because, Prowse said: 'We don't learn about it in British schools.' He did, however, keep the religious content of the story and to some extent heightened that by substituting well-known hymn tunes for Dessau's score for the songs. These featured, for example, 'Onward Christian Soldiers' for Mother

Courage's first entrance and 'Good King Wenceslas' for the Song of Solomon, and included also the scores for 'God Our Help in Ages Past', and 'Abide With Me'.

Perhaps more extraordinary was Prowse's removal, in accordance apparently with his usual practice, of all Brecht's stage directions from the written text, because, he argued:

> One can't impose stage directions on actors in new circumstances. We don't know whether Brecht imagined them and wrote them down for actors to follow or whether he simply incorporated moves from the first production. The job of a director is to re-imagine.

This text without directions, however, did result in some confusions in rehearsal, and was, of course, particularly difficult for the actor (Jane Bertish) playing the dumb Kattrin. Since she has no lines, the interpretation of her role relies very much on the information contained in the stage directions, which are generally more than mere instructions for actors on stage movement. Bertish overcame this problem by using another version of the text in rehearsal and by remembering her earlier performance of the same role (Birmingham, 1978).

The cast for *Mother Courage*, apart from Glenda Jackson and one other actor, comprised regular actors at the Cits, including the usual group of local, non-speaking extras. These were used in the production to create a series of precisely choreographed 'processions of the dispossessed' – soldiers, peasants and refugees – that passed almost unceasingly across the stage throughout the performance. Despite the potential for 'star' publicity, the Cits excluded the name of their leading actor from pre-publicity material and, in keeping with their ensemble policy, simply announced the production in their season's leaflet. At the same time there was no special financial deal for Jackson; everyone in the cast was on the same salary. The production, however, did attract substantial sponsorship, probably owing to its star, from the Goethe Institut in Glasgow, and negotiations with a commercial management for a transfer to London were underway before rehearsals had begun.

Prowse declared that he would not be trapped in this production by inherited notions of what is thought to be 'Brechtian'. He even resisted what he saw as the cliché of marking the episodic structure of the play, which he thought was unhelpful to his own idea of theatrical reality: 'One must find out what is truthful. Going to half lights and having a lot of people scurrying about with pots and pans hasn't anything to do with reality.' In similar vein, he wanted the songs to be delivered by the actors as though they occurred realistically, as if the characters were saying, 'I know a song about that.' This echoes the ideas of Howard Davies and Hanif Kureishi for their RSC production (see p.101).

In contrast to the 1984 version, however, Prowse resisted any attempt by his actors to employ a psychological approach to their roles. In rehearsals his work with the company was almost entirely technical, showing concern with blocking and visual staging rather than with character motivation. He explains this bluntly:

> I'm not very interested if they want to open up their stomachs and show me the [emotional] contents. They must go and find a psychiatrist. Where actors interest me is how they respond to the job in hand. When they make a truthful response – what appears truthful to me – I will do my absolute best to incorporate it within the larger truth of what I'm trying to do.

So the performers were constantly encouraged by Prowse to be simple, not to imagine beyond the text but to play the exact situation, to play the moment. He adds: 'We all know how the characters are feeling because of what they do.' All of these aspects of his direction seem sound advice for a production of Brecht.

On the other hand, the director resisted the idea that a contemporary production of *Mother Courage* could be part of an ongoing political debate. He argued:

> I'm not a German. I'm not in a situation to set up a political discussion, unlike Brecht. . . . I don't think it's as simple as whether you're a communist or not. It's to do with keeping trucking as an artist.

Prowse's non-political line was echoed strongly by his leading actor. This was particularly intriguing as, immediately prior to the rehearsal period for *Mother Courage*, Glenda Jackson had made public her intention to stand as a Labour Party candidate for the British parliament with a commitment to a socialist programme. She thought *Mother Courage* was a great play, but 'not a great political theory. It would be inappropriate to look for contemporary relevance.' Her political perception of the play was limited to its implications for the processes of rehearsal and performance: 'My political interest in it lies in the fact that it is a team play.' And, she added, in express opposition to Brecht's own views: 'It works marvellously because what stays constant is human nature. That doesn't change.'

Jackson's starting point for her portrayal of Mother Courage was the American singer Ethel Merman. This arose from having been told some years before by Lotte Lenya that Helene Weigel, after meeting Merman, had said that Merman *was* Mother Courage; and Jackson knew exactly what that meant: 'Her up-front attitude, bravado, energy. She brooks no argument.' She was also quite clear about the acting style demanded by Brecht: 'The idea of a through-line from the character's point of view is irrelevant. Every character has to be living the moment at the moment.' And if there were times in rehearsal when she was unsure about simply playing the moment, she argued herself back on course:

> When I started on our Act 2, I thought to myself how am I going to show Swiss Cheese's death? And then I thought, that's precisely what you haven't got to do because the meaning of his death doesn't come up until Kattrin's been bashed. . . . You don't have to bring anything from before. That's the antithesis of what Brecht's writing.

Jackson avoided consulting Brecht's dramatic theory, regarding it as 'an excessive kind of baggage' that would only help turn the performance into a 'museum piece'. She was of the opinion that Brecht provided the actor with a huge sub-text but it had to be used truthfully. Her reading of *Mother Courage* told her that what she needed was 'the simplicity, immediacy, and totality of a child', and in this she concurred with the playwright himself. She also appreciated the comic element in the play – 'It's a terribly funny piece of writing. . . . One minute it can be dark as tragedy and the next it's very funny' – and she was instrumental in exploring individual comic effects in rehearsal and in performance. She thought that Mother Courage's humour was based on the fact that she, Courage, believed herself to be in charge of her own destiny: 'She doesn't ever see herself as a victim.' This idea of Courage's perception of herself as strong also meant that, although Jackson highlighted the maternal side of the character (by, for example, helping Swiss Cheese into his coat and haversack and offering a cheek for his farewell kiss), her Courage was quite 'rough' physically (and comically) with her brood. She punched Swiss Cheese, for example, when she discovered that Eilif had enlisted in the army behind her back but with his brother's knowledge.

Jackson relished the freedom and creative opportunity that Prowse gave her in rehearsal, and he, in turn, acknowledged his reliance on her imaginative contribution to the production:

> She knew exactly how she could do it. Her responses were always entirely truthful. I then had to use them truthfully. I listened to her instinct and was well rewarded.

On the other hand, there were key moments of the play when their instincts clearly pulled in different directions. The most significant of these was in Scene 3, when Courage is confronted by the dead body of her son, Swiss Cheese, and has to deny knowledge of him. Initially there was a practical problem in rehearsal over revealing the son's face. Prowse wanted Jackson herself to pull off the sack covering him and she wondered herself, and with good reason, 'if asking her to do that is asking too much'. However, she agreed. Discussion of Courage's reaction to seeing her son's face was also conducted in terms of physical action and Jackson experimented with various gestures and pieces of stage-business. Many of them were decidedly histrionic and out of keeping with the rest of her performance. The most extreme, which survived into the performance, involved the lifting of her skirts and beating her breast with large, wing-like movements, then collapsing forward at the waist, before coming up into a standing position with head thrown back and mouth open. This was, in effect, the Jackson version of the famous Weigel 'silent scream' (see p.33). Prowse had other ideas about the moment:

> I know she should just stand still, as though she's a dead woman, but perhaps it's difficult for an actress to do that. I was very tactful and kept saying, 'I want to see your face'. [Her action] was a failure of taste, of aesthetics.

It may have been a failure of taste, but it was also a failure by the director and the actor to consider the socio-political significance of the moment, to find the *Gestus*.

The problem had possibly come about through the importation of a 'star' into an established, ensemble company. Prowse was clear enough about the differences between Jackson and the rest of the company. He said she 'is not a team-player. She's a star, which is an entirely different thing from being an actress.' And that difference, in status, experience and attitude, made itself felt in rehearsals. Interaction between the leading actor and the others was occasionally uncomfortable and was not helped by the amount of influence the star was able to exert over crucial decisions. For example, at Jackson's suggestion, it was decided that dumb Kattrin should not make inarticulate noises in her desperation to communicate, despite Brecht's own stage-directions and the references to her noises in the dialogue. Jackson gnomically argued: 'Kattrin should be an invisible character, because that is what her mother has worked to make her all her life', and all references to Kattrin's noises were subsequently removed from the play. But this decision meant that Jane Bertish had to work hard, often against the odds and without some of the assistance Brecht had provided, to avoid senti-mentalising the character.

Prowse acknowledged that integrating a performer of Jackson's status and charisma had not been easy. He maintained it was because the other actors were overawed: 'Anybody who is *that* good at their job does tend to be rather frightening.' But perhaps it was not only the actors who were intimidated.

That was, however, only part of the problem. After all, it was clearly recognised at the Berliner Ensemble that Helene Weigel, who performed Mother Courage over 200 times, was herself a star performer. But the crucial point is that a team or ensemble can be created successfully only on the basis of a shared view of its purpose – why the group is performing that particular play in that given situation. It also needs, as was seen in the previous case study of *The Good Person of Sichuan*, a consensus of opinion on the company's approach to the text. While Prowse was undoubtedly right to discourage his cast from developing a rigidly psychological line in their characterisation, there was often insufficient and sometimes con-flicting guidance given on what kind of approach to performance might be appropriate. When one actor asked in rehearsal if his character was 'real', he was told: 'Yes, he has a function.' When another enquired if he should 'hold back emotionally', he was told to play it 'normally'. The actor playing Swiss Cheese was told, variously, to play him as 'stupid' and 'like a pumped-up cartoon'. And when the actor playing the Chaplain wanted to know 'what "alienation" meant', he was told firmly that it was irrelevant and that 'it was just Brecht's strategy for controlling the Romanticism of his day'. One member of the cast, who has appeared in over seventy productions at the Cits, including playing Brecht's Puntila, put the directorial problem simply: 'The trouble is Philip can only work in pictures. He doesn't communicate well with actors.'[9]

Disjunctions in acting approach and style showed up in other ways, too. Jackson herself acknowledges that she is reluctant to make direct contact with an audience, whereas the experience and preference of many actors at the Cits in this regard are the opposite, and certainly several of the cast clearly longed in the production to play more 'out front' than was encouraged. This was particularly evident during the work on the songs. The actor playing Yvette, Roberta Taylor, for example, found the director's request for her to perform 'realistically' The Fraternization Song, which is written essentially as a cabaret-style number, very difficult to fulfil. Perhaps unfairly, the director indicated that he thought she was 'hiding behind doing it as a number', but his attempts to repress her instinct for a broader mode of performance never quite succeeded. In this way there was a general unevenness, an inconsistency of style in the overall performance of the play.

It is arguable that several of these problems were in effect the result of Prowse's placing insufficient emphasis on the social and political reality of the play. While outwardly the cast looked convincingly like poor peasants and weary soldiers, there were many moments of contradiction in the performance that betrayed the actors' limited grasp of the characters' true social situation. Take, for example, the second scene of the play, in which the Cook bargains with Courage over the price of a capon and shows her the piece of rather elderly meat that he intends to cook if her price is too high. He finally buys the capon, but then, in this production, the actor threw away the old piece of meat. This is hardly the action of an army cook, who is likely to be severely punished by his commanding officer for waste and whose instinct anyway will be to eke out his resources shrewdly. This is a small but characteristic example of a failure of grasp of socio-economic detail.

In effect, the lack of political focus in the production overall resulted in an interpretation of *Mother Courage* as a play about the suffering caused by war rather than one about the immorality of trading off war. This was reflected, in the performance, by the frequently over-casual exchange of money for goods between Courage and the soldiers, the half-hearted bargaining over the capon in Scene 2, and insufficiently serious attempts by Swiss Cheese to hide the stolen cash-box under his coat when he runs off in Scene 3. Indicatively, the play had been three weeks in rehearsal before Jackson was given Courage's purse, surely the most telling (and necessary) of props.

As significantly, there were times when the focus in a scene was misplaced because of the director's tendency to create stage images for visual effect aimed at eliciting an easy emotional response, rather than in order to make the social dialectics of the particular episode clear. A key example occurred in Scene 5, when Mother Courage is asked to donate some of her stock of officers' shirts as bandages for the injured, while Kattrin rescues a baby from a ruined house. Brecht's purpose in this 'split' scene is to demonstrate again (as in Scene 1) that Courage is torn between guarding her precious commodities, which are her livelihood, and protecting one of her children from the dangers of war. In this production the focus was almost entirely on the personal narrative of Kattrin's rescue of the baby, aided by the gathering of the onlookers at the ruins and the underplaying of Courage's protest about the tearing of her shirts. Thus the key moment of decision for Courage was lost in the crowd's sympathetic response to Kattrin's successful rescue. A socio-political demonstration of a dilemma brought about by war became, therefore, a sentimental triumph of caring and courageousness. When criticised for this by the present author, the director agreed there was a problem here but laid some of the blame at Brecht's door for providing 'a rather muddled scene'. He added: 'I was glad enough to come out of it with a clear point made. I didn't really mind which one.'

A sentimentalised reading of Kattrin was evident elsewhere in the production, for example, in the character's key scene, Scene 11, in which she climbs onto the roof of the peasants' house to warn the people of the nearby town by her drumming that the soldiers are coming to attack them, and then is herself shot. Brecht actually acknowledged that this scene was moving for the audience but that does not mean sentimental. In this production, the scene was unfocused at the outset because of the casual way in which the soldiers arrived at the peasants' house, thus failing to convey a sense of threat and obscuring their intention to take the peasants by surprise. More importantly, when Kattrin attempts to alert the town, her concentration should be almost entirely on that and not, as it was here, on the soldiers' efforts to force her down and to disguise the sound of her drumming. Brecht indicates very specifically (in the stage directions that had been removed here) those brief moments when Kattrin is to react to the soldiers. To be fair to the actor, she had received little directorial help in this scene.

In the production's final sentimentalising of Kattrin, at the end of Scene 12, her dead body, left centre stage as her mother departed in pursuit of the army, was subjected to a gentle fall of snow. This was followed by soldiers, some carrying wreaths as though for a memorial service, marching (or goose-stepping) across the stage to the tune of 'Abide With Me'. Then finally Courage took up the harness of her (depleted) wagon and began her slow exit. Again, the effect was a triumph of sensibility over sense, to the disadvantage of the production.

It was, then, an overall lack of attention to Brecht's socio-political purpose, an absence of trust in the text, perhaps, and the substitution of an overriding concern for visual and emotive effects that resulted in a production that lacked real moral bite. There were strong portrayals of both the central and supporting roles – Jackson's performance was described by Michael Billington of *The Guardian* (7.5.90) as 'predictably fine' in its presentation of 'the trucculent individualism of an insubordinate spirit' – but the whole epic kaleidoscope was insufficiently rooted in social reality. The production became an essay in visual style, and for the audience an essentially aesthetic, apolitical experience. A number of reviewers focused on Prowse's deployment of the continuously passing peasants, refugees and wounded soldiers as indicative of this overladen interpretation. John Peter wrote in *The Sunday Times* (15.5.90): 'all this bustle simply detracts from the eloquent simplicity of Brecht's stage picture', and Benedict Nightingale of *The Times* (7.5.90) agreed, remarking that it was a case of 'the backstage upstaging the downstage'.

No one would claim that there is only one way to present Brecht's plays and, as Michael Coveney wrote in his review of the production, one welcomes Prowse's challenge to 'misplaced reverence . . . in order to tackle him anew' (*The Observer*, 15.5.90). But in effect this was another case (like those at the National Theatre and the RSC) of the play being overwhelmed by the scenic vision. Furthermore, the ensemble approach of the Citizens Theatre which is their house style was subverted in this production into furnishing a star vehicle for Jackson, so that ironically the experience of the 'little' people in the Thirty Years War was echoed in Glasgow by the disempowerment of the 'little' actors in the production.

A postscript: in the summer of 1990, the Citizens' production of *Mother Courage* transferred to the Mermaid Theatre, London, having been bought out by a commercial management. As the soldiers, in Nazi-style uniforms, marched across the stage in the final scene singing:

> With all its luck, its dangers and its fears
> Seems like this war is dragging on and on
> It could well last another hundred years
> Where will the people be when it is won?

the armed forces of Europe and America were preparing for the Gulf War, to fight over the spoils of oil and prove both history, and the need for Brecht, alive. Within a year, Glenda Jackson had been elected to the British parliament. It is to be hoped that, first in opposition, her experience of playing an 'insubordinate spirit' will be useful there.

THE RESISTIBLE RISE OF ARTURO UI
AT THE NATIONAL THEATRE, 1991

The third case study takes us back to the Royal National Theatre, where this production of *The Resistible Rise of Arturo Ui* opened in the Olivier Theatre on 2 August 1991. The director was Di Trevis, whose background and theatrical outlook would suggest her as one of the most appropriate contemporary directors of Brecht in Britain today. After reading for a degree in social anthropology, Trevis went straight into the acting company at the Citizens Theatre, Glasgow, in 1971. There she appeared in three Brecht productions, including *St Joan of the Stockyards*, in which she played the lead (see Chapter 3). She claims that, being a Trotskyist at the time, she fervently shared the viewpoint of Joan, and that her enjoyment of performing Brecht stemmed from 'seeing the mechanics of theatre put on the stage, and everyone knowing that it's all a performance. I'm simply not interested in naturalism.'[10] When playing Joan, however, she was concerned about 'alienation' and remembers the director, Robert David MacDonald, giving her helpful advice:

I don't think Brecht meant you to act any differently. It's just the way the story is told that's different. Within the acting of it he wants you to be as truthful and unshowy as possible.

In 1980 Trevis gave up acting to become a director and in the early 1980s she undertook two productions of Brecht at the Contact Theatre, Manchester. These were *The Mother* (1984) and *The Resistible Rise of Arturo Ui* (1985), both of which plays she subsequently directed for the National. She summarises her views on the playwright in a forthright and sensible fashion:

I find Brecht's views of the world a sound analysis. Nothing has happened that has changed my mind, Berlin Wall or not. But to really understand Brecht you have to go to the poetry. . . . Then you understand that all the time he's tussling with the conflict of living in the East and wondering whether the experiment is working.

Trevis's production of *The Mother* at the National was under the auspices of the theatre's Education Department and was classified as a 'workshop presentation'. However, it had in the leading role Yvonne Bryceland, the very experienced and much admired South African actor, whose name had been previously connected with, amongst others, the plays of Edward Bond. Trevis was aware that Bryceland worked from 'a very real emotional centre' and decided that she would leave her to create the role in her own way, while she, as director, 'set the production up so the bones of the play were exposed'. She has evidently continued to subscribe to MacDonald's view (above) that in Brecht it is the overall production that provides the political perspective and the theatrical distance, rather than the individual actor's style of performance which can remain relatively realistic.

During the rehearsals for *The Mother*, Trevis tried to establish the physical aspects of the staging very carefully. All the actors remained on stage throughout the performance, sitting at the sides when not performing, and they were encouraged to move 'simply but formally' in and out of scenes. The design was simple, utilising the Brechtian half-curtain in conjunction with projected slides to announce each episode. Trevis was

> pleased to find that this worked exactly as Brecht said it would: the audience knew what was going to happen so they could be concerned with how it came about. If you see at the beginning of the scene that the Mother's son is shot crossing the border, you look at it as the last scene in their lives together. That's quite different from wondering if he's going to get shot.

In her first production of the play at Contact Theatre, Trevis had tried to 'update' the political references by using contemporary footage of the miners' strike in Britain (1984), but decided the second time around that the play did not need to be made 'relevant' so overtly. (This was an issue that was to come up again in connection with *Arturo Ui*.)

Many reviewers of *The Mother* at the National praised the production for its clarity, and Michael Billington declared it to be 'one of the strongest things to come out of the South Bank all year' (*The Guardian*, 7.11.86). He also noted that the production was sponsored by the international petroleum company, BP, and thought that Brecht would have enjoyed the irony. Such sponsorship was, of course, a sign of the 1980s, as discussed at the beginning of this chapter.

For the National, the script of *Arturo Ui* was supplied by the British playwright Ranjit Bolt, who, since he is not a German-speaker, worked from a literal translation. Trevis wanted to place proper emphasis on the musical aspects of the play because she perceives 'Brecht's theatre is music-theatre'. So a musical score was specially composed and arranged by Dominic Muldowney, who brought together the world of the Chicago depression and that of the great German cultural heritage by pastiching the work of Hitler's favourite composers, including Wagner, and splicing with this, as a recurring theme, the popular American tune, 'Buddy, can you spare me a dime?'. The German cabaret was also evoked by including in musical settings Brecht's introductions to scenes and by having these performed by a Master of Ceremonies. Trevis's view was that Brecht

> needs actors who can really bear to sing and who know that the words are very important. The plays are impoverished by not using the music, but you can't make them into sub-Lloyd-Webber musicals.

The role of Arturo Ui in the production was taken by Antony Sher, his second Brecht, and one of a small handful of dramatic roles he had long wanted to play. Sher, a Jewish South African, had gone straight from drama school in London into the company at the Everyman Theatre, Liverpool, when Alan Dossor was director. The actor recalls the impact on him of working in that company:

> I was politicised by being at the Everyman, because it was a theatre designed for its community, left-wing theatre. It wasn't just doing plays as entertainment, it felt that theatre had something to say.[11]

Sher's two-year stint at Liverpool included his first Brecht play, *The Good Person of Setzuan* (discussed in Chapter 3), in which he played Wang. During rehearsals for that production Dossor gave Sher what he remembers as a great lesson about acting when he persuaded him: 'that I could have something to say as an actor. I didn't just have to be the vehicle of the play and the director.'

One of the reasons Sher wanted to play Ui was the palpable influence on him (as on Bill Paterson) of seeing Leonard Rossiter's playing of the role (in 1968):

> I was knocked out by it. . . . It was vividly comic though I remember being terrified by the end. His 'living cartoon' appealed to me as an artist as well. . . . I could draw his outline.

The memory and Rossiter's reputation were, to some extent, to haunt Sher when he came to tackle the role himself. In the meantime, he worked at the Royal Court Theatre, played major roles at both national theatres and made several West End appearances, including an award-winning performance in Fierstein's *Torch Song Trilogy* (1985).

Sher's roles for the RSC included Molière's Tartuffe, the Fool to Michael Gambon's King Lear, the lead in David Edgar's *Maydays*, and Shakespeare's Richard III; as the latter he won a number of 'Best Actor' awards. He had by then established himself as an actor with a reputation for fierce intelligence, great dedication and considerable range over both comic and tragic parts. Sher's commitment to detailed research and his personal and emotional involvement in his roles were nowhere more evident than in his Richard III. His idea that in order properly to present Shakespeare's 'bottled spider' he should appear hunched over two crutches, led him into extensive research on different forms of physical handicap and their associated psychological effects. His book, *Year of the King*, which is an account of his creating the role of Richard, gives great insight into his attitudes to acting and into his creative processes. The book includes a selection of his own sketches of people and images that fed into his work on the role and makes clear that Sher works not only from an emotional response to a text but also in both technical and physical ways. Just as significantly, perhaps, in view of the issues raised in this book about the insecurity of actors' employment and the lack of genuine ensembles in Britain, Sher's account of his 'Richard' year makes only too apparent the hustling and negotiation that actors are obliged to undergo, even those in the relative security of the RSC, where information on casting is often gleaned, it seems, from rumour, first night parties and lunches at select restaurants. None of this is conducive to the creation of a collaborative and open way of working amongst the members of a theatre company.

During the protracted negotiations over *Richard III*, Sher proposed that he should also play Arturo Ui in the same season (1984), noting that Brecht's play makes frequent reference to Shakespeare's. Sher could then have played the two monsters together, (hunch)back-to-back, as it were. The idea was rejected, but Sher was understandably delighted to be offered the role at the National some years later. He had worked with Di Trevis before (on *The Revenger's Tragedy*, 1989) and approved her way of directing, which he accounted for as an amalgam of two 'contradictory influences'. He saw that Trevis's experience at the Citizens Theatre had given her a 'great sense of the theatrical', while on the other hand her association with the director Peter Gill had taught her to be 'precise, honest and faithful to the text'.

The rest of the cast for the production of *Arturo Ui* was mostly experienced National actors, a number of whom had appeared in Brecht before, and, as with other 'large company' productions, there was some dissatisfaction about the smallness of parts that many of them had. However, Trevis set about making her group of actors into as near an ensemble as she could. They had, in the National's terms, a short rehearsal period, seven weeks, but for the first two weeks each day started with a company movement session, relating either to the physical violence depicted in the play or to the 'Italian mannerisms' appropriate to the characters. Movement sessions then led into improvisations that usually connected with the subsequent rehearsal of particular scenes. One veteran actor, Michael Bryant, opted out of these sessions, an action probably unhelpful to the creation of company feeling. However, both Trevis and Sher emphasised the important contribution this actor made elsewhere in the production by giving acting advice to younger members. Sher himself learned from Bryant, too:

> He's one of the most experienced Olivier [Theatre] actors. During the technicals he was talking very well about how to play that space, how that theatre demands open positions, and watching him was very educative.

Appropriately, Bryant played the old, 'ham' Actor who instructs Ui in how to move and make speeches. However, he himself was less than enthusiastic about performing Brecht and was dismissive of the playwright's achievements, saying: 'He was just lucky!'[12] Even allowing for the deliberate flippancy of this remark, it represents a defensiveness with regard to Brecht that is relatively typical of many British actors.

Text work on *Arturo Ui* began with rehearsals in which the actors read parts other than those they were to play, not, as with Gaskill and *The Caucasian Chalk Circle* in 1962, in order to contemplate a re-casting of the role, but to develop a company understanding of the whole play. Temporary interchange of roles was followed by a rough 'moved' reading in the actors' own roles. Many actors commented on and admired the way Trevis pushed them to work hard, created a disciplined yet encouraging atmosphere and paid great attention to textual detail even in the early stages of rehearsal. That so many of the cast should find these aspects of her approach unusual or worthy of comment raises questions about both the techniques of other established directors and the attitudes to the creative process of many British actors.

As has been indicated, Trevis was clear about the relationship between Brecht's politics and the performance of his plays. For her the matter was entirely straightforward:

> there's no point in doing Brecht and not expressing the political viewpoint. The whole form is about revealing the forces that are making human beings behave as they do and showing that they are not the subjective creatures guided by the whims of fate. I think Brecht was obsessed with what robs people of their humanity.

This view, however, did not lead Trevis into 'heavy' political dicussions with her cast, though she did explain to them the theatrical fashions to which Brecht's work had been a reaction, what she called 'the emotional wallowing, that terrible sentimentality' of the German theatre of the 1920s. It was unnecessary in Trevis's view for actors to consult Brechtian theory since she thought that the 'modern *theatrical* acting style' (as opposed to 'Method' acting), a style that most British actors now adopted, was exactly what was required. Like Sam Wanamaker, she believed that British actors had a natural understanding of the function of Brechtian irony. Nevertheless, she was ready to guide her actors away from 'sentimental characterisation' and she made it clear that the songs had to be sung by the actor as performer, and not in character. At a general level, she saw it as the director's responsibility to create a production that 'exposes the play's arguments and doesn't fall into some terrible unthought out naturalism'.

The leading actor agreed with his director on this recipe and did not himself adopt a special approach to performing Brecht:

> I wouldn't know how to play a character in an alienated way. I don't know what that means. The same rules apply, as far as I'm concerned to whatever you're acting. You've got to get in there as much as

possible . . . and then either the production or the play itself will create a kind of style.

He did, however, have a political commitment to performing the play, one which had its basis in his South African and Jewish background. He made comparisons between Hitler and Eugene Terreblanche, the leader of the AWB, the Neo-Nazis in South Africa:

When I watch him I can see most clearly how the Hitler phenomenon works. I find him totally charismatic. He's blessed with a fabulous voice, his religious conviction flows and it's utterly captivating.

This experience was to be fed directly into the final scenes of the play.

There were a number of stimuli for Sher's interpretation of Ui, but one of his early ideas remained important for him: that Ui should be awkward physically, and aggressive, like a fist-fighter. He began drawing sketches that related the character to the Scorcese-Capone-Mafia world, explaining that

The boxing imagery came from the film *Raging Bull*. . . . We wanted to start them [Ui and his gang] as street thugs, in the way the National Socialists were street thugs. They fight with their fists.

Out of this developed Sher's first-half, shifty, nervous Ui, who feinted blows at both real and imaginary opponents and even at one point appeared with a towel around his neck, pugilist-style. But this was not just two-dimensional character. Sher wanted to show the way Ui 'travelled' in the course of the play:

I was very interested in his whole journey. I thought the Actor's scene could *change* Ui, quite completely. He doesn't just learn a few Hitler gestures, he transforms.

The director, too, favoured this concept. In rehearsal she also stressed a parallel idea: the importance of telling the story, of foregrounding the narrative so that the audience could witness the gradual gaining of power by both Ui and others. Furthermore, the spectators should see that such power is made to seem respectable. Trevis explained:

I wanted this production to be about the respectable veneer the acquisition of power is given. A gangster becomes a perfectly reason-able person. All the work I did with Antony was about how Ui is perfectly reasonable; he can't help but shoot these people because otherwise they would do great harm.

The clarity of the narrative and the 'framing' of the events for Brechtian distance were aided by the design of the set and costumes. The set comprised a huge, raked and raised central revolving stage, the outer ring of which was separate and could, therefore, turn in the opposite direction

145

to the inner section (quite a technical challenge to the actors in getting on and off). The revolves were used not only to facilitate scene changes, but to re-position scenes in order to give the audience a different perspective. For example, during the court scene the positions of the judge and the accused were reversed (from upstage/downstage to downstage/upstage) for the giving of sentence, so that the audience found itself aligned with the judge and hence implicated in the decision. Upstage of the revolves, there was a dark, false backwall that contained a slide screen, at either side of which were black, skeletal towers that suggested tenement buildings. The stage was open into the wings but the whole set (and play) was provided, when required, with the framing device of a huge, marble-effect proscenium arch with Ui's name enscribed across the top. This was flown in and out, accompanied by a mobile scaffolding rig of lights that included 1930s film-style lanterns. The director explained that with the arch and the lights she wanted to suggest a 'traditional' production of Shakespeare, or the 'idea of a production that isn't'. (The media lights were complemented at a theatric level by a constant posse of reporters that contributed to the sense of Ui manipulating the events publicly for his own propaganda purposes.)

Brecht includes a scene (14) in which Ui has a nightmare and the ghost of the murdered Roma appears to him – a pastiche of Richard III's dream before the Battle of Bosworth. For this scene the production team constructed a crown-topped circular tent and an enormous duvet that covered almost the entire downstage area. Sadly, the scene was cut after the previews (as it was from the original Berliner Ensemble production) because the director felt it spoiled the rhythm of the second half of the play. The dwarfing of Ui by objects, however, was a very successful 'running gag' in the show. In particular, there was a huge, throne-like chair that was put to good comic use by Sher in the scene where he is taught by the Actor to move like Hitler.

Scene changes were made a performance feature by accompanying them with music and by the actors' creating business and starting scenes before a set was entirely positioned, in part, of course, to keep up the pace of the performance. In addition to onstage slides of images of the Nazi period, huge legends appeared around the auditorium, making clear the analogies between the characters in the play and their Nazi counterparts. Some critics thought this over-fussy or unnecessary, but Trevis defended the idea on the grounds that the production was intended for a young audience, who, she feared, would not be familiar with the historical details.

The costumes in the production were effectively used to assist the narrative reading of the play by means of colour coding for the different groups and factions. Ui's first costume was an ill-fitting suit with very tight trousers that led the eye to oversize 'bovver boots', and, as his power grew, his clothes became larger and more opulent, so that by the end he had acquired an oversize black leather coat, as befitted the Führer. There was even a witty reference to the scene in *The Life of Galileo* in which the Pope is dressed by his bishops (Scene 12). Here (in Scene 7), Ui was helped into his clothes by his henchman during one of his public speeches.

Unfortunately, as with the National's production of *The Life of Galileo* (see Chapter 4), there were problems with the building of the set. At a very late stage it was discovered that the central revolve had been made to the wrong dimensions, presumably because of poor communications between production staff. This resulted in a whole day's delay in beginning the technical rehearsals in the theatre, which were, in any case, very complicated. The first public preview began half an hour after the rushed completion of the technical rehearsals, that is, without a dress-rehearsal.

But, despite such problems, Trevis's achievements with the production were considerable. She created careful stage pictures and moments of stillness to highlight significant points in the play when power was being gained or exploited by characters or factions, and many of these stage pictures were clear demonstrations of Brechtian *Gestus*. For example, Old Dogsborough was given a badge by members of the Cauliflower Trust and it was 'stabbed' onto the lapel of his coat to pre-figure his subsequent murder (Scene 2). On another occasion, Ui took a mirror and false moustache from the Actor's case, in order to transform himself into Hitler and was momentarily tempted by the stage crown in there (Scene 6). And at the height of his power, and with topical reference, Ui ruffled the hair of a small boy standing near him, exactly as Saddam Hussein had done to a small English child in full view of Western television cameras during the hostage crisis in the Gulf War.

The production took to heart Brecht's statement that the play is a 'pantomime' and exploited the opportunity to provide a wide range of comic effects, including the highlighting of Brecht's references to *Richard III*. An elaborate joke entailed Ui's first entrance, when Antony Sher came on upstage with two sub-machine guns and, as he walked down towards the audience, he momentarily used them as two crutches in the manner of his Richard III. There were also simple, visual jokes, such as members of the Cauliflower Trust's standing solemnly round a single, solo-spotted cauliflower placed centre stage; Ui looking at a cauliflower as though it were a skull and he were Hamlet; and a delightful, comic double-act involving the two lawyers engaged in the trial of Fish. There were more elaborate comic sequences, which either started or gradually became macabre, even grotesque, such as a complete company tap-dance routine that opened the second half; or a manic (and sustained) attempt by Ui to erect a deckchair while trying to exert his power over Old Dogsborough; and a grotesque wooing of Betty Dullfeet, in which Ui licked the tears from her face before laying her on a coffin to kiss her (with shades of Richard III again, this time in the famous scene with the widowed Lady Anne).

147

The comic aspects of the show were praised by the critic Irving Wardle, who admired Sher's 'sustained comic virtuosity' and remarked that the production 'releases Antony Sher into a character he was born to play' (*The Independent*, 11.8.91). There was inevitably a tendency among reviewers to make comparisons between Sher and his notable predecessor, Leonard Rossiter, and they were divided in their choice of favourite. Benedict Nightingale in *The Times* thought 'Sher touched something Rossiter tended to miss. If he was less funny, he was more menacing, more evil' (10.8.91). There were some criticisms of the translation, the reviewer for *The Independent* suggesting that the second half of the play was less successful than the first because 'Bolt is wonderful with tightly controlled comic verse, but when the stylistic restrictions are relaxed his powers drain away' (11.8.91). While a few critics, such as Michael Coveney in *The Observer*, objected to the slogans, slides and music in that the historical parallels were 'ponderously spelt out' (11.8.91), Michael Billington wrote that the production conveyed well 'the debased theatricality of fascism' (*The Guardian*, 10.8.91). *The Independent*'s critic also debated the issue of the play's contemporary relevance and suggested that the visual material might have included 'some tasteful shots of Baghdad'.

Trevis had originally considered making many more references to contemporary tyrants as a way of placing the play more explicitly in the 1990s, but she was concerned that this would lead to what she called 'woolly political thinking' by the audience. She supported her decision to avoid contemporary references (other than the one Hussein image mentioned earlier), by quoting the critic James Fenton:

> He says, talking of the RSC production of *The Greeks*, it would have reminded you of the Bader-Meinhof group, had they not been dressed as the Bader-Meinhof group. I think people can make their own connections.

In retrospect, Trevis had come to feel less satisfied with the play itself and wondered if 'the gangster analogy is a bit too thin to sustain such a very important subject'. Sher was inclined to agree and suggested that if Brecht had had the chance to do a production of the play himself, he would have re-worked and simplified the text. He was also unsure about the translation in that it was, he considered, 'too faithful to Brecht'. Overall Sher's experience of performing Ui had been a disappointment to him. He suspected the role lacked an important dimension.

> People told me about Ekkehard Schall doing acrobatics in the Berliner Ensemble production and I constantly wondered why. Then I went home after the first preview and said: 'Tonight I understand why Schall did acrobatics – because the play doesn't. The whole experience is people waiting for this thing to happen and it doesn't quite'.

Sher had also come to the conclusion that the National production was too 'reverential' in its approach and that, if they were to start again, he would propose they should cut the text in order to

> make it punchier, play it faster and more lightly and find a way towards a 'living cartoon' – like Blakemore's production, like Rossiter. It needs that clarity of a cartoon. That way one could score the comic points and the terror more dynamically than we're able to do.

In the present writer's opinion, the production was rather overladen: slides and legends in the auditorium, accompanied by posed stage pictures, were over-elaborate at times, and the set itself was occasionally too fussy and busy. But there was an energy and a clarity in both the story-telling and the creation of the socio-political meaning that combined with a sense of fun and sheer enjoyment in performing that was faithful to the spirit of Brecht. Sher's performance of the central role was dynamic, bold and yet subtle, expressing a skilful blend of satire and menace. And as Di Trevis forcefully put it:

> Of all the Brecht plays, this is the one for the moment. The only legitimate, admirable political position is to be anti-fascist. . . . O.K. the solution Brecht thought was going to be the solution has turned out not to be. So what's new about that? It doesn't mean we should give up trying.

SUMMARY

While these three case studies do not represent all early 1990s' British productions of Brecht, they do, in many ways, demonstrate a recurrent series of problems and issues. The first production, *The Good Person of Sichuan*, shows a lack of both political and aesthetic understanding of the play. In that case, the director seemed determined to ignore not only the playwright's social-didactic intentions but also the performance demands of the text. Warner's declared directing method, which was supposed to allow and encourage actor input, was thus undermined by her pre-rehearsal decision to discount Brecht's political stance and by her subsequent lack of clarity on and understanding of the appropriate performance techniques for *The Good Person*. Despite noting that, for example, Brecht's 'opium' theme made possible connections with contemporary culture, Warner did not succeed in making the play speak more specifically to its audience. This was due in part to the rejection of the opportunity for the company to think through the socio-political implications of the text, and in part to the (consequently) unclear staging of key scenes (such as those in the opium factory and in Shen Te's shop). Perhaps as significant was the director's misunderstanding of the function of emotion in Brecht's plays. In seeking a kind of heightened naturalism (that was not grounded in social reality), Warner produced a mostly sentimental and unfocused interpretation.

In the production of *Mother Courage* the focus on the aesthetics of performance at the expense of the political heart of the piece led to the staging being more important than the social implications and meaning of the text. This was particularly disappointing in view of the considerable experience at the Citizens Theatre of presenting Brecht. However, Prowse's strong interest in design led him to create a series of visual 'moments' which distracted from and blurred the significant points in the story. Here, too, there were problems in ensemble playing: the company's collaborative tradition was subverted so that in this case the production became merely a star vehicle.

The third case study, of *Arturo Ui*, comes much closer to being an authentic Brechtian model. The politics were given central significance, not only in drawing meaning from the text but in creating an appropriate working method for rehearsal. Trevis's understanding of the socio-political intentions of the play led her to create clear stage pictures (through, for example, careful application of the concept of *Gestus*), and a strongly articulated narrative. A sense of fun infected the whole production while allowing the serious meaning, the menace, to come through. The comic aspects of this interpretation contributed, too, to the appearance of an ensemble, for, given the limitations of the National Theatre context, Trevis largely succeeded in facilitating the company's working in a collaborative way that manifested itself in a genuine enjoyment of performance. Some reservations remain with regard to the over-faithful approach to the text itself. As Sher suggested, a bolder editing job might have been helpful to both the narrative simplicity and the political clarity, and a sparer text could also have granted the actors a greater freedom in their playing.

In Chapter 6 these issues of social and theatrical politics in relation to productions of Brecht plays will be discussed further. In particular the focus will be on examining how and in what conditions British Brecht might be revived and developed in the last decade of the twentieth century – and even beyond.

6

PERFORMING BRECHT IN THE TWENTY-FIRST CENTURY

Dinosaurs came later

When I was a kid I went quite often to the Music Hall, saw people doing monologues, jokey material, singing songs, all those Brechtian things. . . . I went straight from the Music Hall to Brecht and my plays. It was only later that I discovered people like Rattigan and Coward. It was like having been in a world where there were quite advanced creatures like swans and giraffes, suddenly coming across dinosaurs. For me, dinosaurs came later.

(Edward Bond)[1]

In this final chapter, the views of some contemporary theatre practitioners will be scrutinised, views that have a bearing on performing Brecht's plays in the late twentieth century, and that might offer insights into possible approaches to his work for the next century. As Edward Bond, the epigraphist above, has said on a number of occasions: 'One should begin from his [Brecht's] deliberations and ruminations on theatre but not stop there.'[2] In order to consider how to revive the (Brechtian) 'advanced creatures' of Bond's pre-dinosaur age so that they have new meaning for contemporary theatre, one must first examine and assess the ways in which their environment has changed.

BRECHT AND THE POSTMODERN

In many ways the dinosaurs still rule in British theatre in the late twentieth century, in the form of the escapist musical, the safe and well-made play, and the hermetically-sealed, non-disturbing comedy, the staple fare not just of London's West End but of many provincial theatres. Between these dinosaurs of the establishment theatre and the new postmodern creatures of the avant-garde that have emerged from the swamp, there is a huge gulf. This might prompt some theatre practitioners to ask themselves for whom are they currently creating their performances, or, as importantly, who will be the audiences of the future. 'Dinosaur theatre' assumes there is no need for change, that audiences will continue to crave conventional and familiar lyrics set to hummable tunes; whereas postmodernist theatre is possessed by the knowledge that there have been changes in some audiences' aesthetic expectations and perceptions, and in the function of theatre itself and in its place in contemporary culture, and that all these factors allow, or require, a remodelling of theatrical forms. (And there is, admittedly, a chicken/egg problem here.)

Postmodern practitioners of the mid-1990s seek to exploit the fact that spectators are now capable of 'reading' sophisticated, complex and multi-layered performances through their drawing on an extensive experience of watching television, films and pop videos. Current, avant-garde theatre forms are built on the knowledge that framing, juxtaposition, montage and collage are artistic concepts and events instinctively understood by their contemporary audience. The postmodern breaking of the traditional theatrical codes and conventions has resulted in new definitions of performance, in particular in its characteristic foregrounding of 'actuality' in the theatre (at the expense of 'imitation'). This new emphasis makes different demands on the actor (who becomes the 'performer' of an event rather than the interpreter of a character) and seeks to invest the spectator with a series of changed perceptions of the relationship between the stage and the auditorium. As indicated in Chapter 5, it is arguable that in some ways postmodern theatre is anticipated in part by the Brechtian dramaturgy. As Elizabeth Wright points out in her book, *Postmodern Brecht*:

> The epic idiom . . . has become the universal language of contem-
> porary theatre, irrespective of its ideological origin. The techniques of
> montage, of epic narration, of diverse visual and auditory effects, are
> used far more radically than they are in Brecht's own plays.
>
> (Wright, 1989, p.113)

However, the origin and *purpose* of much of this kind of contemporary theatre is likely to be apolitical. While recognisably Brechtian techniques may be used in a radical way *theatrically* speaking, they are not commonly used directly to raise an awareness in the audience of socio-political issues. On the other hand, Wright argues Brecht's *Lehrstücke* qualify as post-modern pieces. This, she claims, is partly owing to their anti-narrative structure (which is seen as a postmodernist as well as modernist feature) and partly because of the particular relationship they set up between the audience and the performance:

> The spectator needs to be drawn into the production process in order
> to experience the shifting and contradictory choices of stage subjects/
> objects. The work of engaging the audience is not done on the stage
> via specific V-effects, but pressure is put on the audience to co-

produce in order to avoid the unpalatable alternative of placing her or himself in a psychotic position or abandoning meaning.

(Wright, 1989, p.109)

There is, indeed, a sense in which the resistance of postmodern theatre to the imposition of any one, dominant meaning on a performance can be seen as a (Brechtian) dialectical tactic. However, there is still to be considered the question of the intended function of such postmodern theatre. Is it purely an aesthetic experience or can it also entertain a socio-political debate with some, if not all, of the audience? And, for our purposes here, what impact does this new form of theatre and its changed view of the audience and the performer have on approaches to presenting Brecht now? Postmodernism presses on us the need for a radical re-think of how to perform Brecht in the late 1990s, a search for an alternative approach to that of regarding Brecht as a 'classic'. We now need to find ways of presenting Brecht that both recognise his historicity and his continued relevance to contemporary culture. As Paul Walsh pertinently reminds us in his discussion of Brecht's own approach to 'classic' texts:

> Within the domain of modern Western eclecticism . . . a lack of personal commitment is called versatility, while acquiescence to authority is masked as a sincere respect for the intention of the text. Brecht sought to free actors and directors, and their audiences, from such hierarchies of power embedded in tradition by replacing acquiescence to authority with personal commitment to exploring and elucidating in production the relationship between past culture and present function.
>
> (Kleber and Visser, 1990, p.105)

Heiner Müller, the German playwright who became a writer/director at the Berliner Ensemble in 1990, put the point more aggressively in an article in *The Independent* (14.1.93) when he suggested that to produce Brecht without criticising him was treason. And one way of 'criticising' Brecht that he advocates is to re-work the play-texts themselves, so that they can communicate effectively to a changed audience and achieve the inter-textuality that is a hallmark of the postmodern, artistic experience.

A NEW VIEW OF *THE LIFE OF GALILEO*?

It has been noted several times in this book that one of the key problems or challenges for British productions of Brecht has been the provision of suitable translations of the text. A 1994 production of *The Life of Galileo* at the Almeida Theatre, London, offers a recent perspective on this and on a number of related issues. David Hare, the socialist playwright who 'came of theatrical age' in the late 1960s (see Chapter 3), provided a script for the production. He worked from an academic's literal translation of the original German, since he himself has no competence in the language. However, he did not perceive this as a difficulty (though others might), more especially since his primary aim was to simplify the text so that the production would tell the story more clearly and speedily. This led Hare to cut the text of, or reduce in theatrical scope, a number of the large-scale scenes: for example, Scene 5, in which Galileo's household has to flee the plague, was cut entirely; the Carnival scene (10) was reduced to a puppet-show; and the dialogue in the final scene was cut in order to highlight the image of Andrea's crossing the border with the hidden copy of Galileo's *Discoursi*. Hare argued that his simplifications also eliminated some of Brecht's overloading of the arguments, the tendency of the playwright to present all sides of an issue:

> One of the disadvantages of intellectual playwrights like Brecht is that they feel compelled to embody answers to the possible objections to their plays. . . . The full Galileo text is weighed down with qualifi-cations . . . I wanted to take one clear line: a man who finds himself morally, ethically unequipped to deal with the consequences of his own genius. By taking that line through I stripped off a lot of the accretions.[3]

In addition, the clarity of Hare's narrative line was aided by cutting a number of minor characters and conflating others. According to Jonathan Kent, the director, this helped the production to focus the audience's attention on characters who, though appearing only in one scene, had an important contribution to make to the main arguments of the play. It also served 'to make the play more personal, to ensure a debate in which positions are passionately held, acted with a real passion, a commitment to an idea'.[4] David Hare developed this point by explaining that he saw Brechtian theatre as being passionate in a particular way (echoing, in fact, the views of the Berliner Ensemble actor Ekkehard Schall quoted earlier):

> More than any other playwright he can make *ideas* emotional rather than characters emotional. You can be moved by ideas in Brecht. There's a sensuality of ideas in his writing. . . . At the heart of Brecht is the notion that you should be thinking and feeling at the same time.

Behind Hare's assumption that it was appropriate to 'strip down' the text in this way for a contemporary audience was his awareness that the political context for this 1994 version was vastly different from that which existed even during his (Hare's) own early career, let alone Brecht's in the 1950s. He explained, in an interview with the present writer:

> There is no longer 'socialist drama'. Political theatre now can't rely on the ready-made structure, a common ideology that was understood.

So political writing now has in some way to be affirmative about common action, common values. We've got to create a contemporary political theatre out of the wreckage of Thatcherism.

Hare also wanted the production to avoid the use of what he regarded as outmoded Brechtian theatrical conventions: 'it was time to scrape the accumulated production methods off Brecht. It was an attempt to try and find Brecht the playwright free of what I feel to be the clutter.' He and the director, therefore, agreed that the production should use a simple unified set that could effect transitions quickly and that they would avoid, for example, the cliché use of slides and obvious demarcation and explanation of ensuing scenes. Hare is, however, scornful of all those Western critics who assumed that the breaching of the Berlin Wall rendered Brecht's work politically redundant. On the contrary, he associates with Brecht's plays 'a strong sense of theatrical unfinished business'.[5]

Hare's reduction of the number of characters in *Galileo* led to a strong feature of the production, which was the casting in those surviving 'one scene' roles, of experienced and well-known actors, some of whom actively welcomed the opportunity to play 'cameos' (despite the low and equal pay policy that pertained at the Almeida). This was a far cry from the complaints by actors about the smallness of Brechtian roles at the National Theatre and the RSC, as discussed in Chapters 4 and 5 (see pp.98, 108–9, 126), and it gave the production at least a *sense* of an ensemble through 'equal weight' of playing. The title role was taken by Richard Griffiths, an experienced actor of both straight Shakespearean and modern comic roles. He had already appeared in four British productions of Brecht, including the RSC's version of *Days of the Commune* (discussed in Chapter 4).

Griffiths admitted, in an interview with this writer, that, when he was approached to play Galileo, his 'heart sank'.[6] His previous experience of British Brecht led him (like others before him) to fear that the plays were inevitably 'heavy and pedantic and grey'. He was also aware, however, that the spirit of Brecht had probably been misunderstood, and he had moved towards a view on how the actor might find a way through 'alienation':

> Originally I found the arguments for the *V-Effekt* unbelievable. I have a suspicion now that Brecht was trying to get at complete realism without actors tearing a passion to rags. There's a difference between bullshitting a passion and being passionate.

The production was Jonathan Kent's first experience of directing Brecht, though he had appeared as an actor in the Citizens Theatre version of the same play (1971) and again in the production of *The Good Person of Setzuan*, featuring Janet Suzman (1977) (see Chapter 3). Kent saw Griffiths as good casting for Galileo because, he said in words recalling those of Hare (and Schall) quoted earlier, of Griffiths's 'ability to make abstract ideas

155

concrete and real and human'. The actor's own view was that he was not appropriate physically for the role because he was too big (larger even than Charles Laughton), but that he could find a suitable acting technique by drawing on his classical acting experience, experience which was reflected especially in his 'vocal expertise'. He claimed, however, that his working-class background did not determine that he shared Brecht's ideology. Instead, the main challenges in playing the part lay in its 'sheer unrelenting nature' and in the demands made by the rhetorical nature of Brecht's dialogue on the actor's line-learning: 'poetic prose needs great accuracy if it is to work properly'. So his 'investment' in the role appeared (to him) to be largely technical.

Jonathan Kent was as concerned as his translator/adaptor, David Hare, to maintain a fast-moving pace in the performance, as this, he emphasised, would assist the comic nature of the piece: 'I wanted it to be light on its feet, aesthetically pleasing . . . to have *Spass*.' The director had seen the National Theatre production of *Galileo* (1980), discussed in Chapter 4, which he thought was 'epic bordering on the lumbering'. He wanted to avoid

> things and people trundling forward to tell us what to think and hectoring and finger wagging . . . I'm not interested in theatre that preaches. The politics are complex . . . I tried to make the play as clear as possible rather then doctrinaire.

There was, according to Griffiths, much discussion during rehearsal of the political agenda of the piece, but in retrospect he felt there had been insufficient rehearsal time fully to integrate and express the socio-political ideas of the text in the performance. (The Almeida budget allowed for only three weeks of rehearsal.) For Kent the final result 'was too cool. It didn't have the relish I had hoped for.' (It is possible that the scene design contributed to the production's coolness: a light-coloured wooden construction that opened and turned swiftly and silently, and gave the impression of being detached from the human beings on the stage. The set did, however, assist the achievement of performance 'flow' that matched what Hare had provided in his simplified version of the text.)

Michael Billington's review of the production, punningly headlined 'Speed of the Hare', admired the drive of the story-telling and added pertinent praise for the way Hare's translation drew attention to the political debate within the play: 'it highlights the notion that disinterested rational enquiry is always politically subversive'. He also paid tribute to Griffiths's unsentimental portrayal of

> the multi-facetedness of Galileo: the sensual life lover, the silky ironist, and, above all, the moral coward prepared to sacrifice others, but not himself, to the diligent pursuit of truth.
>
> (*The Guardian*, 18.2.94)

Although the leading actor did not share Brecht's ideology, and despite his predominant concern with the technical challenges of the role, Griffiths did commit himself to ensuring the moral questions in the play were clearly expressed. Some evidence for that commitment, apart from the passion and clarity of the performance itself, came in a speech he made as part of a lunchtime debate on the comparative significance of nuclear physics and theatre held at the Natural Science Museum in London during the production's run. In answer to his 'opponent' in the debate, a professor of nuclear physics, Griffiths said: 'Art is essentially about revealing itself to an audience; whereas science is a creature of dark corners of secrecy'.[7]

The Almeida production of *The Life of Galileo* was, on many counts, very successful, not least in that it attracted a large number of young people in its audience. Kent regarded the youthfulness of his audience as particularly pleasing because of the need to build a new audience for contemporary theatre. But this production of British Brecht now appears a rare event on the current theatrical scene: a strongly performed, coherently and clearly expressed interpretation of a Brecht text, played by a (relatively) evenly balanced cast of expert and experienced actors. Its jettisoning of the 'accretions' of 'Brechtian' production style, its finding of a workable balance between the ideas in the text and the feelings expressed through performance – between analysis and catharsis – and its re-working of the text for narrative and theatrical clarity all constitute an appropriate model for would-be presenters of Brecht's plays in the late twentieth century. But the production did not, perhaps could not, go far enough. This was an *ad hoc* company mounting a production of a complex play in three weeks. Necessarily the focus had to be on textual clarity, and there was recourse to simple (and sometimes very static) blocking. And for the leading actor, the main challenge was the great task of learning such a large (as well as subtle) part. The production was highly competent but, although it seems to have made good contact with its young audience, it was unlikely to have developed in any extended way insights in that audience into the moral and political concerns of the play.

TRANSFORMING THE AUDIENCE

At the heart of any reassessment of contemporary methods of playing Brecht is the re-definition of the relationship between performer and spectator. Such an engagement, of course, is in the true spirit of Brecht, for, as Frederic Ewen reminds us, Brecht

> believed it necessary to develop the art of the spectator, no less than that of the writer or actor. He regarded the audience as a 'producer' . . . to transform the theatre, therefore, meant also to transform the audience.
>
> (Ewen, 1970, p.201)

Again, we are reminded of the autonomy of the 'reader' of postmodern art. A view of the audience's responsibilities lay at the centre of all Brecht's efforts to 'distance' the audience from their 'primary emotions' so that they might maintain an intellectual (as well as emotional) engagement with the issues of the play.

As discussed above, some contemporary audiences now view the play from aesthetic perceptions different from those appropriate to conventional theatre, and practitioners performing Brecht now have to take such new perceptions into account. Previously effective theatrical techniques that are inscribed in the texts either have to be jettisoned, as was Hare's practice at the Almeida, or they have to be re-shaped.

Another British socialist playwright, David Edgar, proposes that the conventional approach to Brecht in Britain, which is based on an understanding of the theory of 'epic theatre', needs, for example, to be leavened with 'the carnivalesque'. In his book, *The Second Time As Farce* (1988) he refers to Bakhtin's views on medieval carnival and suggests that this form with its 'utopian radicalism' provides an alternative basis for contemporary political theatre. Edgar then concludes:

> What I suppose most of us are striving for, is a way of combining the cerebral, unearthly detachment of Brecht's theory with the all too earthy, sensual, visceral experience of Bakhtin's carnival, so that in alliance these two forces can finally defeat the puppeteers and manipulators of the spectacle.
>
> (Edgar, 1988, p.245)

Edgar's own attempts to exploit the features of carnival (for example, large crowd scenes and interaction between performers and audience in the same space) within the contemporary theatre form are perhaps best seen in his *Entertaining Strangers* (1985), the community play he wrote at Ann Jellicoe's instigation. In the quotation above he is, of course, proposing a more emotional experience for the theatre audience than that usually associated with Brecht.

But the notion of political carnival is rejected by Howard Barker, the British playwright who has coined the term 'Theatre of Catastrophe' to characterise his own radical form of dramatic writing. Barker argues for the return of tragic theatre, a theatre that (unlike 'carnival') is not intended to re-establish the *status quo* (make life bearable through a safe and controlled venting of anti-establishment feeling) but that will displace, radically, an audience's understanding of reality:

> A carnival is not a revolution.
> After the carnival, after the removal of the masks,
> you are precisely who you were before. After
> the tragedy, you are not certain who you are.
>
> (Barker, 1989, p.12)

This idea of tragic theatre is not conventionally Aristotelean (giving the gods their due) and it in no sense precludes humour. Barker's plays include not only extraordinarily disturbing, even horrific, events but also extended passages of a special kind of rhetorical wit and striking scenes of mordant, sometimes grotesque, comedy. In his contribution to the current debate about the nature and role of the audience, Barker maintains that a unified, collective experience of a play is neither desirable nor possible (and he thus aligns himself with the postmodernists):

> It is the audience who constructs the meaning. The audience experiences the play individually and not collectively. It is not led, but makes its own way through a play whose effects are cumulative. The restoration of dignity to the audience begins when the text and the production accept ambiguity. If it is prepared, the audience will not struggle for permanent coherence, which is associated with the narrative of naturalism, but experience the play moment by moment, truth by truth, contradiction by contradiction.
>
> (Barker, 1989, p.36)

The last sentence there has strong overtones of Brecht's view that the audience is required to participate actively in the construction of the meaning from a deliberately episodic and contradictory form contrived by the playwright and developed in the performance. Barker does not, however, follow Brecht in trying to create an (intellectual) objectivity in the spectator. His project is to restore power of a different kind to the performer. The latter is intended to operate 'not as demonstrator of a given thesis' but as someone who allows, even encourages the audience 'to abandon its moral and intellectual baggage and permit itself the greater freedom of an imaginative tour, essentially a de-stabilising experience' (Barker, 1989, p.80). Thus Barker provides his audience with an emotional, and possibly cathartic, experience, as well as an intellectual one, but the emotion is not one of simple empathy with the tragic plight of the play's protagonist.

An even more radical concept of the transformed audience is presented by Augusto Boal, the Brazilian theatre practitioner who has had a growing influence on alternative theatre in Britain since the publication in English in 1979 of his seminal book, *The Theatre of the Oppressed*. In anticipation of Edgar, he 'had long responded to the idea of the activated spectator as manifested in Brecht and Brazilian carnival' (Schutzman and Cohen-Cruz, 1994, p.113), and in the foreword to his book Boal makes his own view on the inseparability of art and political stance clear: 'Those who try to separate theater from politics try to lead us into error – and this is a political attitude' (Boal, 1979, p.ix). He then goes on, in Chapter 3, to analyse and criticise Brecht's 'poetics', and to set out his own theatrical programme. This takes on Brechtian notions of the function of art but then moves beyond them in offering theatre as a 'tool' to ordinary people, wherever they may be, for the analysis of the political options open to them. The intention of this kind of theatre is to provide a theatrical experience that is able radically to change people's lives by giving them the opportunity to try out or rehearse alternative behaviour in their lives. 'Theatre of the Oppressed' is, he says, 'a rehearsal for the revolution' (Boal, 1979, p.122).

Crucially, the theatrical form he develops, which he calls Forum Theatre, breaks down any remaining barrier between the performer and the audience, by encouraging the audience not only to respond to the perform- ance, but to participate actively in the creative process, by becoming what Boal terms 'spect-actors'. In Forum Theatre the spect-actors offer their personal experiences of 'oppression' for enactment on the stage by the performers and are then cajoled into joining them in exploring the scenes and situations from their lives and in discovering possible solutions to problems and challenges posed. Thus the didactic form of Brecht's epic theatre is developed into experiential learning, and Boal takes the Brechtian notions of education through participation, on which the *Lehrstücke* are based, a radical but logical step further.

Forum Theatre 'performances' are guided by an outside figure, whom Boal calls the Joker, whose task is to facilitate the process of revelation, discovery and enactment (by, for example, encouraging the interchanging of roles), and, as importantly, to provide social analysis. The kind of performance that results does, of course, beg questions of definition. Is it political theatre? Participatory, creative drama for adults? Or psychotherapy? Boal tries to resist such categorisation, declaring: 'politics is the therapy of society, therapy is the politics of the person' (Schutzman and Cohen-Cruz, 1994, p.99).

In another of his theatre forms, which he calls 'Invisible Theatre', Boal merges actor and spectator in a more inextricable way, blurring even further the distinction between theatre and life. Here a group of actors plays out a pre-rehearsed situation in a real setting without the onlookers (who might become participants) knowing that what they are witnessing is, in fact, theatre. The intention, again, is to effect some kind of socio-political change. As Boal puts it:

> The invisible theater erupts in a location chosen as a place where the public congregates. All the people who are near become involved in the eruption and the effects of it last long after the skit is ended.
>
> (Boal, 1979, p.144)

In this bringing together of theatre, drama, politics and social 'healing', Boal makes actual use of dialectics rather than merely dramatising dialectical possibilities. Furthermore, in his work with actors Boal stresses the signif- icance of the body and physical expression as primary tools in uncovering and revealing the ways in which 'masks of behaviour' are imposed on people by social conditioning. (See Boal, 1992.) So, as with Brecht's *Gestus*, the actions and gestures of the body are, for Boal, determined by social relationships and attitudes, and he develops a theatre strategy that foregrounds this idea.

All these re-uses of Brechtian motifs, together with the underlying socialism they serve, have led to Boal's being described by Mady Schutzman as a 'Brechtian shaman'. While acknowledging the contradictions in such a label, she explains that it:

> suggests the collective de-mythologising, de-ossifying aspect of Boal's work – a kind of group interactive therapy (the shamanic element) confronted by a structural and dialectical alienation demanding dialogue between actor and role (the Brechtian part).
>   (Schutzman and Cohen-Cruz, 1994, p.151)

In many respects, then, Boal's ideas here accord with those of Brecht. He does, however, have a different view on the function of catharsis in relation to the theatre audience, seeing it as a powerful force for the subversion of oppressive social structures. Whereas Brecht thought that catharsis resulted in audience inaction, a mere self-gratification and indulgence in empathetic feeling, Boal believes it has the power 'to encourage imbalance thus kindling the urge for further deeds and action' (Boal, 1992, p.237). But of course Boal's audience members have the opportunity to become 'spect-actors' and, therefore, experience catharsis of a different kind, personally and not vicariously. In that sense they are indeed similar to the performers of Brecht's *Lehrstücke*, in which participants undertake different roles in order to gain a full understanding of any given situation before making decisions that determine the play's outcome. Yet Boal's technique of Forum Theatre has a further dimension in that the spectator can become actor and then spectator again. This provides a 'distance' and perspective not available to the *Lehrstuck* performer.

Boal's connections with and acknowledged debt to Brecht are strong and significant, but, as importantly, he has developed the latter's ideas in a specific and influential way that not only retains something of Brecht's socio-political intention but also offers new possibilities for the development of the actor/audience relationship in more traditional settings. This is not to suggest that audience members might be encouraged to rush onto stage during more conventional modes of theatre, but that a greater awareness of audience responses and respect for that interaction on the part of the performers would be helpful in the contriving of other, contemporary theatre performances. Pertinently, in his book *Games for Actors and Non-Actors* Boal describes the kind of actors he considers necessary for successful Forum Theatre and how they should relate to their audience:

In certain African countries the people measure the talents of the singers by the extent to which they can seduce their audiences into singing along with them. That is what should happen with good Forum Theatre actors. In their performances there must not be the slightest trace of the narcisssism so commonly found in *closed* theatre shows. . . . The actors must be dialectical, must know how to give and take, how to hold back and lead on, how to be creative. They must feel no fear (which is common with professional actors) of losing their place, of standing aside.

(Boal, 1992, p.237)

Boal's concept of the good performer as one who is unafraid of devolving some of his/her power to the audience provides a useful perspective from which to view contemporary modes of performance in general and for British production of Brecht in particular.

A similar view of the necessary readiness to relinquish power by the actor to the audience is endorsed by the Italian director Eugenio Barba, who has, like Boal, exerted considerable influence on British alternative theatre practitioners both through the work of his Denmark-based company, Teatret Odin, and through his writing. Barba conceived of a dramatic activity he called 'Third Theatre', in which the company's work would provide the basis for a form of 'barter' with the community in which they were living and/or working. This means, Barba explains, 'the exchange of our theatrical presence – training, performances, pedagogical experience – for the 'culture' of other theatre groups or communities' (Barba, 1986, p.44). The sharing of skills with the community is itself built on the company's approach to actor training, which includes a four-year apprentice system for young performers and a programme of daily physical exercise and improvisation for the company in general. Barba, like Brecht before him, rejects naturalistic forms of performance and draws on, among other traditions, those of Eastern theatre. But Barba is concerned to have more than an aesthetic impact on his audiences and strives to 'transform the "barter" from a cultural phenomenon into something that will leave a mark on the political and social situation of the place' (Barba, 1986, p.13).

Most of Teatret Odin's performances are created through improvisation by the actors, and although the final versions are 'fixed' as a kind of text, the performers remain 'interactive' with their audiences by constantly responding, during performance, to the spectators' reactions. Furthermore, the company's work is built on a striving towards mutual respect and a sense of equal status between performer and spectator – an impulse that, as has been suggested, is often lost, overlooked or scorned in more traditional theatre forms.

Barba also has a form of subversive theatre, similar to Boal's Forum Theatre, that involves the active participation of the audience members.

The director calls this 'secret theatre' and explains that the purpose of this kind of performance, which focuses on particular issues suggested by the audience participants, is 'to dissect the forces governing human and social realities' (Barba, 1986, p.176). Odin's whole concept of theatre is, in fact, more a way of life than just a kind of socialist art and it is almost inevitable, therefore, that the company is organised as a fully collective ensemble. Barba is forthright about this in his book on the company's work, *Beyond the Floating Islands*:

> We are trying to construct a theatre where people are not pawns pushed around by an absentee director as is the case in the cultural industry. Each member of our group must clearly understand his place within our little society and be responsible for his share of all the work there is to be done: physical, technical, administrative, as well as artistic.
>
> (Barba, 1986, p.202)

The company's social responsibility, moreover, is taken further. As Clive Barker puts it in his essay on 'Alternative Theatre/Political Theatre', the value of Barba's Third Theatre

> lies not in its performances alone but in the social relationships built up inside the company and between the company and the outside world. He takes further Brecht's injunction to remain a 'foreigner' in one's own society, creating an a-social situation in which people pursue socially, through theatre, the dream of building their own lives.
>
> (Holderness, 1992, p.39)

Indeed, it was Barba's awareness of Brecht's experiences as a foreigner and in exile that prompted him to create a show with Teatret Odin called *Brecht's Ashes* (1980). This was largely based on Brecht's songs and poems, and Barba explains:

> We empathized with his experiences as an uprooted man, a man in exile. We were confronted with his disenchanted intelligence, his cunning, the shrewd actions which he used to protect what was essential for him: intellectual independence, discerning vision, doubt, an individual voice.
>
> (Barba, 1986, p.217)

Barba places great significance, in a Brechtian way, on showing the individual in his/her social and historical context and on rendering distinctly not only the interaction between that individual and his/her society but the concept that there is a constant evolution of the relationship between the two.

Such Brechtian preoccupations are reiterated in the work of Edward Bond, who, as noted in Chapter 2, might be described as the 'British

163

Brecht'. A more detailed examination of Bond's views on Brecht and on his own post-Brechtian, dramaturgical and theatrical practice may, therefore, provide a final perspective on late twentieth-century productions of Brecht in Britain.

BRECHT AND BOND

There are clear and forceful parallels between Brecht and Bond in terms of their political commitment, their theatrical skills as playwrights, poets and directors, and their determination to practise and preach the idea that art must have a social function. Recognition of Bond's contribution to the further development of a Brechtian form of theatre lies behind the continuing popularity of his plays on stage in Germany, and promoted the decision by Peter Palitzsch, long-time director at the Berliner Ensemble, to direct a new Bond play, *Olly's Prison*, at the Theater am Schiffbauerdamm in 1994.

For the Berliner's rehearsal of this play Bond supplied notes to the director, which explain in a general way the theatrical intentions behind his play-writing and his ideas on how key moments in his work should be performed. The ideas he expresses in the notes constantly echo Brecht, such as his concern to clarify the way he, as playwright, uses repeated stage images, patterns of movement and physical objects to clarify and forward the narrative:

> This is a basic strategy of the play – a constant hammering and whispering at patterns which give rhythmic, dramatic development to the story – they are used almost as Wagnerian *leitmotiven*, except that they are rational as well as emotional impulses.[8]

That last phrase draws attention to his emphasis (in common with Brecht) on both thinking and feeling. As early as 1972, in the introduction to his re-writing of the Shakespeare play *Lear*, Bond had explained his sense that there was no antagonism between them in art:

> I am not interested in the old dichotomy between reason and emotion. I mean the rational psyche to be fully emotional. It's its relationship to the world which is rational. . . . It means that emotions are, in fact, more pronounced and full.
>
> (Hirst, 1985, p.133)

He does not, in fact, see the inclusion of the expression of strong emotions in theatre as a great shift from the practice of Brecht. In an interview with the present writer, Bond commented that the most emotionally charged productions he had ever seen were those directed by Brecht himself, but he explained (chiming with David Hare above) that the emotion generated on stage was of a different kind and had another purpose from a simple triggering of sympathetic feeling for the characters:

164

The productions were profoundly moving and emotionally disturbing, but not in the sense that you were captured and paralysed by the
emotion. The emotion seemed to be all the time placing the responsibility on you. It wasn't that the actors were experiencing the
emotion *for* you; they were showing you something that demanded
an emotional response, as well as understanding.

Furthermore, this kind of emotional response by the audience to
performance does not, in Bond's view, lead to catharsis, except in a
re-defined (non-Aristotelian) sense: 'for me catharsis is a new idea that can
change you, but to get to these new ideas is often a very emotional
journey'. He always strives in his work, which he terms 'rational theatre', to
link feeling to reason. Indeed, he juxtaposes emotion and reason for
dialectical effect.

Bond, therefore, strives to challenge his audiences, and to unsettle them,
not only intellectually but emotionally, too. In order to achieve this in his
own plays he employs what he calls 'aggro-effects' (a term that clearly
echoes Brecht's *V-Effekts*), which he sees as being a way of sharpening and
extending (even reversing?) Brecht's own 'distancing' technique:

> Sometimes it is necessary to emotionally commit the audience –
> which is why I have aggro-effects. Without this the *V-effekt* can
> deteriorate into an aesthetic style. Brecht then becomes 'our Brecht'
> in the same sloppy patriotic way that Shakespeare becomes 'our
> Shakespeare'. I've seen good German audiences in the stalls chewing
> their chocolates in time to Brecht's music – and they were most
> certainly not seeing the world in a new way.
>
> (Hirst, 1985, p.133)

Bond's aggro-effects comprise carefully choreographed moments or
images that are deliberately disturbing or even puzzling to an audience. As
he puts it, they are 'moments where the known experience frays over into
something which cannot be pinned down to very common usage, but is
somehow suggestive of the experience' (Hay and Roberts, 1980, p.50). An
example of Bond's use of an 'aggro-effect' would be the 'curious buzzing'
made by the gang of youths as they exit after stoning the baby in *Saved*
(Scene 6), and used there to underscore their inhuman behaviour. More
recently, in his notes on *Olly's Prison* for the Berliner Ensemble, Bond
draws attention to another example of an 'aggro-effect', the moment when
a female character puts four lumps of sugar into her tea:

> The modern actress must show hell by the way she handles and drops
> into the cup the four lumps of sugar. If the modern theatre can't
> accomplish these things it can't speak of our times to the people who
> have to live in them.

Janelle Reinelt, in her chapter on Bond in *After Brecht*, explains the impact of aggro-effects on the audience's perception of a character: [they] 'often allow a character to break rationality, forcing the spectator to confront the limits of logical characterisation' (Reinelt, 1994, p.78). This technique thus might be compared to the sustained physicality (and, therefore, 'distance') of the Brecht/Weigel 'silent scream' in *Mother Courage* (see p.33), or the shifts from reality to non-reality when Shen Te becomes Shui Ta by the application of a mask. For the Berliner production of *Olly's Prison*, Bond proposed that at times the actors' own faces should be used as a kind of 'mask', and he stressed that the performers should try neither to exaggerate nor to disguise what is intended to be a non-naturalistic technique:

> Notions such as 'masks' . . . have to be acted – but they should not become 'performance art' or be reduced to naturalism. It is merely necessary to denote their oddness and not explain it away by 'normalising' the acting.[9]

He then goes on to emphasise that the actors need to be absolutely precise in their handling of objects and in creating images through gesture, warning that if the performers reduce these actions to 'generalised' physical action, this allows the audience to be less precise in their perceptions than they should:

> it signals to the audience that they may think in clichés. And so the subtlety of their imaginations will be 'switched off' – the audience will respond in a merely generalized (that is, half aware) way.

Bond's theatre texts, which comprise his 'rational theatre', are multi-layered, and are carefully constructed via a combination of what he calls text, sub-text and meta-text. Texts still have sub-texts, he assumes, 'because they cannot be written wholly objectively' (Bond, 1990, p.243). His 'meta-text' is the overall intended aesthetic, emotional and intellectual impact of the whole play on the audience and is designed to be broken into units, which might be images, moments of action or even whole scenes, called 'Theatre Events'. As he explains in his 'Notes on Post-Modernism', Theatre Events (or TEs) are:

> a means [for the audience] of analytical understanding. They make clear the cause and consequence of events, collecting the diffuseness of real life into illustration and demonstration – not dogmatically or symbolically but still in units of conflict.
>
> (Bond, 1990, p.243)

Through this technique of TEs, Bond intends to draw the audience's attention to significant moments in the production and to promote their analysis of the socio-political situation of which the moments themselves form a part. In this respect the purpose of the technique is not dissimilar to

Brecht's use of *Gestus* and 'dialectical alternative', though Bond is more inclined to employ *non-realistic* ways of highlighting, such as the signalling use of slowed-down action or of unexpected and unexplained images and sounds. He also makes it clear that he believes that his technique of Theatre Events assists in the production of meaning in a theatre that can no longer rely on Brechtian 'alienation':

> Brecht would be saying all the time, 'Alienate it, because although there is no meaning in you, there will be a meaning that is self-existent in society'. This is what I disagree with because I don't think there is any rational enlightenment or obvious meaning in the world outside. You have to put meaning in it. You have to make it.[10]

Thus Bond's technique of TEs frames events so that they acquire new meanings rather than, as with Brecht's *V-Effekts*, 'merely produc[e] space round things, incidents, so that an audience may reflect and consider'. Furthermore, this transformation of *V-Effekts* is necessitated, Bond thinks, by the fact that contemporary audiences cannot be treated as a 'mass' (in the way Brecht at one time may have conceived of an audience), but as individuals; audiences now are 'fragmented'. But even Brecht, Bond argues, began to see the audience as individuals and, in order to find for his epic theatre an appropriate impact in the communist state of East Germany, he was impelled to redefine his theatre as 'dialectical':

> Brecht can say, 'Alienation will work in the theatre I am writing about because there is a strong political party out there'. Brecht is always writing for an audience of the Party. . . . Once Brecht was in a society that called itself socialist, he actually then started to abandon that rather schematic form of theatre and started talking about other forms of theatre.

Bond's own efforts to create a form of rational and political theatre for our 'postmodern' times have led him, naturally, to define the kind of actor and performance techniques appropriate to them, and these ideas may provide some useful insights into possible ways of performing Brecht now. As indicated at the beginning of this chapter, Bond's seminal and formative experiences of performance were, like Brecht's, at the 'cabaret', or its British equivalent, the Music Hall. Thus Bond's concept of an actor has always been that of a performer with a wide range of expressive skills: including comic, musical, direct address of the audience, and the ability to ring swift changes of tempo and mood. He frequently refers to the late Frankie Howerd, one of his favourite British comedians, noting the way in which Howerd 'played with' an audience and turned the spectator into a co-performer:

> the extraordinary thing was, one realized in a sense one was performing a dance with him. You weren't sitting there listening, he was

reacting to you all the time. You knew what the climax was, he knew what the climax was, but you worked together for it.

(Coult, 1977, p.73)

Watching Howerd perform persuaded Bond that the relationship between the actor and the audience should be one of equals, that the spectator had to be an active participant in the theatrical event, and that the essential style for the performer was that appropriate to story-telling (in true Brechtian tradition). When directing his own play, *The Woman*, a version of the Trojan Wars, at the National Theatre (1978), Bond explained to the company the kind of acting he wanted and stressed the importance of story-telling and its function of liberating the emotions of the performer.

> A concept, an interpretation (of the situation not the character) must be applied to an emotion, and it is this concept or interpretation or idea that is acted. This relates the character to the social event so that he becomes its storyteller. When this is done, emotions are transferred to the surface. Instead of being hidden in the heart or the gut (or other corners of the bourgeois soul) they go to the hands, feet, face, head and become living creative energy. Then the actor is freed to interpret the situation.

(Hirst, 1985, p.43)

Although this suggests an 'externalised' approach to performance, Bond wants to avoid in his work the reduction of characters to caricatures of class function because, as he says, 'that can only confirm audiences in what they already know . . . learning is a more subtle experience'. He, therefore (in common with Brecht before him), gives due weight to human psychology in character portrayal, but only inasmuch as its presentation leads to social understanding on the part of the audience:

> In order to understand history, to understand economics, to under-stand why people behave as they do, you have to look at their psychology. . . . If you can make that psychology clear then its deviousness becomes a good paradigm for understanding anyone else's psychology. I think Brecht would see the truth in that.

Bond also concurs with Brecht on the issue of character inconsistency, on actors' honestly playing the contradictions inherent in a role rather than imposing a psychological coherence. His poem *Advice to Actors* makes this plain:

> Actors
> Don't try to make your character possible
> Men do things that ought not to be possible
> Don't say 'he'd never do this'
> Men don't behave in expected ways

168

> Don't make the character one man
> Unfortunately a man is many men
> Don't worry when an action isn't consistent
> Men aren't consistent
> Ask why they're not consistent
>
> (Bond, 1980, p.99)

But, as Bond knows too well, actors do not easily take this or other advice, and a political playwright/director is always faced with the inherent instinct of the actor to become more interested in the character *per se* than in its functioning within a broader social perspective:

> The problem is always to make actors interpret roles as social roles or social functions, to ask not 'Who am I?' but 'What am I?', not 'Who does this action?' but 'What is this action?', to define themselves in relation to other characters, to consider the nature of the action rather than the nature of the self.

In fact, this may be a problem not just of the natural tendency of actors to invest in the inner landscape of their roles but also the result of the kind of actor-training common in Britain which often focuses too much on the performer as individual and his/her role as the limited sphere of proper interest and neglects the development of a capacity to analyse the super-objective and function of the whole play. After watching student actors at the Royal Academy of Dramatic Art working on one of his plays, Bond remarked:

> There was a gap between the play and them. They didn't know how to *use* the play, they didn't know what the play is there for, or why the play was written . . . I think in acting they're still taught to be themselves in some way, to disappear into themselves. I think on stage they are having a fine old time, but nothing is really happening, except for them. So we have to watch something that we are not quite part of.

The crucial issue is how we can ensure that both the contemporary performer and the audience for Brecht (and for Bond and other political theatre) are fully engaged, emotionally and intellectually, in the legitimate theatrical experience offered to them by such drama. There is a high degree of agreement between the contemporary practitioners considered here on how socio-political theatre can be effective in our fragmented world. There is agreement, too, on the need for creating a closer and more 'balanced' relationship between the performer and spectator and for stimulating the spectator actively to participate in the creation of the performance's mean-ing, by offering a more emotionally as well as intellectually disturbing form of theatre than that offered by its more conventional counterparts. A significant aspect of what we might call this 'rediscovered' Brechtian form is the greater emphasis on creating an emotional as well as social impact on the audience through a range of techniques. These might include the sensual release of 'carnival' (Edgar), the destabilising catharsis of tragedy (Barker), the empowering participation of the 'spect-actor' (Boal), the shared respect of 'barter' and exchange (Barba), and the dialectical analysis and emotional power of non-realistic 'aggro-effects' and 'Theatre Events' (Bond). We need now to examine how feasible are such intentions and ideas for productions of Brecht's plays on the contemporary British stage.

THE WAY FORWARD FOR BRITISH BRECHT?

In 1993 Heiner Müller said: 'In the last ten or fifteen years the Berliner Ensemble tried to make Brecht kosher for socialism, and he's not kosher, he is a subversive' (*The Independent*, 14.6.93). The argument in this book has been that in the West, and in Britain in particular, Brecht has been treated too often as a 'kosher' classic, thus largely avoiding the implications of his work both for socialism and subversion. And, as discussed in earlier chapters, British practitioners have too often fallen into the trap of imitating a 'received' Brechtian style rather than striving properly to understand and adopt his actual working methods and theatrical and social purposes.

John Willett usefully summarises the main obstacles to good 'Anglo-Brecht' in a chapter titled 'Ups and Downs of British Brecht' (in Kleber and Visser, 1990). The obstacles Willett observes include: 'self-importance' (i.e. of the actors); designers' 'love of spectacle' (coupled with a lack of skill in its effective deployment); 'strained topicality' (directors' making the play contemporary whatever the cost); 'Anglicization' ('Cosy for the actors, but disastrous for the play'); actors' 'mangling the verse' (lacking trust in the words to convey the meaning); 'having the translation done by well-known writers, unaccustomed to Brecht's original language' (Kleber and Visser, 1990, p.87). Willett's objection to the actor's 'self-importance' paradoxically relates to the contemporary problem for the British performer of the scarcity and insecurity of employment which encourages the actor to ensure that his/her current performance is 'noticed' by resorting to theatrical techniques that serve to draw attention to his/her performance rather than contributing to the overall impact and meaning of the production. A contributory factor here also, of course, is the British actor's lack of the opportunity to work in ensembles, where non-self-centred methods of working and performing by the actor might be developed over a long period. Job insecurity also leads to the concession by the actor of too much power (and responsibility) to the director. All of these issues have been discussed in previous chapters.

Willett's 'love of spectacle' refers to the current trend, especially in London, for what is often described as 'designer's theatre', in which (like

170

the actor) the director and/or designer draws critical attention to a production (and his/her talent) by means of an over-elaborate, and sometimes inappropriate, dependence on visual statements and spectacular staging. Here, too, the situation is exacerbated in British theatre by the predominance of freelance practitioners in both directing and design, artists who are often by definition and training part of a theatre 'team' for no more than the duration of a single production. Membership of an ensemble for the director and designer, like the actor, can offer not only security, but also the opportunity to develop with the other team members both a shared theatrical language and a set of common goals, a practice in which the personal ambitions of the individual operate in line with, and not counter to, those of the rest of the team.

Willett's notion of 'strained topicality' is in part a criticism of attempts to 'update' Brecht (such as have been discussed in previous chapters). The crucial point here is that adaptation is not 'treason' (to use Müller's word), provided, that is, that the actions of the characters in the play are placed in their historical, social and economic context and evolution. Brecht's own example is before us with regard to tackling anew another's creative efforts. For him, the archetypical adapter/reviser, not even his own work was sacrosanct:

> I rewrote *Mann ist Mann* ten times, and presented it at different times in different ways. . . . In studying an interesting book we must 'look back', we re-read passages in order to grasp them entirely, and so too in the theatre. Revisiting a play is like re-reading a page of a book. Once we know the contents of it, we can judge more closely of its meaning.
>
> (*B on T*, p.80)

Willett's criticism of 'Anglicization', of translations by writers without knowledge of German, and of actors mangling the verse, are, of course, closely linked by his informed understanding of Brecht's dramatic language in its original form. The difficulties of effective translations of Brecht's plays have been noted in previous chapters. Over the last forty or so years a wide range of translation methods has been adopted by British practitioners: from the faithful and literal, almost word-for-word, versions, to the radical adaptations that have included substantial re-writing. There is no simple answer to the problem of establishing a translation text, but *actors* need to be made aware of the intentions and functions of Brecht's (and the translator's) choices of language in order to use the text effectively, much as they would with Shakespeare. They can then be encouraged to develop a mode of delivery that exploits the inherent 'distancing' and comic effects of the structures, rhythms and unusual vocabulary (at least of the original) and avoid the tendency to 'naturalise' the language in performance.

In summary, what is required for the re-invention of the theatre of Bond's 'pre-dinosaur' age (when Brechtian theatre was deemed natural and relevant) for this new age? First, changes are needed in the British theatrical context. As Michael Billington reminds us in an article on the National Theatre and the RSC: 'Policy . . . is the people you work with and in the theatre permanence is a measure of quality' (*The Guardian*, 1.2.95). Without the greater security and longer-term employment of companies (as in the Berliner Ensemble), British theatre practice necessarily limits the exploratory and open processes of rehearsal and inhibits the creation of shared aesthetics and a common performance language. This is not to suggest that some kind of dulling uniformity should be imposed on individuals in such a company, but that there has to be an acknowledgment by all concerned of the ways in which individual skills and talents can contribute to the whole business of production. Barba stresses this point when writing of the process of creating his company:

> It is often thought that a theatre group has unity because its members resemble each other. On the contrary: it is necessary to look for reciprocal differentiation in order to achieve totality.
>
> (Barba, 1986, p.14)

Such respect for the individuality of the performer would also entail recognition within the professional theatre of the need for actors to deploy both an intellectual and an emotional approach to performance. Indeed, the integration and/or the dialectical opposition of thinking and feeling in the performer should be seen as crucial to the development of post-Brechtian theatre. Respect must also extend to the audience, the members of which should be regarded as equals, as educated and individual participants in the creative process of performance, not as people to be flattered or wooed into passivity.

The changes in the organisation and structure of British theatre suggested above would, of course, be particularly appropriate for working on Brecht. Such changes would help actors and directors to tackle his texts anew, to adapt, re-write and re-work them so that the 'dead hand' of performance clichés, dramatic theory and outmoded notions of Brechtian 'style' might be shaken off. Brecht's texts need to be re-made so that they are again challenging and uncomfortable, as well as able to furnish what Brecht would call 'five pennyworth of fun' (*B on T,* p.7). Given such changes in the theatrical context and a fresh approach to Brecht's texts, we then would get a performer who fulfils a number of criteria. First, the performer would have the personal qualities of charisma, energy and emotional depth, and the technical skills characteristic of a good story-teller: that is, clarity, timing, imagination, observation and the ability to establish a rapport with an audience. Second, the performer would be by nature and inclination a collaborative artist, sensitive to the work of others, and able to function as part of a team that shares a view of the overall theatrical purpose of the enterprise. Third, the performer would have a social perspective on his/her art, to see it as part of social change; as Bond would say, a performer who knows what his/her art is *for*.

For the British performer of Brecht, most of these *personal* requirements would pose no especial problems. As has been noted in previous chapters, many actors in this country already have an innate Brechtian sense of irony in their role-playing, built on, among other things, the tradition of playing Shakespeare and other classics, and of telling a complex story on a relatively bare stage. Furthermore, the popular tradition of Music Hall, variety theatre and pantomime, and their contemporary equivalents in 'alternative comedy', have heightened an awareness of and developed skills in the handling of an audience through direct address. And the recent developments in postmodern theatre that exploit the actor's own self, his/her reality, bring the contemporary performer close in key ways to Brechtian ideas of performance. Thus the postmodern actor, in the characteristic, avant-garde theatre piece, is frequently required to contribute to the collective story-telling in his/her own person rather than maintain a continuous engagement with a fictional character. It is not without significance, of course, that some of the best British performers of Brecht (in the opinion of the present writer) have been either 'natural' comedians (Leonard Rossiter, Michael Gambon), and/or have developed their performance skills in the essentially Brechtian form of Theatre-in-Education (Bill Paterson, Maggie Steed), and/or have inherited a strong sense of personal and political commitment to socialist theatre (Janet Suzman, Antony Sher). And these are all actors who, in the Boalian sense, are not afraid of losing their status in relation to an audience, or of opening up themselves to new possibilities in the dynamic between performer and spectator. As Edward Bond told the Berliner Ensemble in 1994:

> We can still trust our audience – provided we have made it possible for them to trust us: and that means understanding what we do – understanding it fully – and not resorting to the empty trickery which comes so easily to theatre. But theatre is capable of making profound mistakes only because it deals with profound things: and that is theatre's chance – and its justification.[11]

NOTES

INTRODUCTION

1 See 'Cultural Policy and Academy of Arts', *B on T*, p.266
2 'Actors reply to Brecht', *New Theatre*, Vol.5, No.10, 1949, p.15

1 BRECHT AND THE PERFORMER

1 Esslin, M. 'Brecht and the English Theatre', *Tulane Drama Review*, Vol.11, No.2, 1966, p.159
2 Barthes, R. 'Seven Photo Models of *Mother Courage*', *Tulane Drama Review*, Vol.12, No.1, 1967, p.44
3 Brecht, B. 'On Chinese Theatre', *Tulane Drama Review*, Vol.6, No.4, 1961, p.133
4 Brecht, B. 'Notes on Stanislavsky', *Tulane Drama Review*, Vol.9, No.2, 1964, p.165
5 Marowitz, C. 'Talk With Tynan', *Encore*, Vol.X, No.4, 1963, p.13
6 Chaikin, J. 'The Actor's Involvement: Notes on Brecht', *Tulane Drama Review*, Vol.12, No.2, 1968, p.149
7 Brecht, B. 'Notes on Stanislavsky', *Tulane Drama Review*, Vol.9, No.2, 1964, p.160
8 Ibid., p.161
9 'Dialogue: Berliner Ensemble', *Tulane Drama Review*, Vol.12, No.1, 1967, p.112
10 Brecht, B. 'Notes on Stanislavsky', *Tulane Drama Review*, Vol.9, No.2, 1964, p.163
11 Capon, E. 'Brecht in Britain', *Encore*, Vol.X, No.2, 1963, p.28
12 Rouse, J. 'Brecht and the Contradictory Actor', *Theatre Journal*, Vol.36, No.1, March 1982, p.36
13 Weber, C. 'Brecht As Director', *Tulane Drama Review*, Vol.12, No.1, Fall 1967, p.103
14 Rouse, J. 'Brecht and the Contradictory Actor', *Theatre Journal*, Vol.36, No.1, March 1982, p.31
15 Weber, C. 'Brecht as Director', *Tulane Drama Review*, Vol.12, No.1, 1967, p.112
16 Capon, E. 'Brecht in Britain', *Encore*, Vol.X, No.2, 1963, p.28
17 'Dialogue Berliner Ensemble', *Tulane Drama Review*, Vol.12, No.1, 1967, p.112
18 Brecht, B. 'Notes on Stanislavsky', *Tulane Drama Review*, Vol.9, No.2, 1964, p.163

19 Honneger, G. and Schechter, J. 'An Interview with Ekkehard Schall and Comments by Barbara Brecht', *Theater*, Spring 1986, p.35
20 'Dialogue Berliner Ensemble', *Tulane Drama Review*, Vol.12, No.1, 1967, p.117
21 Honneger, G. and Schechter, J. 'An Interview with Ekkehard Schall and Comments by Barbara Brecht', *Theater*, Spring 1986, p.35

2 PERFORMING EARLY BRITISH BRECHT

1 MacColl, E. 'The Grass Roots of Theatre Workshop', *Theatre Quarterly*, Vol.3, No.9, 1973, p.58
2 Ibid., p.63
3 Page, M. 'The Early Years at Unity', *Theatre Quarterly*, Vol.1, No.4, 1971, p.64
4 'Brecht and the British Theatre: A Brief Symposium', *Encore*, Vol.III, 1956, p.27
5 Brown, I. 'Mother Courage and Her Children', *International Theatre Annual*, No.1, 1956, p.29
6 Wanamaker, S. 'The Brecht Revolution', *International Theatre Annual*, No.1, 1956, p.121 and following. All subsequent quotations from Wanamaker taken from here
7 Devine, G. 'The Berliner Ensemble', *Encore*, Vol.VI, 1956, p.11
8 Capon, E. 'Good Woman of Setzuan', *Encore*, Vol.X, 1956, p.33
9 Hall, S. 'Beyond Naturalism Pure', *Encore*, Vol.8, No.6, 1961, p.12
10 Bond, E. 'On Brecht: a Letter to Peter Holland', *Theatre Quarterly*, Vol.8, No.30, 1978, p. 35
11 'Teaching is for Schools: An Interview with Robert Bolt', *Encore*, Vol.VIII, No.2, March 1961, p.26
12 'Gaskill in Germany: William Gaskill talks to *Plays & Players* about directing in Munich and Hamburg', *Plays & Players*, April 1973, p.30
13 This and subsequent quotations from an interview with present author, 5 December 1989
14 Milne, T. 'And the Time of the Great Taking Over', *Encore*, Vol.IX, No.4, 1962, p.22
15 Ibid., p.11
16 Ibid., p.20
17 Ibid., p.45
18 This and subsequent quotations from an interview with present author, 23 May 1990
19 Esslin, M. 'Brecht and the English Theatre', *Tulane Drama Review*, Vol.11, 1966, p.67

3 PERFORMING BRECHT POST-1968

1 W. Stephen Gilbert, Review of *Plenty*, *Plays & Players*, June 1978
2 'Interview with Howard Brenton', *Theatre Quarterly*, Vol.17, 1975, p.8
3 From an interview with present author, 9 November 1986
4 This and subsequent quotations from an interview with present author, 20 May 1992
5 This and subsequent quotations from an interview with present author, 29 October 1993
6 Eaton, B. 'The Liverpool Everyman', *Drama and Theatre Quarterly Review*, Autumn 1982, p.21

7 This and subsequent quotations from an interview with present author, 12 June 1992

8 On BBC Radio programme *Desert Island Discs*

9 From an interview with present author, 18 December 1991

10 From an interview with present author, 8 August 1990

11 This information from an interview with present author, 15 April 1994

12 This and subsequent quotations from an interview with present author, 30 June 1990

13 This and subsequent quotations from an interview with present author, 2 May 1990

14 This and subsequent quotations from an interview with present author, 11 June 1990

15 'Interview with Keith Hack', *Plays & Players*, April 1973, p.34

16 Lecture: 'Brecht at the Citizens Theatre', Goethe Institut, 12 May 1990

17 From an interview with present author, 20 July 1990

18 This and subsequent quotations from an interview with present author, 3 May 1990

19 From an interview with present author, 30 August 1991

20 This and subsequent quotations from an interview with present author, 30 August 1990

21 Esslin, M. 'The Good Person of Setzuan', *Plays & Players*, December 1977, p.12

4 PERFORMING 'CLASSICAL' BRECHT

1 Holland, P. 'Brecht, Bond, Gaskill and the Practice of Political Theatre', *Theatre Quarterly*, Vol.8, 1978, p.24

2 This and subsequent quotations from an interview with the present author, 20 September 1985

3 Mairowitz, D.Z. 'The RSC's *Man is Man*', *Plays & Players*, December 1975, p.18

4 Mairowitz, D.Z. 'The RSC's *Schweyk in the Second World War*', *Plays & Players*, July 1976, p.14

5 This and subsequent quotations from an interview with the present author, 30 March 1994

6 In conversation with the present author, 21 August 1991

7 In response to questionnaire from present author, 1986

8 Interview with Ria Julian, *Drama*, 155/1, 1985, p.6

9 Ibid., p.7

10. 'Mother Courage and the RSC: Malcolm May talks to Judi Dench who plays the title-role', *Plays & Players*, November 1984, p.18

11 This and subsequent quotations from an interview with the present author, 23 May 1990

12 This and subsequent quotations from an interview with present author, 5 December 1989

13 Rehearsals at National Theatre, August 1982

14 Programme note by Michael Bogdanov

5 PERFORMING BRECHT IN THE 1990s

1 This and subsequent quotations from an interview with present author, 7 August 1990

2 This and subsequent quotations from an interview with present author, 5 December 1989

3 This and subsequent quotations from an interview with present author, 5 December 1989
4 This and subsequent quotations from an interview with present author, 12 December 1989
5 'Who's Afraid . . .?: Glenda Jackson Gives Vera Lustig her Views on Acting', *Plays & Players*, May 1990, p.7
6 In the BBC television series, *Elizabeth R*, 1975
7 This and subsequent quotations from an interview with present author, 11 May 1990
8 This and subsequent quotations from an interview with present author 26 May 1990
9 From conversations during rehearsals April/May 1990
10 This and subsequent quotations from rehearsals/interviews with present author July/August and 10 December 1991
11 Interview with present author, 6 December 1991
12 Answer to present author's questionnaire, 1986

6 PERFORMING BRECHT IN THE TWENTY-FIRST CENTURY

1 This and subsequent quotations from an interview with present author, 25 June 1993, unless stated otherwise
2 From a letter to present author, 30 October 1994
3 From an interview with present author, 11 May 1994
4 From an interview with present author, 11 May 1994
5 Almeida Theatre programme
6 From an interview with present author, 30 March 1994
7 At the National Science Museum, London, 23 March 1994
8 Unpublished notes, 13 October 1994
9 Unpublished notes, 13 October 1994
10 Letter to present author, 30 October 1994
11 Unpublished notes, 13 October 1994

BIBLIOGRAPHY

Ansorge, P. (1975) *Disrupting the Spectacle: Five Years of Experimental & Fringe Theatre in Britain*, London, Pitman.

Arden, J. (1977) *To Present the Pretence*, London, Methuen.

Banks, M. (1984) *The British Theatre and Bertolt Brecht*, Unpublished dissertation, University of Warwick.

Barba, E. (1986) *Beyond the Floating Islands*, New York, PAJ Publications.

Barker, H. (1989) *Arguments for a Theatre*, London, John Calder.

Bartram, G. and Waine, A. (eds) (1982) *Brecht in Perspective*, London, Longman.

Benedetti, J. (1982) *Stanislavski: An Introduction*, London, Methuen.

Benjamin, W. (1977) *Understanding Brecht*, trans. Bostock, A., London, NLB.

Bentley, E. (1968) *The Theory of the Modern Stage: An Introduction to Modern Theatre and Drama*, London, Penguin.

—— (1981) *The Brecht Commentaries*, London, Methuen.

—— (1985) *The Brecht Memoir*, New York, PAJ Publications.

Billington, M. (1972) *The Modern Actor*, London, Hamish Hamilton.

—— (1988) *Peggy Ashcroft*, London, John Murray.

Blau, H. (1982) *Take Up the Bodies: Theater at the Vanishing Point*, Illinois, University of Illinois Press.

Boal, A. (1979) *The Theatre of the Oppressed*, London, Pluto.

—— (1992) *Games for Actors and Non-Actors*, trans. Jackson, A., London, Routledge.

—— (1995) *The Rainbow of Desire*, trans. Jackson, A., London, Methuen.

Bond, E. (1980) *The Worlds with the Activist Papers*, London, Methuen.

—— (1990) 'Notes on Post-Modernism', in *Two Post-Modern Plays*, London, Methuen.

Bradby, D. and Williams, D. (1988) *Director's Theatre*, London, Macmillan.

Braun, E. (ed. & trans.) (1969) *Meyerhold on Theatre*, London, Methuen.

—— (1982) *The Director and the Stage*, London, Methuen.

Brecht, B. (1961) *Helene Weigel: Actress*, trans. Berger, J. and Bostock, A., Leipzig, VEB Edition.

—— (1964) *Brecht on Theatre*, trans. & ed. Willett, J., New York, Hill & Wang.

—— (1965) *The Messingkauf Dialogues*, trans. Willett, J., London, Methuen.

—— (1976) *Poems 1913–1956*, eds Willett, J. and Mannheim, R., London, Methuen.

—— (1979) *Diaries 1920–1922*, ed. Rauthum, H., trans. Willett, J., London, Methuen.

—— (1990) *Letters 1913–1956*, trans. Mannheim, R., London, Methuen.

—— (1993) *Journals 1934–1955*, ed. Willett, J., trans. Mannheim, R., London, Methuen.

Brook, P. (1972) *The Empty Space*, London, Penguin Books.

Brooker, P. (1988) *Bertolt Brecht: Dialectics, Poetry, Politics*, London, Croom Helm.

Brown, I. (1956) *Theatre 1955–56*, London, Reinhardt.

Browne, T. (1975) *Playwrights' Theatre*, London, Pitman.

Bull, J. (1984) *New Political Dramatists*, London, Macmillan.

Burton, H. (1967) *Great Acting*, London, BBC.

Callow, S. (1984) *Being an Actor*, London, Methuen.

Chambers, C. (1989) *The Story of Unity Theatre*, London, Lawrence & Wishart.

Chaplin, C. (1964) *My Autobiography*, London, Bodley Head.

Coult, T. (1977) *The Plays of Edward Bond*, London, Methuen.

Coveney, M. (1990) *The Citz*, London, Nick Hern Books.

Craig, S. (ed.) (1980) *Dreams and Deconstructions*, London, Amber Lane Press.

Davies, A. (1987) *Other Theatres*, London, Macmillan.

Demetz, P. (ed.) (1962) *Brecht: A Collection of Essays*, New Jersey, Prentice Hall.

Dexter, J. (1993) *The Honourable Beast*, London, Nick Hern Books.

Dickson, K. (1978) *Towards Utopia: A Study of Brecht*, Oxford, Clarendon Press.

Drews, W. (1965) *Die Schauspielerin Therese Giehse*, Berlin, Henschel.

Duerr, E. (1962) *The Length and Depth of Acting*, New York, Rinehart.

Edgar, D. (1988) *The Second Time As Farce*, London, Lawrence & Wishart.

Elsom, J. (1976) *Post-War British Theatre*, London, Routledge.

Esslin, M. (1959) *Brecht: A Choice of Evils*, London, Heinemann.

Ewen, F. (1970) *Bertolt Brecht: His Life, His Art, His Times*, London, Calder & Boyars.

Eyre, R. (1993) *Utopia and Other Places*, London, Bloomsbury.

Findlater, R. (1981) *At the Royal Court*, London, Amber Lane Press.

Fuegi, J. (1972) *The Essential Brecht*, Los Angeles, Hennessy & Ingalls Inc.

—— (1987) *Bertolt Brecht: Chaos According to Plan*, Cambridge, Cambridge University Press.

Gaskill, W. (1988) *A Sense of Direction*, London, Faber & Faber.

Goorney, H. (1981) *Theatre Workshop Story*, London, Methuen.

Gorchakov, N. (1968) *Stanislavsky Directs*, trans. Golding, M., New York, Greenwood.

Gray, R. (1976) *Brecht the Dramatist*, Cambridge, Cambridge University Press.

Grossvogel, D. (1962) *The Blasphemers: The Theater of Brecht, Ionesco, Beckett, Genet*, Cornell University Press.

Hall, P. (1983) *Diaries*, London, Hamish Hamilton.

Hay, M. and Roberts, P. (1980) *Bond: A Study of His Plays*, London, Methuen.

Hayman, R. (1969) *Techniques of Acting*, London, Methuen.

—— (ed.) (1975) *The German Theatre*, London, Wolff.

—— (1983) *Brecht: A Biography*, London, Weidenfeld & Nicholson.

Herbert, J. (1993) *A Theatre Notebook*, ed. Courtney, C., London, Arts Books International.

Higham, C. (1976) *Charles Laughton*, London, W.H. Allen.

Hiley, J. (1981) *Theatre At Work*, London, Routledge.

Hirst, D. (1985) *Edward Bond*, London, Macmillan.

Holderness, G. (ed.) (1992) *The Politics of Drama and Theatre*, London, Macmillan.

Itzin, C. (1980) *Stages in the Revolution*, London, Methuen.

Jacobs, G. (1986) *Judi Dench*, London, Futura.

Jacobs, N. & Ohlsen, P. (eds) (1977) *Bertolt Brecht in Britain*, London, TQ Publications.

Kershaw, B. (1992) *The Politics of Performance*, London, Routledge.

Kleber, P. (1987) *Exceptions and Rules: Brecht, Planchon, and The Good Person of Szechuan*, Frankfurt, Lang.

Kleber, P. and Visser, C. (eds) (1990) *Re-interpreting Brecht: His Influence on Contemporary Drama and Film*, Toronto, Cambridge University Press.

Littlewood, J. (1994) *Joan's Book*, London, Methuen.
Lyon, J.K. (1982) *Bertolt Brecht in America*, London, Methuen.
McGrath, J. (1981) *A Good Night Out*, London, Methuen.
Marowitz, C. (1961) *The Method As Means*, London, Jenkins.
—— (1986) *Prospero's Staff: Acting and Directing in the Contemporary Theatre*, Bloomington, Indiana University Press.
Marowitz, C. and Trussler, S. (1967) *Theatre at Work*, London, Methuen.
Marowitz, C., Milne, T. and Hale, O. (eds) (1965) *The Encore Reader*, London, Methuen.
Nathan, D. (1984) *Glenda Jackson*, Tunbridge Wells, Spellman.
Needle, J. and Thomson, P. (1981) *Brecht*, Oxford, Blackwell.
Ott, F.W. (1979) *The Films of Fritz Lang*, New Jersey, Citadel Press.
Patterson, M. (1981a) *The Revolution in German Theatre 1900–1933*, London, Routledge.
—— (1981b) *Peter Stein*, Cambridge, Cambridge University Press.
Piscator, E. (1980) *The Political Theater*, trans. Rorrison, H., London, Methuen.
Rees, R. (1992) *Fringe First: Pioneers of Fringe Theatre on Record*, London, Oberon Books.
Reinelt, J. (1994) *After Brecht: British Epic Theater*, Michigan, University of Michigan Press.
Rowell, G. and Jackson, A. (1984) *The Repertory Movement*, Cambridge, Cambridge University Press.
Samuel, R., MacColl, E., Cosgrove, S. (1985) *Theatres of the Left 1880–1935: Workers Theatre Movements in Britain and America*, London, Routledge.
Schechter, J. (1985) *Durov's Pig: Clowns, Politics and Theater*, New York, Theater Communications Group.
Schutzman, M. and Cohen-Cruz, J. (eds) (1994) *Playing Boal*, London, Routledge.
Sher, A. (1986) *Year of the King: An Actor's Diary*, London, Methuen.
Speirs, R. (1982) *Brecht's Early Plays*, London, Macmillan.
Stanislavski, C. (1924) *My Life in Art*, trans. Robbins, J.J., London, Methuen.
—— (1937) *An Actor Prepares*, trans. Hapgood, E., London, Methuen.
Suvin, D. (1984) *To Brecht and Beyond: Soundings in Modern Dramaturgy*, Sussex, Harvester Press.
Tatlow, A. (1979) *The Mask of Evil: Brecht's Response to the Poetry, Theatre and Thought of China and Japan*, Bern, Lang.
Thomson, P. and Sachs, G. (eds) (1994) *The Cambridge Companion to Brecht*, Cambridge, Cambridge University Press.
Tschudin, M. (1972) *A Writer's Theatre: George Devine and the English Stage Company at the Royal Court 1956–1965*, Bern, Lang.
Tynan, K. (1964) *Tynan on Theatre*, London, Methuen.
Völker, K. (1979) *Brecht: A Biography*, trans. Nowell, J., London and Boston, Marion Boyars.
Wardle, I. (1978) *The Theatres of George Devine*, London, Cape.
Whiting, J. (1966) *On Theatre*, London, London Magazine Editions.
Wiles, T. (1980) *The Theater Event: Modern Theories of Performance*, Chicago, Chicago University Press.
Willett, J. (1959) *The Theatre of Bertolt Brecht*, London, Methuen.
—— (1984) *Brecht in Context: Comparative Approaches*, London, Methuen.
Wintour, C. (1980) *Celebration – 25 Years of British Theatre*, London, W.H. Allen.
Witt, H. (ed.) (1975) *Brecht As They Knew Him*, London, Lawrence & Wishart.
Wright, E. (1989) *Postmodern Brecht: A Re-Presentation*, London, Routledge.

INDEX

187